RAILWAYS
OF
ZIMBABWE

RAILWAYS
OF
ZIMBABWE

The Story of the Beira, Mashonaland
and Rhodesia Railways

ANTHONY H. CROXTON

(with additional material by Anthony H. Baxter)

David & Charles
Newton Abbot London North Pomfret (VT)

British Library Cataloguing in Publication Data

Croxton, Anthony H.
   Railways of Zimbabwe.——New ed.
   1. Railways——Zambia——History
   2. Railways——Zimbabwe——History
   I. Title   II. Croxton, Anthony H.   Railways of
   Rhodesia
   385'.096894   HE3459.Z/
ISBN 0-7153-8130-X

First published as Railways of Rhodesia 1973
Second edition, retitled Railways of Zimbabwe, 1982

Printed in Great Britain by
Redwood Burn Limited Trowbridge Wiltshire
for David & Charles (Publishers) Limited
Brunel House Newton Abbot Devon

Published in the United States of America
by David & Charles Inc
North Pomfret Vermont 05053 USA

For
Carolyn and Philip

Contents

List of Illustrations

LIST OF ILLUSTRATIONS

*Photographs not acknowledged to
source were taken by the author or
are from his collection*

LINE ILLUSTRATIONS IN THE TEXT

MAPS

Coat-of-arms of the British South Africa Company
as used by the Beira, Mashonaland and
Rhodesia Railways

Coat-of-arms used by Rhodesia Railways
since nationalisation

Introduction

THERE can be few extensive railway systems which have owed so much to the dreams, foresight and drive of one individual as did the Beira, Mashonaland & Rhodesia Railways. It is entirely thanks to Cecil John Rhodes and his British South Africa Company that the closely connected territories of Bechuanaland, Southern Rhodesia and Northern Rhodesia—to give them their pre-independence names—became served by a series of railway companies that linked these countries with Beira on the east coast and with the Cape in the south.

It has become rather the fashion in recent decades to decry and criticise the political and financial planning of that great Empire-builder who aimed to colour red so much of the Victorian map of Africa. While his Cape-to-Cairo Railway was never to reach fruition, it was Rhodesia Railways (as the title became) that opened up a great span of land-locked territories in the centre of the continent. Though Cecil Rhodes did not live to see his railways develop deep into Rhodesia, his vision had seen them stretching far to the north. In a letter from Bulawayo in September 1900 he wrote: 'The object is to cut Africa through the centre and the Railway will pick up trade along the route.'

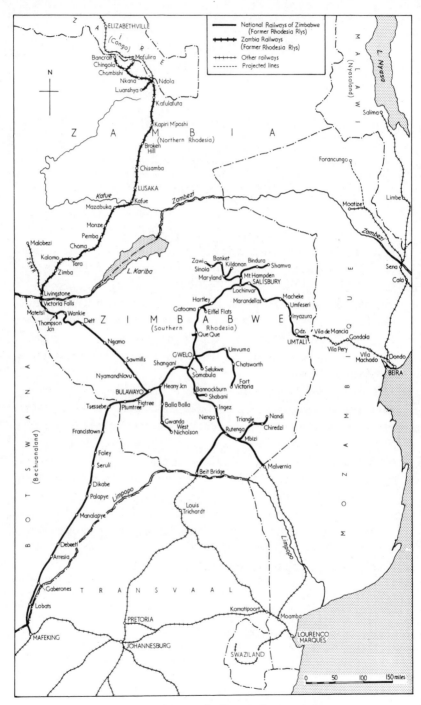

Map of the former Rhodesia Railways system

CHAPTER 1

The Beira Railway

It was in September 1890 that the Pioneer Column organised by
Cecil Rhodes reached Salisbury and so added Mashonaland to the
British Empire. With the prospect of gold and other mineral
developments, the column had been followed by many adventurous and optimistic spirits looking for an early fortune in the
newly-won territory between Fort Victoria and Salisbury and even
further north. As claims were staked and the need for mining
equipment and the day-to-day necessities of life grew, the early
settlers realised that transport by ox waggon over rough tracks
and great distances would be a slow and costly process, even if
the oxen could escape disease from the tsetse fly. A railway from
the coast to speed up the development of Mashonaland was the
constant demand in the bars and homes in the little township of
Salisbury, and over the camp fires of the prospectors. 'What is Mr
Rhodes doing about it?' was the question.

Rhodes with his powerful 'Chartered Company', by which name
the British South Africa Company was generally known, had not
been idling—he was far too dynamic a person for that. His un-
successful efforts to acquire territory east from Umtali into Manicaland had led to the treaty between the Portuguese and British
governments, dated 11 June 1891, under which the Portuguese
agreed to construct a railway line between the Pungwe river and
the British sphere of influence, with docks, quays and other
installations at the port of Beira. By Royal Decree in July 1891
the Mozambique Company was granted the right to undertake the

work and, in turn, under a contract dated 11 September 1891, this company gave the concession to Henry T. van Laun, with the approval of the Portuguese government.

Then it was that Cecil Rhodes decided to make a personal visit to Beira and travel inland up the Pungwe river to see for himself the kind of country to be surmounted. He had already obtained a good idea of the terrain from the most noted hunter of his time, Frederick Courtney Selous, on whose advice he placed much reliance. Selous, then at the age of forty, had an unrivalled knowledge of Central and East Africa and had travelled extensively through Manicaland between the coast and Umtali. In 1890 Dr Jameson (later Sir Starr Jameson) had been sent by Rhodes to travel from Umtali to the sea and after various mishaps had reached the Pungwe river and travelled thence by boat to Beira. Jameson saw enough of the mouth of the Pungwe to realise that here was a perfect port for the future, with no bar to block its entrance and ample anchorage for large vessels.

Rhodes was at Beira on 26 September 1891, and after the river trip to Mapandas his party made their way through the forests and over the escarpments to Massi Kessi (as Macequece was first spelt) and on to Umtali, which he reached on 9 October. He thus gained a knowledge of the country through which a railway could be built and this was to serve him well when the actual route was being decided.

The next step was for the Chartered Company to promote the Beira Railway Company, which acquired the railway concession from Mr van Laun for £10,000, paying also £5,000 for survey plans. Van Laun and two Mozambique Company representatives joined Alfred Beit and Rochfort Maguire on the board of the Beira Railway, the company eventually being constituted on 12 July 1892. The Beira Railway Company was peculiar in that the liability of its shareholders was limited by guarantee and it issued no share capital for cash. Having an authorised capital of 600,000 shares, it issued 295,000 to the Mozambique Company in part payment for the concession to build the line. The remaining 305,000 shares were offered as a bonus to subscribers for the £250,000 A debentures at a rate of twenty shares for every £20 of debentures. These 6 per cent debentures were secured on the first seventy-five miles of railway from Fontesvilla.

The successful raising of capital was mainly influenced by the London banking firm of d'Erlangers, the head of which, Baron Frederic Emile d'Erlanger, had taken a great liking to George and Harry Pauling and had helped them with their railway contracting work in Africa. Later, the baron and the Paulings formed the London & Paris Exploitation Co to finance contracts, mainly in Africa, while the d'Erlangers were closely associated with Rhodes in the financing of his railway projects in Rhodesia.

While these diplomatic and financial negotiations were in progress Alfred Beit on behalf of Rhodes, through his agent, Major Frank Johnson, called for tenders for the construction of the first section of the railway from Mapandas on the Pungwe river, later to be known as Fontesvilla, to Mandigoi some seventy miles inland. As early as 1 July 1891 the famous railway contractor, George Pauling, who had already built railways in Cape Colony and elsewhere and was well-known to Rhodes and Beit, made an offer to build a 2ft gauge 'steam tram line' seventy miles in length at an estimated total cost of not more than £70,000. In the letter from George and Henry Pauling to Major Johnson making this offer, it was stipulated that all permanent-way material and rolling stock was to be supplied and landed at the point from which the line was to start, in time for the beginning of work and for continued track-laying at a rate of one mile per day from 15 September 1891. The enclosure to this letter from Paulings, detailing the interesting estimate of costs, is given in Appendix A. Pauling had never been near this part of Mozambique at the time and can have had only the most sketchy of maps to which to refer. He would, however, have had the opportunity of consulting with Sir Charles Metcalfe who, with Sir Douglas Fox and Sir George Bruce, had been appointed consulting engineers for the construction of the railway. Sir Charles was an old friend of Cecil Rhodes from his Oxford days, and had already helped him with railway development in the Cape.

Besides Pauling, other contractors had competed for the job of building the Beira Railway, but Alfred Beit decided to award the contract to Pauling & Co. George Pauling then engaged Alfred L. Lawley, one of his competitors, to manage the contract as he knew him to have no fear of fever, which was so bad in the low-lying country beside the Pungwe. It was Lawley's drive and personal strength that enabled him to overcome the enormous difficulties that beset the contractors during the construction of this pioneer railway line starting from the river-bank camp at Fontesvilla.

At this time Beira, which came on the map as the future gateway to Rhodesia, was described as a narrow strip of sandbank with monotony only broken by the occasional low galvanised-iron house, an evil-looking saloon or a so-called hotel. There were no roads, only sand tracks, and no wharves or means of landing cargo from ships in the roadstead. Lack of finance had dictated starting the railway at Fontesvilla rather than at Beira itself, some thirty-five miles away, so construction material had to be transhipped to lighters at Beira and towed along the winding Pungwe river by tugs brought by Pauling from East London and Delagoa Bay.

At Fontesvilla a construction camp was formed and in September 1892 work began, the contract then being for seventy-five miles of line. Pauling had spread it around in Salisbury that he would recruit any local white labour he could, as many men were known to be out of work, and some fifty went down to Fontesvilla in the early days of the contract. Surveyors and engineers were sent out from England in charge of Harry Pauling, the brother of George, but he only remained to see the survey work properly started. E. R. Mansergh took charge of the actual survey, while Lawley had control of the construction itself.

Fontesvilla was intensely hot and, being on the river bank, was most unhealthy so that malaria and blackwater fever soon claimed many victims among the white employees. The camp was composed of galvanised-iron or pole-and-dagga huts with little or no protection from the swarms of mosquitoes. George Pauling records in his memoirs that when he visited the line in May 1893 he found Lawley at Beira, whence he had been sent desperately ill with malaria, so he put him on board a steamer for a sea trip to restore his health. At the construction site Pauling found practically every employee on the job suffering from fever and in one fortnight six white men died including his book-keeper. Many employees were from Great Britain and of the roughest type, but their experience as platelayers served to train the local labour.

The first rainy season was a very heavy one so that nearly all the flat country was under water, a sign of the troubles that later beset the Beira Railway through so much of its history. Even river transport became a problem when the *Agnes*, one of Pauling's two tugs, got out of the river stream and grounded on a sandbank some distance above Fontesvilla and about seven miles from the normal bed of the Pungwe. The river went down quickly, as was usual, leaving the *Agnes* high and dry in the bush. Three years passed before they had a similar flood high enough to get her away and even then a canal had to be cut for some miles. These heavy floods constantly shifted the sandbanks, and navigation up and down the river was a nightmare and source of much delay and frustration.

From Fontesvilla (now known as Ponte do Pungwe) the first twenty-five miles were across flat grassy country teeming with game and sprinkled with tall coconut and rafia palm trees. It was not until the line had reached beyond Bamboo Creek (later known as Vila Machado) that the ground began to rise much above sea level. Once the Siluvu hills were reached the base camp was moved to a somewhat better locality for living, but it had been a hard slog for the men putting down a railway across such unhealthy country. In the early construction days Lawley had im-ported 500 donkeys to haul waggons, owing to the losses sus-tained with oxen due to sleeping sickness brought on by the tsetse fly. Indian labourers were imported but they did not fare as well as the Shangaan and Inhambane natives and practically all died of disease. The local labourers fortunately proved to be very suitable for railway work and were well content with a shilling a day and food, generally rice, while ample meat was supplied by shooting game. Apart from food, all they needed was a loin cloth, a straw mat and a wooden pillow, and they built well-palisaded huts of rushes or bamboo to protect themselves at night from marauding lions and other wild animals.

For the white employees it must have been largely a matter of luck that some survived, as Pauling states that in 1892 and 1893 they lost 60 per cent of their white staff by death, including all the teetotallers. In Pauling's experience teetotallers did not withstand a fever country as well as excessive drinkers. Fresh vegetables were very scarce, ice was unheard of, and as steamers only called at Beira about once in a month or six weeks, fresh supplies were seldom obtained. Among those who succumbed to fever was George Pauling's cousin, Harry, who died at Beira and had been Lawley's chief assistant. George himself, during a spell on the job while Lawley was recuperating, had attacks of malaria and a mild dose of blackwater: he, however, was *not* a teetotaller.

The line itself was being built in a very austere manner due to shortage of capital funds. It was of 2ft gauge with light track, the rail first being in 24ft lengths of 20lb, and later 28lb, per yard. It would appear that Kerr, Stuart & Co, railway plant suppliers of London and Glasgow, undertook the delivery of much of the material for the early contracts and that prefabricated sections of track were shipped out to Beira to facilitate the laying down of the line. Kerr, Stuart acted as factors and their old records show that an order was placed with the Brush Electrical Engineering Co in July 1892, for the supply of five steam locomotives from their Falcon Engine & Car Works, Loughborough, to George Pauling & Co, Beira.

Not much detail is available about these first engines for use by the contractors on the Beira Railway. Three engines had 7in diameter cylinders and are thought to have been small tank engines. The other two locomotives had 8in × 15in cylinders and it is clear that these were a larger Falcon 'Midge' type of tank engine. They were of the 0—4—0 type, had side tanks, straight lipped-top chimneys and open cabs with wood-fuel bunkers. One of them was named *Rhodes*. The smaller type was a typical contractor's 0—4—0, with large conical spark-arrester chimney, a roof on four supports for a cab and a large oil lamp, and hauled a square domestic water tank mounted on a four-wheel bogie to maintain water supplies on its journey to the railhead.

Initially the wagons used for carrying rails, sleepers and so forth were mainly of the platform design or timber bogies of the bolster type, the bogies being connected with adjustable chains. Hook and link couplings of the Norwegian type were fitted but there was no brake equipment on wagons and only screw hand brakes on the passenger carriages which later came into service.

Work began from Fontesvilla in September 1892 and by the end of November fourteen miles of earthworks were complete and two and a half miles of rail had been run out for platelaying to commence. At this time one locomotive and seven trucks were in use. At Fontesvilla, thirty-six miles of permanent way had already been stacked in addition to 1,700 tons more being discharged at Beira into lighters. A good start had therefore been made but this was before the onset of the rains and floods which, with the inevitable fever, were to cause so much trouble later.

However, the first contract to 75-mile peg was completed in October 1893. This was a remarkable achievement by Lawley as, after traversing the swampy plains during the wet season, he faced a severe climb over the range of hills covered by the dense Amatongas forest. In the last twenty-five miles before reaching the 75-mile peg, the altitude rose from 650ft above sea level to 2,029ft.

The climb through the forest was a succession of curves and in one part the rise could only be surmounted by a series of zigzags into dead-end spurs, with the train having to reverse direction at each halt. With trees rising 200 to 250ft high, the journey must have been indeed an impressive experience on this miniature railway.

Rhodes visited Beira during the construction and travelled with his friend, Sir Charles Metcalfe, the railway engineer, over the railway works and thence on to Umtali. Soon after, arrangements were made for the next section of line to be built to Chimoio, for which a further £250,000 debentures were issued. Work was begun in June 1894 from the 75-mile peg—much later to become the little township of Gondola and a sub-depot of the present

21

railway—and as the plateau was over 2,000ft above sea level and the tsetse fly belt had been cleared, progress was fairly rapid to Chimoio.

During the rains early in 1894 great difficulty was experienced with flooding where the line crossed the Pungwe flats, while up-country between the railhead and Umtali the waggon transport, hauled by donkeys and oxen, battled over roads which were in a deplorable state. One BR locomotive capsized at the Mutchira river bridge and was out of service for over a month undergoing repairs at Fontesvilla, while at one stage the whole line was only open for seven miles and passengers wishing to go up to the rail terminus had to be conveyed by trolley.

By May the *Umtali Advertiser*, a handwritten duplicated weekly newspaper which had been started in January 1894, reported that 'the railway was now running to 65-mile peg and passengers had come through from Fontesvilla to the 75-mile peg in the day without delay'.

For the extension to Chimoio Lawley arrived on the job with 1,200 men and a further 2,000 labourers were expected soon. By mid-June earthworks were complete to eighty-seven miles, except for a one-mile gap where a 43ft embankment and a deep cutting had to be constructed. This embankment was to take four months but the energetic Lawley arranged to convey a locomotive across the gap so that plate-laying could be continued to Chimoio, by which time the bank would be finished and the line linked.

It is related that in May the railway carried 500 tons of freight, apart from construction material, and that about 400 tons were on hand at the 75-mile peg awaiting road transport. To augment the donkey transport a Mr Jagger sent down from Umtali a traction engine which was capable of hauling four trucks of four tons each at four miles per hour. It had a gauge of 9ft with 18in flanges on the wheels and weighed seven tons. This was in the dry season in July and one wonders what effect this machine had on the already deplorable roads. Unfortunately the *Umtali Advertiser* suspended publication for two months due to the non-arrival of printers' ink so the fate of the traction engine is unknown.

In September 1894 an advertisement appeared to the effect

that the Beira Railway was running a passenger train from 75 miles every Wednesday at 6.30am connecting with the 'mail steamer' (*sic*) at Fontesvilla, while a passenger train left Fontes-villa for 75 miles on the arrival of the mail. The journey time by train is given as 9¼ hours. This announcement was over the name of George Pauling, as the line was being operated by the contractors. Indeed, the Beira Railway was run by Paulings, under contract with the railway company, for the entire life of the narrow gauge and only came under railway management when the gauge had been widened to 3ft 6in and the line linked with the Mashonaland Railway between Umtali and Salisbury in 1900.

In November the newspaper contained a BR notice giving rates and fares. Passengers were charged 6d a mile for first class and 3d a mile for third class, while natives paid 1d a mile. If you were dead it was more expensive, as adult corpses cost 1s a mile and children's 6d. Goods were generally charged 1s per ton a mile, though waggons were 2s, and cycles and prams 1d a mile. The overall cost of goods from Beira to Umtali comprised 12s 6d to £1 per ton from Beira to Fontesvilla, including landing charges, £6 a ton by rail to the terminus, and £6 a ton by road waggon—a total of about £13 a ton.

By the end of November 1894 the railhead had reached Chimoio and this was to remain the terminus for well over two years, so achieving a doubtful fame with the many people en route to Rhodesia who had to alight from trains and make their way on foot or by occasional coach to Umtali. The *Umtali Advertiser*, now typed instead of handwritten, reported under the headline 'Ructions at Chimoio' that 'upon the last rails being laid festivities were the order of the day'. Two platelayers had entered into a competition, firing at bottles, whereupon the commandant called out the native police and ordered that the men be arrested and taken to jail. They objected and 'a general hubbub followed', upon which the police were ordered to fire on the railway workers in the course of which the commandant shot a platelayer named Macdonald through the arm and neck. Macdonald was taken down to 75 miles camp where he died. After the affair the native police threw away their rifles and bolted, together with the commandant and some other Portuguese. Two commandants from Beira and Fontesvilla arrived later to enquire into the matter and some days after, Vasconcellos, the Chimoio commandant, who had shot Macdonald, gave himself up to the Beira police. He was later sentenced and sent to Mozambique for two years, to be followed by a move to Angola to serve the rest of his sentence.

By January 1895 trains were running regularly to Chimoio, two or three a day. A daily passenger train left Fontesvilla at 6.30am reaching Mandegos the same evening and Chimoio early next morning. Passengers were advised to provide themselves with provisions for the journey as with the exception of 75 miles station there were no stores at which to buy food. Apart from the lack of eating facilities the standard of travel on the trains was far from comfortable. Kingsley Fairbridge in his autobiography relates his experiences in 1896 when he travelled first class, for which he had a deck chair in an open truck with a tarpaulin over as shade. 'We saw great herds of game and men fired at them from the open trucks', he writes. 'A herd of zebra raced the train and we all shouted at them. Our train did not run off the rails but most trains did, and then the passengers had to get out and push them back again'.

A vivid account by a young lady, Edith Campbell, who travelled from Beira to Umtali in December 1895, appeared in *Rhodesiana*, 1963. She wrote in a letter home:

Landed at Beira and joined the tug *Kimberley*, which steamed 4 miles up the Pungwe . . . and then anchored for the night. Next morning we went on but came bang on a sandbank where we stuck. Breakfast on the tug cost 3s, eggs, bacon, curry and bread with beer or cold water. Later we went on to Fontesvilla. It is on the right bank and is almost a river in itself. A few houses about 3ft above ground level.

Well we started, ten of us in the carriage. The Beira Railway is a queer-looking concern, very narrow and only a couple of carriages and about three engines. The carriages are long narrow things with hard seats on each side like garden seats and 10 inches wide. The train conveniently slackened off for hunters to shoot at each herd of game. Mr Jansen shot a hartebeeste, cut it up and put it on the train. Then on to the 40-mile peg where we had to wait an hour for the Chimoio down train, so a fire was made, steaks were cooked and we picnicked under a big tree. After beer and canned pears for dessert we went on again through lovely forest . . .

At 60-mile peg at 2 o'clock we came to a dead stop, the engine and first truck had run off the line and were lying gracefully on their sides against some rocks; fortunately our carriage stood up . . . The engine driver jumped off in time and dragged the stoker with him. Then help was sent for up and down the line. Next morning a man came along on a trolley with a basket of meat, some gin and beer . . . We had to wait for another engine . . . From 62-mile peg the line is comical, it is a zigzag on the side of a hill and the train is pushed backwards and forwards to get to the top of the hill. I lived in a funk all along that line . . . At Chimoio a man met us and took me to the hotel.

This hotel was a wood-and-iron building close to the little station at Chimoio. It was described as a 'first-class railway hotel' and was run by J. Lawson & Co, which firm later maintained its railway connection when 'Fatty' Lawson held a contract to operate the original dining-car service before Rhodesia Railways started its own catering department.

Percy Shinn, who many years later was to become the catering superintendent on the railways, was another who entered Rhodesia via the narrow gauge. Arriving at Beira, he left in the charge of Capt Dick, whose tug 'as usual ran us on a sandbank where we remained until the stock of liquor was sold out, then he managed to get off and proceed on his journey'. This practice was understood to be a regular one: rather an ironic experience for a future catering manager! Shinn, who was a Londoner, described Fontesvilla to the author as being a 'city consisting of a few mud huts, each hut fitted up with six canvas stretcher beds, and a kind of eating-house where we got some sort of a meal'. Next morning he joined the train to Chimoio, hauled by a wood-burning engine which stopped frequently to take on fuel. There were two passenger coaches 'exactly the same in appearance as the old tramcars in England with a long seat down each side with one's back to the drop windows, beautifully arranged so that the red hot sparks from the engine could fly in and set your clothes alight. Every now and then someone would smell clothes burning and there would be a general post to find who was alight'.

One point on the line between Fontesvilla and Chimoio was called the 'zigzag' where the train reversed back and forward in the Amatongas forest until it reached the top of the escarpment, after which it went on to Chimoio. From this point Percy Shinn had to carry his food and walk to 'Old' Umtali, as owing to the Mashona rebellion of 1896 and to cattle disease there was no animal transport through to Rhodesia.

With the difficulties of navigation along the Pungwe river coupled with the extra handling of cargo into lighters in the roadstead at Beira and the transhipping at Fontesvilla, it was essential to connect the two places by rail. In 1895 the Beira Junction Railway Co was formed with an authorised capital of £62,500 in 250,000 5s ordinary shares and £125,000 in 600,000 5s 6 per cent cumulative preference shares. Of these 249,993 ordinary shares went to the London & Paris Exploitation Co in payment for the concession to build the railway, while the BSA Co subscribed for 423,583 preference shares to provide funds for the improvement of the wharf accommodation at Beira. In addition, £250,000 of 6 per cent debentures were issued.

Once more the contract was placed with Pauling and work began in July 1895 from Fontesvilla with Lawley in charge. The first job was the erection of a bridge across the Pungwe river from the Fontesvilla side, and this was built of timber, as were all bridges on the line between Beira and Umtali in the early days. It was not considered strong enough to carry the 'heavy' BR locomotives working trains but only light contractors' engines; when the through train service came into being, the practice was for a locomotive to propel a carriage at speed on the approach to the bridge so that it would roll across by itself to the other bank where another engine was waiting to couple up. Crossing the Pungwe flats, with the need for frequent small bridges and culverts to take streams and flood water, slowed the work and the thirty-five miles over almost entirely flat marshy country took fifteen months. It must be remembered that the staff were working under very trying climatic conditions and were constantly falling ill with fever. Lawley himself was absent for a time, since he joined Dr Jameson as an active participant in the abortive

Jameson Raid, which was mounted from near Mafeking against Johannesburg to overthrow President Kruger over the New Year of 1896. Lawley was captured and imprisoned at Pretoria until late in May, when he was released and was able to return to his work for Pauling on the Beira Railway.

Much concern was being felt in Salisbury and Umtali over the delay in extending the railway from Chimoio. George Pauling had been persuaded by Rhodes to take office as commissioner of public works in the administration of Southern Rhodesia—the three areas of Matabeleland, Mashonaland and Manicaland had been joined together—under Dr Jameson as administrator. In his new capacity Pauling was placed in charge of all roads, public buildings and railways, as and when they were constructed, while later he also had mines and posts under his control. Large quantities of imported goods had reached Chimoio by rail and had been dumped for clearance by donkey waggon, as owing to an intervening flybelt oxen could not work down from Umtali. No news could be obtained by the general public of the extension of the line and neither Rhodes nor Jameson was available.

In March 1896 the Matabele had rebelled and it was realised by Rhodes that it was essential to complete the line and so give Mashonaland access from the sea. A third issue of Beira Railway debentures for £600,000 was created in 1896 and this enabled a contract to be placed with Pauling & Co for the remainder of the line from Chimoio up to Umtali, a matter of sixty-eight miles, the work beginning in May.

In June 1896 the situation worsened with the Mashona uprising, which led to over one hundred settlers in the outlying districts being killed at their farms or mines. The unsettled conditions caused a shortage of native labour on the railway construction from Chimoio, although this did not affect the extension to Beira. This was completed in October 1896 and the railway concentrated much of its effort on moving food, mules and waggons for Mashonaland, as well as permanent-way material for the last section to Umtali. The ordinary trains on the Beira—Fontesvilla section were now covering the thirty-five miles in $2\frac{3}{4}$ hours, hauling eight to ten trucks with a total capacity of some fifty tons per train. A weekly passenger train left Beira at 5am and arrived at Chimoio, all being well, at about 10.30pm the same day. By the end of 1896 the Beira Railway possessed twenty locomotives and 140 trucks, a batch of new Falcon-built 4–4–0 engines having just arrived.

About this time Lawley had decided on Mandegos (now Vila Pery) as the most suitable point at which to establish a locomotive depot. It was roughly half-way from Beira to Umtali at an altitude of 2,300ft and so climatically suited to working and living conditions for the staff. A repair shed with four engine roads was erected and equipped with the essentials, while a triangle was installed for the turning of locomotives. A photograph of the time shows four Falcon built 4—4—0 tender engines standing outside this shed ready for the road, it being noticeable how well polished the crews kept their engines. The green boiler barrels and the tenders were lined with dark green, and yellow or gold, as were some front buffer beams on which the engine numbers were painted in most instances. Stacks of wood fuel were conveniently piled for loading and gave a generally efficient impression. The wood-and-iron building with its glazed windows is particularly interesting, as about 1905, long after the narrow-gauge line had been replaced, the structure was dismantled and removed to Victoria Falls where it became the dining-hall of the railway hotel.

Beira, too, had acquired a small locomotive shed with but two tracks and a picture shows BR locomotive no 1 standing outside with a group of enginemen and fitters. In another view a very small wood-and-iron station building is seen with a lean-to verandah and oil lamps affixed to the roof uprights. Across the four tracks—three occupied by trains—is a goods shed with narrow platform for loading, while in the background one can discern the bridge across the Chiveve creek with the sheds of the 'Customs' wharf through which much of the imports passed.

By 1896 the T-shaped lighterage pier had been constructed at Beira running out some 250ft into the stream of the Pungwe. On the cross-section three small steam cranes were mounted for off-loading the lighters and loading the cargo into railway wagons, which were shunted along the pier by a small tank engine. It is believed that these cranes were later moved to the new wharves constructed nearer the bridge over the Chiveve creek.

In August 1897 platelaying had reached Macequece (now named Vila de Manica) and refreshment rooms were opened for the passengers arriving at this temporary terminus. The announcement in November that two 'mail' trains weekly were now running was greeted in the Umtali newspaper with 'Bravo, Mr. Lawley!'

Travel comfort had been much improved by the new first-class carriages which Paulings had put into service. These new BR coaches were compartment stock with cushioned seating for four passengers in each section and the old 'tramcar' type carriages were relegated to the third class. While comfort was better a journey could still be full of incident, such as occurred one day in December 1897. The mail train suddenly stopped and all passengers were warned to get out as fast as possible and seek shelter behind the nearest trees as the boiler of the locomotive was about to blow up. Apparently the boiler changed its mind but refused to produce movement by the engine, and it became necessary to get three following goods trains to push the mail into the nearest siding. Here much confusion ensued for some hours (relates the apocryphal story) while the trains were shunted on the crossing loop 'until they could be disentangled from one another and the engine of one of them coupled on to the mail train!'

At Macequece the contractors were faced with the ascent of the second escarpment with a rise in altitude of some 1,200ft in the last twenty miles into Umtali by devious curves, among the towering mountain ranges broken by passes and rushing streams. When the last portion of the rail route was surveyed by Paulings it had been found that the then site of Umtali would be off the main route to Salisbury via the Odzi river, and would have to be served by a branch line. George Pauling recounts that this was essential because a line via Umtali would have needed very heavy and costly work, including a tunnel through the hill crossed by Christmas Pass. In discussion with Rhodes, Pauling suggested that the solution was to move the township of Umtali and lay it out on the site of the present town which was suitably placed for the railway line. At a public meeting attended by Rhodes and Pauling the owners of sites and houses were offered corresponding sites in the new Umtali and given the option of being paid for their existing houses or háving similar buildings put up, free of cost, in the new township. After some discussion this was accepted by the owners of property, and Pauling, with surveyors, selected the site of New Umtali, the present town, with the result that many buildings, mainly wood and iron, were dismantled and re-erected in time for the arrival of the railway.

By early 1898 platelaying had reached Umtali and on 4 February amidst considerable rejoicing the first material train steamed into the station site. This train of open wagons was hauled by one of Paulings' side-tank engines with a tender containing a domestic water tank. The engine was well decorated with flags, branches of flowering shrubs and a slogan 'Now We Shan't Be Long—to Cairo' as it puffed in slowly amid the cheers of a crowd of citizens. Speeches followed but the arrival was informal as it had been decided to hold a Railway Celebrations Week in April. By 16 February the first goods train had arrived and next day seventeen passengers alighted from the first mail train.

The arrival of the railway at Umtali achieved fame with a cartoon in *Punch* on 29 January 1898, which depicted a thatch rondavel as ticket office and a station sign reading 'UMTALI—Change for Rum-Tum-Tali'. The passengers and staff were all shown as Africans of the 'Coal Black Mammy' type.

In an inspection tour about this time Rhodes had recommended that a deviation be constructed in the Amatongas area to eliminate the zig-zag section, which had caused much delay, and the Mashonaland Railway Co's board agreed to meet half the cost of the £5,000 needed for the job. It had already been foreseen that the 2ft gauge line must soon be widened to 3ft 6in as the Mashonaland Railway from Umtali to Salisbury was to be constructed to this gauge to conform with the line already open to Bulawayo from the south. During the same visit Rhodes entered into an agreement to lease the railway refreshment-room at Umtali to Douglas Hudson for two years at a monthly rental of £25. This shows the keen attention of Rhodes to the details of 'his' railways; though not on the board of the Beira Railway he was a director of the newly-formed Mashonaland Railway and was chairman of the Bechuanaland Railway, later to be re-named Rhodesia Railways Ltd.

With the arrival of the line at Umtali no time was lost in transferring workshops, housing and other buildings from Fontesvilla and elsewhere so as to concentrate activities at Umtali. The *Rhodesia Herald* in April 1898 complained that all public traffic had been held up over several days because all trucks were needed for the transfer of Paulings' buildings and plant to their depot at Umtali for the extension of the railway to Salisbury. In the meantime Umtali was determined to have a week of festivities to celebrate the arrival of the railway and a programme of banquets, dances, cricket matches, rifle club events, Caledonian sports, a fancy dress ball and so forth was arranged. The administrator, the Portuguese governor of Manica, A. L. Lawley and his assistants were among those attending some of the functions and doubtless a good time was had by all.

Despite the start made at Fontesvilla as far back as September 1892, the Beira Railway reached Umtali only in February 1898 and thus failed by little more than three months to gain the honour of being the first railway in Rhodesia. This had already been won in October 1897, as the line from Mafeking had been rushed north by Pauling in a record-breaking construction achievement, to alleviate the difficulties of the settlers in Matabeleland who had been faced with the rinderpest outbreak following on the 1896 Matabele rebellion. But railway construction through Bechuanaland had been an easy matter compared with the struggle with floods, fever and mountains met on the way from the coast to Umtali.

In a Beira Railway directors' report of 1898 it is learned that the whole line from Beira 'to the British frontier' was leased to Pauling & Co Ltd for a term of two years at £60,000 per annum. The rolling stock taken over at this time by Paulings consisted of seventeen engines, two first-class and six third-class carriages, ninety open and covered wagons, eighteen pairs of timber trucks

31

(bolster type), nine brake vans, nine 15 ton platform wagons, eleven 'horse boxes' and 150 trucks described as 'various'. It is stated that twenty-eight engines had since been sent out to meet the requirements of the increased traffic, which gives a total of forty-five locomotives. As there is no record of a no 45, it is possible that one unit was used as a replacement for a damaged or scrapped engine.

The carriages provided in the early days of the railway were quite comfortless, being of the open tramcar type with hard seats. Access was gained through centre doors from the open balcony end, with its wrought-iron railings and swing gates, while a metal flap could be lowered over the couplings to enable a passenger to move from one carriage to another. Drop windows and venetian blinds were provided and a water tank with drinking water was installed at one end. The body framing, panels and mouldings were of teak, and the roof was double, with sun screens hanging down over the upper part of the windows. All carriages were carried on two four-wheeled bogies with steel coil springs. The drawgear was the Norwegian type central draw and buffer with hook and link coupling, while two safety chains were fitted at each end of the vehicles. Oil roof lamps were fitted and roof ventilators.

The open-type carriages were originally used for first-class passengers, the third class being conveyed in wagons. Later, when the first-class compartment carriages were placed in service late in 1897, the old coaches were allotted to third-class passengers. One of the first-class carriages is depicted in a delightful photograph of a train standing in a siding with a group of passengers in Victorian attire, their thick voluminous clothes being singularly inappropriate for travel in this tropical climate. These side-door carriages had three compartments large enough for six passengers apiece; but they could only sit up, as the width was insufficient for lying down. The seats and backs were upholstered with buffalo hide and stuffed with horsehair, while the interior finish was generally of better standard.

On the waist panels 'BEIRA RAILWAY' was painted, with 'FIRST' on each door. The third-class carriages, however, had a large '3' placed on the centre lower panel.

All the trucks had wooden bodies, the covered wagons having either wood or corrugated iron roofs, though it was found that wooden roofs were susceptible to fire caused by sparks from the wood-burning engines. Bolster wagons were in constant use carrying rails and baulks of timber for railway bridges, often with sheets of iron and large piping for culverts perched on top to obtain maximum use of the trucks. Unusual loads must have been the 3ft 6in gauge locomotives imported from Cape Town via Beira for the Mashonaland Railway construction, which had to be carried over the narrow-gauge line to be erected at Umtali in 1898. Later on, carriages for the Mashonaland line were shipped out from England in packing cases and it is related that, owing to the size of the zinc-lined cases, it took five days to get them up to Umtali as many of the railway cuttings had to be widened.

Early in 1898 a narrow-gauge private saloon, described as a 'Pullman' car, was brought into use for the frequent journeys of Mr Lawley, 'It contained a bed, table, couch, bath and lavatory and was fitted up in a most luxurious manner', wrote the *Rhodesia Herald,* 'and to anyone who is in constant habit of having to run up to Umtali, a carriage of this description is a necessity'. Though there is no mention of a kitchen, it would seem certain that some form of ice-box was installed for food and liquor to sustain Lawley and his colleagues on their line tours. Unfortunately, no photograph of this early private saloon is known to exist.

Although the Beira Railway did not reach Umtali until February 1898, the whole line had been leased to Pauling & Co for a period of two years from 30 September 1897. To conform with Portuguese law, the railway had to establish a general manager's office in the Mozambique Territory and this was arranged at Beira. Mr A. L. Lawley thereupon became general manager and all notices were issued over his name. A. M. Moore was his chief assistant and George Brand was the traffic manager, while A. E. Wainwright was locomotive supervisor.

In June 1898 Lawley issued a book of *Rules and Regulations to be observed by All Persons in the Service of the Beira Railway Company,* which consisted of forty-eight pages in a booklet sized

3½in by 4½in and printed by the Beira Post Printing & Publishing Co at Beira, East Africa. The copy seen by the author was no 110 issued to Allan Bowes, '1st Class Driver', who bound himself to observe and obey the rules and regulations 'which I have read (or heard read) and understand, and all others that may from time to time be issued for the better government of the Railway', and this had to be signed in the presence of a witness. It is interesting to note that Allan Bowes, who was a driver on the narrow gauge, later rose to be senior locomotive inspector of Rhodesia Railways and retired in 1930. No details are given of the method of train working but drivers were required to have an order before starting from a station and it can thus be assumed that a telegraph order system was used. The speed of trains passing over facing points was not to exceed 4mph, while engines running tender-first on the main line were limited to 8mph. It is probable that the maximum speed was about 20mph.

With good progress being made on the 3ft 6in gauge Mashonaland Railway to Salisbury it soon became apparent that the change of gauge at Umtali entailed serious delay and expense in transhipping goods, while the narrow gauge itself limited the quantity of traffic that could be handled efficiently. In March 1899 a cable from Rhodes brought the news to Umtali that he had arranged a contract for widening the gauge of the Beira Railway for the full 222 miles. For this work £900,000 in 5 per cent first mortgage debentures at 95 per cent guaranteed by the Chartered Company were issued and the contract was placed with Paulings. As well as widening, it entailed realignment to ease the worst of the heavy gradients.

In May 1899 Duncan Bailey of the Gloucester Carriage Co travelled out from England to inspect some carriages supplied to the Mashonaland Railway and he has related his experiences of the Beira Railway in extracts from his diary, which he handed to the author. On Beira itself he wrote:

> The roads were all sand, with tram rails about 20in gauge running along on which the boys pushed trucks and little trollies. In places there were footholds of asphalt. It was nearly all canteens; the only business places were the shipping and railway

office and the bank. The post office was a dirty little wooden crib. The only lights were wax candles, stuck in their own grease on the desk. The stamps, having no gum, had to be stuck on by the sender. In the middle of the town was a creek, which was a large sheet of swampy water. I cannot describe the flatness of this part; one could see nothing at any distance.

The railway shops were very fair, with a concrete floor. Almost the first thing I saw was a coffin lying in the road, and one day I saw three funerals. A very unhealthy place owing to malaria—the insurance company at Home would not insure my life.

Such was the reputation of Beira in England, and in view of the high death rate among the railway construction staff it is no wonder. Duncan Bailey set out from his 'hotel' to catch the Saturday train to Umtali and noted:

At 6am I got down to Beira station signboard—I say signboard because I did not know I was at the station until I was told. The express mail train was due to leave at 8am and it left at 8.25. The train consisted of nine wagons, seven full of coal (on top of which the black boys sat), one with timber, and a covered wagon full of cases of whisky. Behind were two carriages and a brake van. There was only one class (1st Class) or riding in open wagons. The gauge was 2ft but it varied an inch or so in places.

Over the 30 miles up to Bamboo Creek the country was nothing but swamps. . . . When the Siluvu hills are reached, right up 4,000ft to Umtali the scenery is magnificent, the little railway winding over gorges and through lovely valleys. There were few bridges, but one I noticed was of timber, the sleepers being about 3ft apart with nothing between them, and the rails held on with nails in places.

In the carriage in which I travelled, marked 1st class, the cushions were all to pieces, and a panel out here and there. The sparks (which at night were a sight in the forests as the engines burnt coal and wood) came through the cracks in the carriage roof, and it was a marvel how the vehicles kept the rails.

About every hour the train stopped for water at tanks, or for wood, which was kept in heaps along the line. At 12.30 noon there was a jolting and a stop. We got out and I heard from a driver that he and his mate, taking a goods train on one trip, went back three-quarters of a mile to shoot some buck, and nearly all drivers carried a gun.

At this stop we found the front wagon off the line with three axle-boxes broken to bits. The lifting jack was tried but was no good, so the engine was sent on six miles to fetch some boys and water. When they returned in about 1½ hours they unloaded the truck of whisky, put it on the veldt, turned the wagon clean over on its side, and we proceeded after a stop of two hours. We were now in the dark as there was no oil in the roof lamp. At about 12.30 midnight we stopped at Mandegos until about 8.15 next morning. The carriages were not wide enough for a fellow to stretch out his legs, so I leave you to imagine how nice they were to sleep in.

Next day when it was light Bailey found they were on a siding with a few corrugated shanties about, so he went to the Railway Hotel for a wash, fortunately taking a towel and soap.

> Then I had breakfast or at least I tried to eat it, but no go. I gulped down something which I believe was coffee. At 8.15 we restarted, and at 12 noon we stopped and found the front van of timber on fire. This was put out and again we proceeded, reaching Umtali at 3pm. The last 20 miles or so was grand but awful, as the little train rushed round terrible curves just on the edge of steep banks and over rough bridges, which were simply wooden piles with the sleepers laid on, with no ballast or hand-railing, and being hardly as wide as the carriages. Food on the way for four of us consisted of a pot of jam, tins of sardines and German sausage, and lemonade to drink. This little lot, which we had in a box, cost 40s or more.

Such were the impressions of a man used to rail travel in England, but who had never experienced a pioneer railway in 'Darkest Africa' before. When at the age of ninety he chatted with the author, Bailey's journey to Umtali was still vivid in his memory. He had then been head of Charles Roberts & Co, Horbury, for many years, a firm which built many wagons for RR.

Travel over the narrow-gauge Beira Railway was therefore quite a thrilling experience, especially for new arrivals from Britain who described it as a 'toy' railway, as undoubtedly it must have seemed to those used to the British 4ft 8½in gauge or who recalled the famous Great Western Railway's 7ft gauge which had only disappeared as recently as 1892. On the Beira Railway one was lucky to travel in a carriage instead of riding in an open wagon sitting in a deck chair. The latter method gave passengers a much better view of the wild animals and scenery than those cooped up in the small carriages, even though one stood the risk of being set on fire by the sparks from the wood-burning engine. Stops were frequent, for the locomotive to replenish its fuel and water because of the small-capacity tenders, but at these stopping-places gangs of natives were trained to load the cut timber quickly from the large wayside stacks, while overhead tanks held the water supply, being re-filled by well water hand-pumped by natives. The stations were small corrugated iron buildings with a covered verandah and were linked to each other by a two-wire telegraph line on iron poles, which were convenient scratching posts for the elephants in the neighbourhood with disastrous effects on communications for train working messages and so forth.

In the latter part of 1899 the BR had forty locomotives at work, with six trains a day leaving Beira for Bamboo Creek where the loads were split in two for the heavily-graded climb to Umtali. At this time the mail train timetable was:

Mileage	Station or Siding	Arr	Dep	Days
0	Beira		8.00	Wednesdays & Saturdays
18	Dondo	9.40	9.41	
36	Fontesvilla	11.16	11.30	
61	Bamboo Creek	2.00	3.15	
75	Siluvu Hills	4.45	4.46	
85	Inchope	5.36	5.45	
95	Amatongas	7.00	7.05	
116	Mananjebas	8.50	9.00	
129	Gondola	10.05	10.16	
144	Mandegos	11.30		
			8.00	Thursdays & Sundays
154	Chimoio	8.49	8.50	
169	Vandusi	10.04	10.05	
184	Revue	11.20	11.35	
200	Macequece	12.55	1.00	
	Menini	1.54	1.55	
222	Umtali	3.00		

Over the years, several of these names have been changed. Fontesvilla became Ponte do Pungwe, Bamboo Creek was re-named Vila Machado in tribute to the distinguished Portuguese administrator, General Sir Joachim José Machado, KCMG, Mandegos became Vila Pery, while Mananjebas disappeared when the gauge widening and deviations took the new line through Maforga. In more recent years Macequece has become Vila de Manica.

Paulings leased the railway from October 1897 at a rent of £60,000 a year, with a half-share of net profits if they exceeded £40,000. Traffic over the BR in 1895 had averaged £250 a month for passengers and about £3,000 a month for goods traffic, say £39,000 for the year. In 1896 it had risen to £69,000 for the year and in 1897 the first four months brought in £8,400 a month, of which £1,150 was from passengers, giving a total of £100,800 for the full year. Figures for the last two years of the narrow gauge are unfortunately not available, so that one cannot assess the success of the contract Pauling had entered into with the railway company, but it was during this period that the peak traffic occurred with the movement of troops and equipment from the port to Umtali.

For the 222-mile journey from Beira to Umtali the fares were £6 for European passengers and 30s for natives. The ordinary goods tariff was £11 per ton, which compared very well with the cost of cartage by waggon at £27 15s per ton in the pre-railway days when transit time was indefinite and damage en route was frequent.

In the meantime Lawley, who was already busy on the construction of the line to Salisbury, had been deputed by Pauling to carry out the widening of the Beira line and work was begun at once on re-surveying the route. The actual relaying of the line to the wider gauge was started from the Umtali end, so linking with the 3ft 6in line to Salisbury, which had been completed in May 1899. The first forty miles to near Revue were open by November and this meant that one of the two difficult escarpment sections had been completed. A month before, the South African War had broken out, and with the encirclement of Mafeking the railway from the Cape to Bulawayo, opened in 1897, had been cut and Rhodesia was isolated from the south.

Meanwhile, apart from widening the gauge, work had been

proceeding on the replacement of the temporary wooden bridges by steel girder structures. These wooden bridges were susceptible to fire from sparks from the engines, and were not sufficiently strong or wide to take the 3ft 6in track. For the Pungwe river crossing a new steel girder bridge was being built by Wm Arrol & Co at a cost of £30,000, and with its completion the practice of propelling carriages by a 'fly shunt' across the bridge came to an end.

Work was in full swing with the gauge conversion when Lawley and his staff were faced with the decision of the British government to attack the Transvaal, and so to protect Rhodesia with a force of 5,000 troops to be landed at Beira and moved inland by rail. For some unknown reason Bamboo Creek was chosen as the concentration point for the British, Australian and Canadian troops together with their horses and equipment, and a more unsuitable place could hardly have been selected. Notorious for fever, it was surrounded by tropical vegetation, and there were many wild animals in the area. All in all, the influx of this military force at a time when the contractors were striving to complete the gauge widening was not a happy move by the imperial government. Between March and July 1900 Lawley, by superhuman effort, managed to move over the combined narrow and widened lines between Beira and Umtali, en route to Marandellas, a total of over 5,000 troops under General Carrington, with 14,000 tons of military stores, guns and ammunition and 10,000 horses, mules and cattle. While this military traffic was passing, the Beira Railway also had to cope with civil supplies for Rhodesia and with a high tonnage of construction material for widening the line. High praise must be paid to Lawley and the railway staff for coping with this peak traffic over the narrow gauge at a time when the conversion to 3ft 6in gauge was in progress and the point of transhipment was being changed. However, the wide gauge was opened from Umtali to Bamboo Creek in April 1900 and, but for the military traffic, the remaining sixty-one mile section to Beira would have been finished before 1 August when Paulings handed over the completed job to the Mashonaland Railway Administration, which then assumed full responsibility for the management and operation of the whole line between Beira and Salisbury.

By July 1900 Lawley and his staff had moved the great bulk of General Carrington's troops and supplies, and Lawley decided that he would convert the remaining section from Bamboo Creek to Beira from narrow to standard gauge in a matter of a few days, so that no delay would occur to the rest of the military forces. The last sixty miles were divided into three 20-mile sections and gangs allotted to the job. The last narrow-gauge train left Beira on a Thursday morning and after its passage the gangs fell to. It was a simple job to lift and throw clear the light 2ft-gauge track but there were a number of bridges to be re-timbered. The gangs worked well and by sleeping out at the trackside for a few hours each night converted the line through from Beira to 40-mile peg by Sunday morning. In a final spurt the last section was linked by sundown and H. F. Varian tells of the junction at 42 miles, after which the first train slowly passed over the new line. Varian was on an open wagon propelled by the little tank engine *Jack Tar* with Lawley and another standing beside him. With frequent stops to distribute food and drink from the carriage behind the engine, the train made its way to Beira, reaching there later in the evening to be greeted by a large crowd and as much noise as possible from rockets loosed off by ships, dynamite sticks in empty bully beef tins and the yelling of thousands of natives, dancing round the station area.

Next morning, 1 August, an official inaugural train headed by one of the two Mashonaland Railway 4–6–0 main-line engines, decorated with the Union Jack and the flag of Portugal, and hauling a couple of carriages, steamed into Beira again to be received by a large crowd, ready for further enthusiastic celebrations. So the widening of the line to provide a direct unbroken link between the port of Beira and Salisbury was completed by another piece of sterling work by Lawley and his team of Pauling's pioneering engineers and contract workers.

As some reward for their outstanding work, the records of the British South Africa Company show that grants of land for farms were made to various members of the Beira Railway construction staff. Lawley was granted 1,500 morgen in the Marandellas district, while other 1,500 morgen 'farms' along the Umtali—Salisbury line were given to Messrs. A. M. Moore (engineer), P. St G. Mansergh (surveyor), F. Buchan (accountant) and eight others. Most of these men continued to work with Pauling and Lawley on the further railway contracts in Rhodesia which over the years carried the line right up to the Congo.

These grants of land were, of course, at the instructions of Rhodes in appreciation of these pioneer railway contractors. Lawley's first meeting with Rhodes is related by George Pauling, who tells of the peculiarly high-pitched voice affected by Rhodes when he became excited or intensely interested in anything. This first meeting with Lawley was during the construction of the line from Beira to Umtali, when the coach conveying Rhodes and his party arrived three days later than expected, which seems to have affected the temper of the great man. Without any warning Rhodes began to swear and abuse Lawley in front of his staff, his voice rising with the flow of language to a high falsetto note. Lawley thereupon asked Rhodes to say who the hell he thought he was, and told him, in a flood of railway vernacular, not to squeal liked a damned rabbit. Rhodes, astonished at Lawley's unexpected daring, walked off, but returned to enter the train at the last minute as it was pulling off. At a stop for water, Rhodes sent Dr Jameson with an invitation to Lawley to join him in his compartment and upon his doing so, Rhodes, who had calmed down, expressed his regret and asked Lawley to shake hands. From then on Rhodes and Lawley remained the best of friends.

Lawley's close association with George Pauling continued for many years of railway contracting in Rhodesia and later, with the construction of the Trans-Zambesia Railway, was to provide a link between the Beira Railway and Nyasaland (now Malawi). Lawley devoted much of his spare time to Beira, where he established various interests and became known as 'The King of Beira'. One of these ventures was the Savoy Hotel, which became a well-known rendezvous for residents and visitors, with Lawley presiding over parties which he regaled with yarns of the old days. He was a man with a very generous nature, having many acts of kindness to his credit. In one instance a young widow was left in poor circumstances and when her home was sold up in Beira Lawley bought most of the furniture at very much higher prices than it would normally have fetched. Lawley eventually retired to England, where he died at the age of seventy-four. The Savoy Hotel was purchased in 1930, after his death, by the Beira Railway Co and was operated by the railway catering department until 1949.

When the work of widening the narrow gauge was completed, most of the 2ft-gauge rolling stock was stored in sidings close to Bamboo Creek station and was drawn upon over the years for use on other railways. A batch of the Falcon-built 4–4–0 tender engines remained there with grass growing out of the chimneys until 1915 when there was a sudden demand from the South African Railways for narrow-gauge locomotives following the occupation of German South-West Africa. Lawley took the opportunity to sell thirteen of these old Beira Railway engines to the SAR and after rehabilitation nine of them went into service on various lines in South Africa. They became the NG6 class but were always known on the SAR as 'Lawleys' during their service.

Some of the narrow-gauge track was recovered from the old line and in June 1900 the Salisbury Town Council received an offer from a Mr W. C. Coward of the Beira Railway to lay down a tramway system in Salisbury for which he proposed to utilise the old rails, though he admitted that some of them would be twisted owing to the careless way in which they had been thrown into the veld. It is stated that the letter caused some amusement but the council decided against constructing a tramway. In Umtali however, the need for local transport was recognised and narrow-gauge track was used for what turned out to be the only tramway company ever to operate in Rhodesia. It was constructed in 1898 and a four-wheeled 'toast-rack' type tram drawn by a pair of mules provided a service for passengers from the railway station up the main street to the centre of the township, but its chief purpose was the carriage of goods from the railway sheds to the shops and business premises. Flat-topped wagons were used and hauled up the tramway line, an easier method than cartage over the indifferent roadway. To the youngsters of the day it was a joy to 'borrow' the empty wagons and coast down the main street on them to the station area. This tramway was discontinued in 1920.

CHAPTER TWO

The Link with the Cape

RAILWAYS ranked high in Cecil Rhodes' vision for opening up and developing the interior of 'The Dark Continent', and it was from Cape Colony, after his success at Kimberley with the diamond mines, that he planned his thrust to the north. He visualised the linking of Africa with Europe and the rest of the world through ports on the south, east and west coasts, to be followed by a vast expansion of trade and commerce in which communications would be the keynote. A 'Cape-to-Cairo' railway was paramount in his thoughts and, while this was never to be, a trans-continental telegraph system was achieved.

The Cape Government Railway system had reached Kimberley in 1885 with the progressive extension of the Cape Town—De Aar line, and urged on by Rhodes, who had formed the British South Africa Company to develop Bechuanaland and the Mashona and Matabele territories to the north, a railway was put in hand in 1889 from Kimberley to British Bechuanaland. This 127-mile line, which was constructed by the British South Africa Company, crossed the Vaal river at Fourteen Streams and ran on from the then Cape Colony border to Vryburg (then in British Bechuanaland), which was reached in December 1890. On completion, it was purchased and became part of the Cape Government Railways.

During this period much was happening in the north. Lobengula, king of the Matabele, had entered into a peace treaty with Great Britain in 1888, the Rhodes-Rudd Concession covering all mineral rights was granted by Lobengula in the same year, and a Royal Charter had been obtained by the British South Africa Company over the territories later to form Rhodesia. The Pioneer Column organised by Rhodes left Macloutsie, in Northern Bechuanaland, and reached Salisbury in Mashonaland in September 1890 to add that territory to the British Empire. A treaty was signed soon after with the paramount chief of Manicaland to incorporate his territory to the east of Mashonaland. Thus it was that European settlement came to Central Africa as another step in the plan by Rhodes to expand the Empire farther north.

Meanwhile Sir Charles Metcalfe, Bart, who was a partner with Sir Douglas Fox, a leading consultant engineer in London, had persuaded Rhodes to extend the Bechuanaland Railway from Vryburg to Mafeking. Metcalfe and Rhodes had been together at Oxford where they had formed a lasting friendship, and this experienced engineer had given Rhodes much useful advice on many of his projects. The Bechuanaland Railway Co had been formed in London in May 1893 with the backing of the British South Africa Co and, with Cecil Rhodes as chairman, had asked George Pauling to go over the route and tender for the construction of the ninety-six miles of line. Pauling relates that he had some differences with Metcalfe as to the price, but eventually Pauling signed a contract at midnight after a dinner in Cape Town at which Metcalfe and he were the guests of Rhodes. Work was begun in May 1893 and this line was of special significance to Pauling as being the first section of the Rhodesian railway system, with the construction of which he was to have such close connections over the many years to follow.

Mafeking was reached and the line opened in October 1894. To the surprise of Rhodes this line paid well from the first—it had brought the Cape railhead nearly one hundred miles closer to Bulawayo—but Metcalfe could not at first induce Rhodes to go further, although the settlers in Matabeleland were clamouring for rail communication with the coast. Rhodes at that time was concerned with the route from Beira to serve Salisbury and all his financial efforts were devoted to that for a time. However, on 3 August 1894 an agreement was signed by Alfred Beit and

Rochfort Maguire on behalf of the Bechuanaland Railway with the Crown Agents for the Colonies and the governor of British Bechuanaland for the construction of a railway from Mafeking to Palapye and this was confirmed by proclamation no 227 BB on 21 October 1895, shortly to be followed by another proclamation covering construction from Palapye to the northern border of the Bechuanaland Protectorate, now Botswana.

The ninety-six miles of line from Vryburg to Mafeking were of easy construction and boasted at that time a stretch of straight line thirty-three miles long, from a siding named Paradise—possibly so named by the overjoyed engineer surveying the route—this being then the second longest piece of straight line in South Africa. Most of the route was on high plateau, devoid of bush but excellent for stock raising and grain, and was to become popular with farm settlers. From Maribogo through Kraaipan and Maritzani the country was undulating with occasional seasonal rivers which gave trouble when in flood. Kraaipan was later to become historic as being the scene of the first shot fired during the Boer War in 1899 when on 12 October an armoured pilot engine was derailed by the Boers and the British occupants of the ammunition train taken prisoner.

Late in 1895, finance having been arranged, work was begun by Pauling on the construction of the line from Mafeking for the first hundred miles northwards. At the start this work must have been carried out in a somewhat leisurely manner in contrast with Pauling's much speedier construction later on when, as a result of the Matabele rebellion and the ravages of the rinderpest among the cattle, Rhodes pressed for a rapid finish to the job. Pauling had placed his cousin, Harold Pauling, in charge of the contract and he carried out George's promise to Rhodes that the last four hundred miles to Bulawayo would be built in four hundred days. The first section, that from Mafeking to Mochudi, 123 miles, was opened to traffic on 1 March 1897, and from there the remainder of the line was built with extraordinary energy: Mochudi to Palapye, 136 miles, opened on 1 July 1897; Palapye to Francistown, 101½ miles, on 1 September 1897; and Francistown to Bulawayo, 122 miles, on 4 November 1897.

Actually the line had reached the outskirts of Bulawayo on 19 October, when at about three o'clock in the afternoon the first train arrived behind a CGR engine. This construction train consisted of four open trucks, a cattle truck and a saloon conveying Mr and Mrs Harold Pauling, their two daughters, Charles Buchan and R. B. Carnegie, while some of Harold Pauling's horses, timber and other materials were carried in the trucks. The locomotive was gaily decorated with bunting and greenery, while the slogan 'Advance Rhodesia' surmounted by a plaque with the arms of the British South Africa Company was placed across the front of the engine. This plaque had been prepared by Edward Rosher, a young engineer who had been engaged on the survey for the line from the Tati river, near Francistown, to Bulawayo. He has told the author how construction of the formation of the line was often only a day behind him in his surveying and pegging the actual route; such was the speed of work in the later stages. Streams had been crossed by the erection of 'birdcage' or trestle bridges of timber, while the wider rivers, which usually have dry sand beds, except when flowing, were crossed by temporary low-level deviations of the line as can be seen in an illustration. This shows a train crossing the Shashi river with the track partially under water and overturned trucks lying some distance from the line where they had been swept by a previous sudden rise in the river. As the approaches to these low-level river crossings were often on a short 1 in 25 grade, the train's negotiation of a track partly submerged was an adventure for the passengers. (Picture, p 84.)

A missionary at Palapye in 1897 has recorded in his recollections that 'the principal bridges were not built when the rails reached Bulawayo; the train simply ran down the river bank, crossed the sandy bottom, and climbed up the other side as best it could. This switchback arrangement provided a little excitement for those of us who happened to be in the train—we always expected that the train would have to be taken up the bank in penny numbers—but it rarely happened that the carriages had to be uncoupled'. An illustration in his book shows Palapye station as being a small wood-and-iron building raised well up from the ground in very bare veld surroundings. A surprising feature was

47

that home signals were provided as protection at each end of the station. A mixed train of eleven short trucks, four carriages and a van was standing in the station headed by a brass-domed CGR 4–4–0 engine with a six-wheel tender.

Harold Pauling had concentrated on getting the line open to Bulawayo as quickly as he could, leaving the 'frills' to be built at leisure. For the wide rivers, such as the Tati, Shashi and Mahalapye, masons had to be recruited to construct the stone-work piers and buttresses for the steel girder bridges and it was well into 1898 before the bridges were completed. Cranes and boilers for air compressors were erected on the sandy river bed during the dry season and trucks of granite for the piers were shunted down a siding for convenient offloading and for the masons to cut and trim the stone, while bird-caging with wooden sleepers was put up for the launching of the steel spans from pier to pier. The granite for all the bridges was quarried near Plumtree.

The line from Vryburg to Mafeking was laid with recovered CGR 45lb rail on steel sleepers, but from Mafeking northwards 60lb track was installed, except for the last seven miles into Bulawayo for which 45lb was used, as the stock of 60lb had been exhausted. This section was relayed with 60lb rail in 1898. The Cape Government Railways undertook the operation of the new railway as it was handed over in sections by Paulings; and in July 1897 a CGR advertisement referred to the direct route to Mata-beleland, Mashonaland and Barotseland, opening on 1 July, and offering 'Cape Town to Bulawayo in 5½ days' with the following fares:

Cape Town to Palapye by rail 1st Class	£13	10s	0d
2nd Class	£8	16s	10d
Palapye to Bulawayo by coach	£12	0s	0d
Bulawayo to Salisbury by coach	£12	0s	0d

The coach journey was over rough roads behind a team of ten mules and this service was operated by the famous Doel Zeeder-berg. Luggage up to 30lb was allowed free, this being carried on the roof of the coach. By 1 October the rail journey had been extended to Francistown, with a daily coach to Bulawayo at a fare of £7. In actual practice it sometimes turned out that Paulings, for construction purposes, stopped a train with passenger carriages at some earlier station and everyone had to alight with their baggage and go forward in trucks at the end of a material train to the connecting point with the coach service. One pioneer lady has recalled that as a young girl she and her parents, with others of the family, arrived at Gaberones to be ordered off the passenger train, and were then packed into the end of an open truck half-full of sleepers, from which her father strung up blankets to give a little shade for the rest of the journey. No food could be obtained on trains, which stopped at stations such as Lobatsi, Mochudi and Mahalapye where there were refreshment rooms, while at a few points small hotels near the line offered some sustenance. Rugs, pillows and water bottles were necessities for rail passengers in those days.

In completing 400 miles of new railway in twelve months to the date of the arrival of the first train at Bulawayo, Harold Pauling had performed a feat to go down in the annals of railway history. A new era had come to Bulawayo and the occasion was one for festivities. As the line was approaching, a committee was formed to organise the arrangements for a week of celebrations to commence on 4 November, four years after the occupation of the town in 1893, and invitations were sent to distinguished guests in various parts of South Africa and elsewhere.

No less than four special trains for guests were run by the CGR, two trains from Cape Town on 31 October, and one from Port Elizabeth and one from Kimberley on 1 November; all these spent the night at Francistown, coming forward to Bulawayo early on 4 November. An additional special train for the High Commissioner for South Africa, Sir Alfred Milner, had reached Bulawayo hours late on Tuesday, 2 November, and the crowd which had assembled to greet him at the station had gone home, apart from the official welcome committee. The opening day was declared a public holiday and for the following six days all businesses closed at mid-day to enable the townsfolk to attend the many functions on the programme, followed on most evenings by dinners and parties, giving good opportunity for the many 'VIPs' to make appropriate speeches. One great disappointment was the absence of Cecil Rhodes, who was unable to attend owing to an attack of fever, but many references were made to his vision and the energy with which he had pressed on with the development of the latest addition to the British Empire.

For the opening ceremony by Sir Alfred Milner the temporary railway station was decorated with flags, bunting, greenery and a variety of slogans considered suitable for the occasion. These included 'Our Two Roads to Progress' 'Railroads and Cecil Rhodes' and 'Change here for Zambesi', while someone selected some Latin tags as being appropriate. To see 'Pro Bono Publico' and 'Cui Bono' in juxtaposition must have been startling to the Latin scholar. The town, too, was gaily decorated and one thrill was the turning-on for the first time of electric lighting in streets and buildings on the evening before the opening day.

From a dais on the platform Milner read a message from Joseph Chamberlain, then Secretary of State for the Colonies, and after speeches the opening ceremony was followed by the presentation of the Victoria Cross to Trooper H. S. Henderson for his bravery during the Matabele rebellion. An official luncheon took place at the recently built Palace Hotel, where the invited guests sat down to an impressive menu and wine list. It was typical of George Pauling that he should remember the excellent work done by his employees on the construction and a special chef was engaged to prepare the free meals, with drinks, that he gave his men for the week of celebrations.

In May 1897 the Bechuanaland Railway had entered into an agreement with the Cape Government Railways by which the latter undertook to work at cost price the entire line from Vryburg to Bulawayo, taking over sections from the contractors and providing the staff for traffic, maintenance and locomotive purposes. At the same time the services of J. L. Bissett were obtained from the CGR and he was appointed general manager, his duties being to watch the economical working of the line in the interest of the company. A Scottish railwayman, Bissett had joined the CGR in 1881 and became goods superintendent and stationmaster at Kimberley in 1889. By 1896 he had risen to assistant traffic manager and it is apparent that he must then have impressed Cecil Rhodes, who was chairman of the Bechuanaland Railway, for him to be selected as general manager for the next section of the 'Cape-to-Cairo' line.

Bissett initially had an office in St George's Street, Cape Town, but soon after was functioning as watchdog over his CGR colleagues at Bulawayo. Stephen F. Townsend, also from the CGR, had been resident engineer for the construction of the Vryburg—Mafeking—Bulawayo line and in 1898 was appointed at Bulawayo as chief resident engineer, under the consultant engineers, Sir Douglas Fox and Sir Charles Metcalfe. Townsend then moved his temporary offices and quarters for his field staff from Mochudi in Bechuanaland to the railway camp near the station at Bulawayo, an area later to become Raylton, the centre for railway housing and recreational purposes for many decades to come.

Early photographs show how bare the veld was in the vicinity of the railway terminus on the outskirts of Bulawayo. A few mimosa trees and scrub showed green on the otherwise brown and dusty ground. On this high, open and windswept stretch was established the permanent station and other facilities. The station building, a wood-and-iron structure placed on a high-level platform, was a row of offices with a parcels store behind. Close by was a small refreshment kiosk which advertised 'Tea—Coffee—Cocoa, Shandies 6d, Cigars and Tobaccos', while on the other side of the station building was a separate refreshment-room serving meals. This had no verandah and in summer must have been like an oven to sit in.

Goods traffic was at first offloaded on a bank at the 'town' end of the platform until, in 1898, a long goods shed was erected on the Raylton or south side of the railway yard. The first engine shed was a small wood-and-iron building with two tracks, complete with pits, and could accommodate four small 4–4–0 tender locomotives. A lean-to office was provided alongside the shed, while close by was a row of single quarters for the engine crews, within the engine turning triangle. At this time all engines and rolling stock were owned by the CGR as the first batch of Rhodesia Railways 7th class 4–8–0 tender locomotives had not yet come into service, while wagons and carriages were also on order.

For the control of traffic the CGR had placed at Bulawayo an assistant traffic manager W. W. Hoy, who after a short spell in an office at the temporary terminus, moved into the township to open a CGR office in Williams Buildings, where importers could obtain news of their incoming goods. Hoy at that time could hardly have imagined that in 1910 he was to become general manager of the unified railways of South Africa and that in 1928 he was to return to Bulawayo as Sir William Hoy, KCB, Chairman of the Railway Commission of the Rhodesias and Bechuanaland.

In his annual report for 1897 C. B. Elliott, general manager of the CGR, commenting on the opening of the line to Bulawayo, wrote that heavy rains falling shortly after the opening had retarded traffic very seriously. Accommodation for the men was very scanty and the scarcity of what would generally be regarded as some of the absolute necessaries of life was imposing a severe tax upon the staff. Men were compelled to live in box trucks or tents for lack of housing, and 'those who have borne the heat and burden of the day amid special difficulties and drawbacks require very cordial thanks'.

The CGR took over the Francistown—Bulawayo section from Paulings on 15 November 1897, but on the first day communication was interrupted by wash-aways. On 3 December the river at Shashi 'came down', partly destroying the approaches to the temporary bridge, and the line was closed for two weeks. At Bulawayo the permanent station was incomplete and all traffic had to be handled in the veld on the edge of a marsh about three-quarters of a mile from the final terminal. The waggon road to the township soon became cut up by the cartage contractor's transport so that great difficulty was experienced in coping with the quantity of goods. Telegraph communication had not been completed between Plumtree and Bulawayo so that the 63-mile section had to be worked without telegraph, and train arrangements once made could not be altered until the telegraph line was opened throughout in mid-December. Telephonic communication by a station-to-station line of indifferent reliability was achieved in December 1898.

Such were the troubles that the railwaymen of 1897 had to face after the record-breaking construction of the line but they had the satisfaction of having opened a new railway to a new European settlement almost cut off from the world after the rinderpest outbreak had stopped animal transport.

The opening of the line to Bulawayo was followed by a period of consolidation while the bridges, buildings and so forth were completed and the line itself settled down to a commercial undertaking. One mixed and two goods trains a day were run in each direction and trains coming into Bulawayo were heavily loaded with imports for the developing township and the mining activity in the surrounding district. In 1898 thought was soon given by Rhodes and Metcalfe to the extension of the railway system in a northward direction as the financial success of the Bechuanaland Railway had filled Rhodes with enthusiasm for further rail development. While he was anxious to see his 'Cape-to-Cairo' plan go forward, he realised that it was first essential to connect the two towns of Salisbury and Bulawayo by rail.

The Beira Railway had reached Umtali in February 1898, three months after the Bechuanaland Railway had arrived at Bulawayo, and construction from Umtali to Salisbury was proceeding apace. Early in 1899 a survey team under Edward Rosher set off from Bulawayo with ox waggons carrying tents, equipment and provisions for the pegging out of the route to Gwelo and then on to Globe & Phoenix, this being a goldmine at the future township of Que Que. (Picture, p 83.) George Pauling had been given the contract to construct this new extension and the first sod was cut in Bulawayo on 30 May 1899. Pauling expected to have the section completed for traffic in twelve months from 1 November, Harold Pauling being once more in charge of the work. But this was not to be, as in October the South African War broke out and within a few days the main line from the Cape had been cut and Mafeking was besieged. Thus all supplies coming forward from the Cape ports were stopped and the available rails and sleepers brought construction to an end at Insiza, sixty miles towards Gwelo from Bulawayo.

With the extension of the railway into Rhodesia the board of

53

the Bechuanaland Railway under the chairmanship of Cecil Rhodes decided to change the name of the company to Rhodesia Railways Limited from 1 June 1899, and so 'Rhodesia Railways' were born.

At its meeting on 7 November 1899, the board, which then included Earl Grey, Alfred Beit, Rochfort Maguire, J. O. Maund, Capt E. F. Rhodes and Thomas Shiels, decided that the Bulawayo—Gwelo and the Bulawayo—Gwanda sections when completed would be worked by RR instead of the CGR, as had originally been planned, and for this purpose rolling stock was ordered to make up two mixed trains a week for each line. At the same meeting a contract was approved for the supply of sleeping, dining and smoking cars to make up a 'Train de Luxe' to run between Cape Town and Bulawayo, the arrangements being made with the CGR.

For his own railway journeys Cecil Rhodes usually travelled in the luxurious Pullman saloon cars specially built in the United States in 1895 for the De Beers Consolidated Mining Co, one of which was preserved and later presented to the RR; for a time it was in Umtali museum but is now in the railway museum, Bulawayo. Because of the many distinguished personalities and wealthy mining magnates visiting Rhodesia in connection with development projects, Rhodes decided that the long train journey from the Cape should be made as comfortable as possible, and he envisaged a luxury train as a good advertisement for the new country. On his instructions Sir Douglas Fox and Sir Charles Metcalfe designed a train worthy of his ideas and a description said, 'This may justly claim to rank among the finest and most sumptuous of its kind in the world', while another writer considered that the Train de Luxe had an air of solidarity and comfort 'which one seldom expects to find except in a first-class hotel or on one of the large ocean liners'.

Built by the Lancaster Railway Carriage & Wagon Co in England, the train consisted of six coaches, three sleeping-cars, one dining-saloon, one smoking-buffet car and a baggage and guard's van, each vehicle being 56ft long. A spare dining-saloon and baggage van were also supplied. The sleeping-cars had four four-berth compartments and one two-berth coupé, with a washroom, a shower/bathroom and two toilets. The beds were 6ft long and mattresses were stored in cupboards under the seats. The dining-car seated twenty-four passengers, and the buffet car contained a reading-room at one end, complete with lending library, a card room for four people, and a centre bar-lounge compartment with two settees and several armchairs in red leather upholstery. The Stones system of carriage lighting with axle-driven dynamos was fitted to every vehicle, this being the first train in South Africa to be so equipped as the CGR at that time only had dynamo vans to supply electric current. Electric fans were fitted in each compartment and public room, and wine coolers were built into the underframes of the lounge and dining-cars.

Limited to first-class passengers, but with no supplementary fares apart from bedding fees, the train had a frock-coated conductor supervising a team of stewards. In outward appearance it looked impressive—polished teak vehicles with raised brass designations, a coloured British South Africa Company coat-of-arms in a centre plaque on the sides and ornamental curved brass handrails at the entrance gates. Open platforms were provided at each end but the carriages had concertina corridor connections as protection from the weather, the first to be used in Southern Africa.

One can picture the club atmosphere in the lounge car of this train with groups discussing the fluctuations of the share market and the prospects of their latest investment in Rhodesian gold mines over drinks and cigars after dinner, as the Karoo or Kalahari countryside faded from view in the advancing darkness. And how sad that Cecil Rhodes should have died before he had the opportunity to sample his luxury train. The carriages were landed at Cape Town and were erected by the CGR at its Salt River workshops in mid-1901. Owing to the war, their introduction to the through Cape—Rhodesia service was delayed and when the Duke and Duchess of Cornwall visited the Cape in August 1901 during a cruise, the brand-new RR de luxe carriages and van formed the royal train for the journeys between Simonstown and Cape Town. A CGR private saloon set aside for the governor was occupied by the royal couple, but the rest of the party and officials used the RR coaches. Later the Train de Luxe was to accommodate Joseph

Chamberlain and his staff for a tour of South Africa at the end of the Boer War.

The train went into public service in December 1902, leaving Cape Town on Wednesday mornings at 11am and reaching Bulawayo on Saturdays at 8am; it returned south on Sundays at 9am, arriving at Cape Town at 2pm on Tuesdays. It soon achieved a high measure of popularity and one humourist called at the Cape Town offices of the RR to say that if the railway company would erect a billiards table on the train and meet him as regards terms he would be glad to spend his six months long leave aboard it.

Very soon after the beginning of the South African War Vryburg was captured and Mafeking besieged, while at Crocodile Pools (now named Notwani) the bridge over the Metsimasuane river had been blown up by the Boers and the line cut. The defence of Mafeking under the command of Col Robert Baden-Powell is well known and the railway workshops staff helped in producing armaments during the eight months of siege. From the north, two Rhodesian armoured trains were organised to patrol the line and afford protection to the railway gangs on a third train busy on repairs to the track and to the three bridges damaged in the section between Ramoutsa and Gaberones. One 100ft span was jacked up from the river bed and replaced in position by a party of CGR railwaymen while under heavy shellfire.

The armoured trains were equipped in Mafeking and Bulawayo, the locomotives and tenders having steel plating affixed to the sides and top. Open wagons had steel plate or rail protective sides and one wagon held a Maxim gun at one end and a nine-pounder at the other, with branches of trees set up as camouflage. A typical armoured train comprised one armed wagon, a locomotive, water tanks, a guard's van and another armed wagon; two such trains did very good work in keeping open the railway line towards Mafeking. Edward Rosher was withdrawn from being engineer on the Bulawayo—Gwelo survey and worked with the armoured trains; in May 1900 he had the satisfaction of being on the first train to enter Mafeking when the siege was lifted. There he joined Capt J. R. Moore, the CGR engineer who did good work during the defence and was later to become general manager of the SAR.

The war greatly interfered with rail traffic and from October 1899 until the end of June 1900 the line was under the control of the military. In the meantime the shipment of railway material was not slowed up from England and by early 1900 a dump of some 300 miles of permanent-way material for the RR was on hand at Port Elizabeth, while ten 7th class 4–8–0 locomotives and 80 out of the 200 30-ton open trucks on order had arrived. As soon as these were erected the movement of the rails, sleepers and other equipment to Bulawayo was begun, while at the CGR workshops at Salt River, near Cape Town, other wagons were being erected for Rhodesia.

One of the jobs at Salt River was the construction of some trainmen's cabooses for use on the RR. Because of the long distances without established centres of population to provide housing for relief crews, it soon became the practice to haul a caboose next to the engine on all trains, this vehicle having sleeping accommodation, toilet, kitchen and a small dining-room; thus two train crews, each consisting of driver, fireman and guard, could travel on the long round trips, taking alternate turns of duty. This method of working was begun on the 984-mile trip from Mafeking to Bulawayo and back, and later introduced between Bulawayo and Salisbury and to Northern Rhodesia during the early days of the railway's development. With a small coal stove and oil lamps the living conditions in the hot summer months must have been far from comfortable, and the train crews undoubtedly earned their meagre pay, sometimes being away from home for four or five days, or even longer when washaways and other mishaps occurred.

Meanwhile, as permanent-way material gradually arrived at Salisbury from Beira, the work of extending the line to Gwelo and Bulawayo went ahead. Though Paulings were not faced with heavy grades as the line followed the watershed, there were several large rivers to be crossed, such as the Hunyani, Umfuli, Umsweswe, Umniati, Sebakwe and the KweKwe, all of which required major girder bridges with masonry piers, and it was not until

THE
RHODESIA RAILWAYS.
SALISBURY TO GWELO
EXTENSION.

This Extension will be opened for Traffic on June 1 t, 1902, and the Train Service will be as under:

SALISBURY TO GWELO.			Monday Wednesday Saturday	GWELO TO SALISBURY.			Sunday Tuesday Thursday	
			P.M.				P.M.	
SALISBURY	..	.. Dep.	6.30	GWELO	..	.. Dep.	3.0	
NORTON SIDING ..		..	8.40	KWEKWE SIDING		..	5.30	
MAKWIRO SIDING		..	10.32	GLOBE & PHŒNIX		To Arr.	7.30	
			A.M.			Dep.	7.45	
GADZEMA SIDING		.. Arr.	12.25	SHERWOOD SIDING		..	8.55	
		Dep.	12.30					
HARTLEY	..	.. Arr.	1.0	BATTLEFIELDS SIDING		Arr	9.55	
		Dep.	1.5			Dep.	10.0	
GATOOMA SIDING		.. Arr.	2.55	GATOOMA SIDING		..	11.50	
		Dep.	3.0				A.M.	
BATTLEFIELDS SIDING		.. Arr.	4.50	HARTLEY	..	.. Arr.	1.40	
		Dep.	4·55			Dep.	1.45	
SHERWOOD SIDING		..	5.55	GADZEMA SIDING		..	2.15	
GLOBE & PHŒNIX		.. Arr.	7.0	MAKWIRO SIDING		..	4.0	
		Dep.	7.15					
KWEKWE SIDING		..	9.40	NORTON SIDING		..	5.50	
			P.M.				P.M.	
GWELO	..	.. Arr.	1.0	SALISBURY ..		.. Arr.	8.0	

FARES.

From		Class				From		Class			
		1	2	3	Native			1	2	3	Native
		s. d.	s. d.	s. d.	s. d.			s. d.	s. d.	s. d.	s. d.
SALISBURY TO HARTLEY..	..	28 6	19 0	9 6	6 3	GLOBE & PHŒNIX TO HARTLEY ..		26 3	17 6	8 9	5 9
,, ,, GLOBE & PHŒNIX		54 9	36 6	18 3	12 3	,, ,, ,, GWELO ..		15 9	10 6	5 3	3 6
,, ,, GWELO ..	..	70 6	47 0	23 6	15 9	,, ,, ,, SALISBURY ..		54 9	36 6	18 3	12 3
HARTLEY TO SALISBURY.		28 6	19 0	9 6	6 3	GWELO TO GLOBE & PHŒNIX ..		15 9	10 6	5 3	3 6
,, ,, GLOBE & PHŒNIX ..		26 3	17 6	8 9	5 9	,, ,, HARTLEY ..		42 0	28 0	14 0	9 3
,, ,, GWELO ..	..	42 0	28 0	14 0	9 3	,, ,, SALISBURY ..		70 6	47 0	23 6	15 9

Children under 3 years of age free; over 3 years and under 12 years half-fare. Natives in batches of 20 or over, travelling from Salisbury will be charged at the rate of half-penny per head per mile.
For particulars respecting Goods and Parcels Rates, etc., apply to the Station Masters, or to the Traffic Superintendent at Umtali.

C. WIBBERLEY, Manager.

Umtali P. & P. Co.

Poster advertising Salisbury to Gwelo extension, June 1902

1 June 1902 that the section between Salisbury and Gwelo was opened for traffic. The last section over the rolling plains from Gwelo to Insiza did not take long to complete and a link-up was effected on 6 October, to be followed by the through working of traffic between Salisbury and Bulawayo from 1 December 1902.

As was quite common on such occasions, the opening of the line between Bulawayo and Gwelo was not without incident. Mrs J. M. Hardman travelled on the first 'passenger' train to Gwelo which left at 4am on a dark morning and the passengers were accommodated in a covered truck with an oil lamp swinging from the roof. Two plank seats along one end and a pile of mail bags at the other gave some seating in the truck for the thirty-five men and three women passengers. They had been told that the train from Gwelo would be met about half way, at Insiza siding, but when the train got there nothing but bush and trees were to be seen. By then everyone was hungry. Some native passengers had come prepared and were boiling water in a paraffin tin and into this Mrs Hardman put about a quarter pound of tea, half a pound of sugar and part of a tin of condensed milk, the remnants of her supplies for her journey from the south. With this tea and a few sandwiches the pangs of hunger were relieved. After some two hours' wait the driver decided to go ahead and about half way further on they met the train from Gwelo. Then began the argument as to what was to happen next, as the Gwelo train held orders to cross the train from Bulawayo at the siding at Insiza. Evening came on and the trains still waited until a whistle sounded and a second train arrived from Bulawayo. This had been sent out with wood and water as it had been thought supplies must have run out. Then, after a further long discussion, the Gwelo train backed into Gwelo with the two trains from Bulawayo following and the journey ended about 10pm. So was opened the Bulawayo—Gwelo line and the link with Salisbury completed.

Metcalfe, who had been charged by Rhodes with the task of supervising the development of the Rhodesian railway system, knew full well the desire of Rhodes to carry the line of rail north-wards in his aim for Cairo. He had first the idea of striking north-west from Gwelo towards Kariba gorge, for there coal had reportedly been found. Metcalfe was a practical engineer and not an idealist; his aim was a railway that would earn its way. However, on examination, the coal near Kariba was shown to be very inferior and Metcalfe persuaded Rhodes against this route, which would also have been expensive and difficult to construct.

A little earlier another coal discovery had been made in the Wankies area, some 200 miles north-west of Bulawayo on the way to the Victoria Falls. The Wankie coal concession had been sold by the Mashonaland Agency Ltd to the Wankie Coal, Railway & Exploration Co in 1900 and preliminary reports were extremely satisfactory. At that time coal was becoming essential for the development of the country, which could no longer exist on the cutting of its timber to feed the furnaces of its mines and railway locomotives. By 1901 the Rhodesia Railways board under its chairman, Cecil Rhodes, had decided that a new railway should be constructed from Bulawayo through the Wankie district to tap the colliery, and thence to Victoria Falls and the crossing of the Zambesi river. Apart from the coal traffic to be picked up, the route was an easier one than a crossing of the Zambesi lower down where it broadened out over a wide and deep valley with steep escarpments on either side. Decades later the attraction of the 'cut-off' by a crossing of the great river to shorten the rail route between Salisbury and Kafue, in Northern Rhodesia, was to be a fairly frequent object for closer investigation by both the railway company and the government, but nothing has come of it.

Once again Paulings were called upon to construct a new section of the RR and work began in 1901 on the first 161 miles of easy going to Mambanje, which it was hoped would be reached in eighteen months' time. This line ran through sand veld, well wooded with mopani and teak, and with the exception of the vicinity of the Umgusa river was of easy grading. As elsewhere, 60lb round-top rail was laid on steel sleepers, while the two main bridges over the Umgusa and Gwaai rivers were substantial steel and masonry structures. An exceptional feature of this line was the 'long straight' of seventy miles from near Gwaai to Dett, which at the time of construction was probably the longest stretch of straight railway track in the world. In later years, when electric headlights had been fitted to locomotives, it was possible to stand at Dett station at night and see a train in the distance an hour or so before it arrived. The line was partially in forest and the country teemed with game, from small antelope to giraffe and elephant, while the roar of a lion often caused anxiety to the train staff when waiting at a crossing place.

While construction proceeded from Bulawayo to the north, reconnaissance of the route forward from Mambanje to Wankie and thence to the Victoria Falls had been in hand. Edward Rosher recalls that the heavily graded section between Dett and Wankie was some of the toughest country he had ever encountered for survey work and that it was reputed to be Livingstone's 'Valley of Death'. It was often a case of crawling on hands and knees along game trails to get through the bush and forest to reach a suitable spot where the bush could be cut back enough to allow instrument work to be done for the next traverse. No easy job in country abounding with lion, elephant and other game, apart from the malarial mosquito, all of which made camp life far from enjoyable.

By March 1903 the line had been opened as far as Mambanje and, despite the difficult country, Paulings had the next section to Wankie available to general traffic on 1 December 1903. The magnet of Wankie coal had been a strong one and in 1902 the development of no 1 Colliery, as it was later to be known when a second shaft was opened, had been urged on, so that when the line actually reached Wankie under construction conditions in October 1903, it was possible to run the first train of coal south. From then on it was very soon possible to cease importing coal into Rhodesia, and this provided an increasing flow of traffic over the railway system to Bulawayo and beyond, which was a useful balance to the imported goods from the Cape and from Beira.

While extension of the main line north was in progress the RR board gave Pauling the contract for the early construction of two branch lines to serve goldmining discoveries. One was from Gwelo to Selukwe and was twenty-three miles long; sidings were installed at Guinea Fowl and Surprise, while a water tank in Sebanga Poort met the need of locomotives. Initially built to serve gold-mines, the branch was later to meet the heavy demands of chrome ore mines at Selukwe and elsewhere along the line, a traffic that became most impressive in the mineral exports of Rhodesia. This branch was opened to traffic on 25 August 1903. On the same day another branch line, that from Heany, seventeen miles from Bulawayo, was opened as far as Gwanda to serve other goldmining propositions.

While Paulings undertook the construction of the Gwanda line, Edward Rosher was appointed district engineer at Heany to over-see the contract for the RR. Bridges were at first built with bird-caging timber supports until the stone abutments had been erected after the line was open. For his inspection work, Rosher had one of the first motor-propelled trolleys on the RR. As can be seen from the photograph on p 84 this was a very primitive affair with a driver's seat in front and a seat for another passenger behind, with a canvas awning on a light metal frame. A petrol engine made by de Dion Bouton provided the power when it worked, but it was somewhat erratic and there were times when the occupants had to get off and push it home.

It was during the construction that Rosher one evening heard uproarious laughter coming from the tent of his assistant engineers. These two men had both had mishaps in their early lives, one having lost a forearm and the other his leg below the knee, and both used false limbs, which in 1903 were simple in design. They had been out shooting for the pot and on return had sunk into deck chairs to rest. After a while they called their native servant and the one-legged engineer asked him to pull off his boots. On doing so off came one leg, whereupon the other engineer jumped up and offered his hand to the startled native who had fallen over backwards with the boot and leg. The servant grasped the proffered hand and it too came away! That was too much for the native who, letting out a scream, made off into the bush and was never seen again.

A couple of years later Rosher was still at Heany Junction as district engineer for the main line to Gwelo and the Gwanda branch when, returning home one afternoon, he met the railway doctor coming down the path from his house. The doctor had a wide grin and said, 'I must congratulate you'. 'What for?' asked Rosher. 'You have a boy and a girl'. 'No joking now, doctor, the matter is too serious'. 'You have a daughter and TWO boys'. The much overcome Rosher took some moments before he could ask how his wife was. The occasion was historic as the Rosher triplets were the first white triplets to be born in Rhodesia.

The South African War was drawing to a close when news came of the death of Cecil Rhodes at his seaside cottage at Muizenberg on 26 March 1902. The passing of the founder of Rhodesia and the mainspring of its railway development was a sad loss. His expressed wish was to be buried on a kopje he named 'World's View' in the Matopos Hills and for the long journey from the Cape to Rhodesia the CGR and RR were closely associated. A special train was formed to convey his body and the principal mourners and it is ironic that the carriages of Rhodes' Train de Luxe, in which he had never travelled in his lifetime, should be available for the long journey north. The composition of the funeral train was as follows:

De Beers private Pullman saloon
CGR bogie coach no 521
RR buffet car no 7
RR sleeping-cars nos. 2, 3 and 1
RR dining-car no 5
RR luggage van no 8
CGR bogie coach no 549

For much of the journey the train was hauled by CGR locomotives nos 240 and 242. Between Kimberley and Vryburg, as a protective measure because of raids by parties of Boers, an armoured bogie wagon was attached next to the engines, while from Mafeking to Palachwe (Palapye) two armoured trains, one ahead and one behind, escorted the funeral train as a precaution where the line ran close to the Transvaal border. The train safely reached Bulawayo on 7 April and at the station the bier was transferred from the private coach to the gun-carriage on which it was eventually carried to the Matopos for the funeral service.

At a meeting of the board of the Mashonaland Railway in London on 11 August 1902, the vacancy of chairman was filled by J. Rochfort Maguire in succession to Cecil Rhodes. Maguire had personal knowledge of Rhodesia and was to visit the country several times in his capacity as railway chairman.

One last direct connection with Cecil Rhodes was the construction and opening, on 4 November 1903, of the nine mile branch line from Westacre Junction, seventeen miles south of Bulawayo, to Matopos. This little line was built in the terms of Cecil Rhodes' will, so that 'the people of Bulawayo may enjoy the glory of the Matopos from Saturday to Monday', and the cost of construction was borne by the Rhodes trustees. Trains left Bulawayo on Saturday afternoons at 1.40pm and, with a brief stop at Westacre for the guard to 'sign the train book', arrived at Matopos terminus at 3.25pm. The load usually consisted of two or three carriages and a van. As passengers normally spent the weekend at the hotel at the terminus, which had also been provided by the trustees, the empty train worked back to Bulawayo at 4.10pm. Early on Monday mornings the empty coaches were again hauled out to Matopos and at 6.30am the weekenders set off for Bulawayo; they were due in at 8.15am, in time to get to work after a quiet weekend in the country, for a fare of 10s first class and 5s second class return.

The track used was 45lb rail recovered from the Vryburg—Mafeking section of the main line and so only small locomotives were used and a restricted speed applied over the branch itself. A goods shed and cattle ramp were erected at Matopos and later on a railway agent was appointed to maintain some control, but the trains were worked by RR enginemen with a CGR—later SAR—employee as guard.

In later years the timetable was altered so that passengers could go out on a Sunday morning train to Matopos for a day's picnic and return the same evening, and this became very popular in the days before motorcars usurped the slow rail journeys. Eventually the passengers were only a few natives and the train ran on Tuesdays, hauling odd trucks of mining or farming supplies and

Page 65 (*above*) Beira Railway 2ft gauge no 1, 0–6–0 or 0–4–2, at Beira, c 1899; (*below*) narrow-gauge mixed train behind BR 4–4–0 no 9 at siding, c 1895

Page 66 (*above*) Mandegos loco shed with Falcon-built 4–4–0s. This shed later became Victoria Falls Hotel dining-room; (*below*) Beira Railway Falcon 4–4–0 no 24 with six-wheel tender after repaint

produce, with occasional lots of cattle. Finally, on 1 June 1948, the last train ran and the branch line closed down, being replaced by a railway lorry service over the Bulawayo main road. Soon afterwards the track was lifted but its formation survives over much of the route. A cairn with plaque has been placed at the terminus to commemorate the line.

CHAPTER THREE

The Mashonaland Railway

In 1895 the Salisbury Chamber of Commerce and the Chamber of Mines petitioned Cecil Rhodes for the early construction of a railway to link Umtali with Salisbury and so give through rail connection with the port of Beira. Resolutions addressed to Rhodes, demanding a promise of the railway reaching Salisbury in two and a half years from 1895, had not brought a satisfactory reply, but in November 1896 during a visit to Salisbury Rhodes met a deputation and promised that the railway would be built, though not before May 1898.

Rhodes kept his word and on 13 April 1897, the Mashonaland Railway Co was incorporated in London with the immediate object of constructing the railway from Umtali to Salisbury. For this, 450,000 £1 shares were issued and 5 per cent debentures for £1,150,000 were guaranteed as to interest by the Chartered Company for twenty-two years. Rhodes was elected chairman of the Mashonaland Railway and no time was lost in pushing ahead with this new railway. Six locomotives and 100 trucks were ordered in letters from the British South Africa Company to Paulings, who had been given the contract for the construction of the line, and on 11 January 1898 work began from Umtali where material had been arriving over the Beira Railway.

George Pauling placed Lawley in overall charge of the Umtali— Salisbury construction and his assistant, A. M. Moore, was appointed as resident engineer. It was these three who, on a recent trip of forty-eight hours over the Beira Railway, had drunk between them 300 bottles of German beer, for which Pauling admits a particular partiality. Railway construction was evidently thirsty work, but as Pauling had averred, teetotallers could not stand up to the fever encountered in the country through which the line passed.

Leaving Umtali on a down grade, the new line twisted its way through the hills and valleys until it reached the first real obstacle, the Odzi river. This wide river was originally crossed by a wooden bridge in the construction days but, following upon an inspection by Rhodes, the MR board arranged to substitute an iron girder bridge, which was completed just before the line was opened through to Salisbury. Hardly was this job finished than the river rose in flood and one of the piers was washed away. This damaged pier was rebuilt at the expense of Pauling & Co.

From Odzi the contractors were faced with an almost continuous climb, as the line rose from near 3,000ft at the river to a summit of 5,418ft at Eagles Nest near Headlands. Small rivers and hills abound in this area which was to become decades later a prosperous farming district for maize and tobacco. The line then dropped in sweeping curves to Macheke before facing another climb to its highest point—later to prove to be the highest on the whole of the Rhodesian railways—of 5,538ft close to Marandellas. From there the railway was easily graded, mainly downhill, until it reached Salisbury, 170 miles from Umtali.

Good progress was made with construction and one of the foremen on the earthworks was T. W. Rudland, who was later connected with many railway contracts in Rhodesia. In four months fifty miles of earthworks had been completed and three miles of track had been opened from Umtali. At the workshops established by Paulings in Umtali the first two 3ft 6in gauge locomotives had arrived and by May 1898 had been tested under steam, while the erection of the next two locomotives had begun. These arrived from Beira over the then narrow-gauge line, as did wagons for the construction trains. Umtali was rapidly developing into a railway centre with both temporary and more permanent housing being erected for the contractors and railway staff, mainly in an area close to the station, which had appropriately been named

Paulington. The station itself was built on a shelf cut in the sloping side of the valley. It was a wood-and-iron building and no platform was provided for passengers, who climbed up and down from the track. The site was a difficult one and the line was on a curved approach rising to the station and yard from each end. At the Salisbury end the line made a sharp right-hand curve as it left the station and at once crossed the Melsetter road by the first rail-over-road bridge in Rhodesia. The locomotive shed and offices, small wood-and-iron buildings, and a triangle were on the right-hand side, with small railway houses and single quarters close by, while on the left-hand side were placed the mechanical workshops. Access to both the shed and workshops was by tracks taking directly off the main line and this situation prevailed, with merely locks on the points, for many years. On one occasion the facing points from the main line were left set for the shed, and the Salisbury mail train, steaming hard up the bank swung over them; fortunately it found the running shed track empty and ran straight through and back on to the main line at the far end.

The track was laid with 60lb rail on steel sleepers and while all the bridges were initially built of timber it was soon decided, in the light of experience on the Beira Railway, to replace them by permanent girder structures with masonry piers. Work went on apace, the only major interruption being a serious accident which occurred on 21 November 1898 thirty-three miles from Umtali, when a locomotive and several trucks were derailed through excessive speed on a curve. The driver, fireman, a timekeeper and four natives employed by Paulings were killed, while native commissioner Ross and his wife, another couple and eighteen natives were injured. The passengers were all travelling in trucks on a construction train operated by the contractors, who were sued for damages by one of the passengers. Paulings defended the case on the grounds that it was not a public railway and the claimant failed to obtain damages. This was Rhodesia's first serious railway accident.

At a directors' meeting in London on 29 March 1899 it was agreed that Cecil Rhodes should be appointed managing director of the railway company in South Africa, a generic term covering

Rhodesia. It was also decided at the same meeting to make enquiries for suitable men to be engaged as general manager and assistant general manager, so that they would be ready to take over the line from the contractors in October 1899. On 1 May tracklaying was completed into the terminal station of Salisbury and this was soon followed by the formal opening of the Mashonaland Railway which provided a ready excuse for festivities in the capital. The opening took place at Salisbury on 22 May with the arrival of two trains from Umtali conveying the Governor of Sofala and Manica and his staff, with a number of visitors from Beira and Umtali, including Mr Lawley representing Pauling & Co.

The two trains, each composed of two new carriages and a goods guard's van, were hauled by the 4–6–0 tender engines purchased from the Cape Government Railways and taken over as nos 1 and 2 of the Mashonaland Railway. Each engine had been specially painted for the occasion, no 1 being named *Cecil J. Rhodes* and embellished with a Scottish thistle emblem on the wheel splashers. The locomotives were gaily decorated with flags and slogans reading 'Salisbury—Umtali', 'Advance Rhodesia' and 'Now we Shan't be Long to Cairo', while the carriages were also adorned with slogans such as 'Track follows Flag' and 'Pro Bono Publico.' (Picture, p 83.) To meet the trains was a gathering of dignitaries including the Administrators of Mashonaland and Matabeleland, the British Resident and Bishop Gaul, who with the townsfolk gave three cheers as the trains steamed in. As the Governor of Manica stepped off his saloon the British South Africa Company's police band struck up the Portuguese national anthem and the reception council greeted its guests. Three days of general holiday were declared for Salisbury, with festivities in the market hall, races, military displays and sporting events, and there is little doubt that the new railway was well toasted by everyone. Even the children were treated to a free train ride to Ruwa for a picnic and sports.

The four passenger coaches used on the two opening trains were the first to be purchased for the Mashonaland Railway and had an interesting history. Strangely enough they had been built by the Gloucester Railway Carriage & Wagon Co for the metre-

gauge Sao Paulo Railway in Brazil, which line had been constructed by Pauling & Co. Owing to some financial difficulty,
however, though the carriages had been dismantled and packed in
zinc-lined cases for shipment, they were never despatched to
South America and lay in the Gloucester works until they were
offered to the Mashonaland Railway. Glad to get speedy delivery
of four suitable carriages, the offer was accepted and after suitable alterations they were re-packed and shipped to Beira. It took
five days for them to be conveyed from the port to Umtali over
the narrow-gauge BR, as many of the railway cuttings had to be
widened to allow the large cases to pass. In April 1899 they had
safely reached Umtali where the carriages were assembled in the
somewhat pioneer workshops, though they were described as 'very
good for a place like this' by Duncan Bailey who, as a young man
of twenty-three, was sent out from England by the Gloucester
company to check on their assembly and running condition.

Bailey gave the author extracts from his diary, from which one
gleans illuminating impressions of the pioneer days:

> Arrived at Umtali at 3pm (28 May 1899) and went to the
> Pauling Hotel—a corrugated-iron building called after the rail-
> way contractors. Had a bedroom, across the yard, corrugated
> iron, of course, and called for a bath. After a time this arrived
> in a biscuit tin, the water being the colour of coffee. My room
> had two broken windows, two chairs, a bed, a little table for
> washbasin, toilet set, one enamel jug and bowl, and a saucer for
> soap dish. The weather was extremely cold.
> Next day I found the railway shops very good for a so-called
> town with one dust road, with shanties here and there, just
> planted down on the veldt. There were six oil street lamps stuck
> on poles. I looked round one of the carriages and found it very
> roughly re-erected.
> The huts in which the railway boys lived were about 10ft × 5ft
> made of corrugated iron. In each were about a dozen boys with
> two fires going—how they lived in the smoke I can't think.
> There were a lot of tame baboons at the huts. To go round at
> night with no lights was a queer experience; one could easily
> get lost 100 yards away.

Bailey travelled in one of the new carriages from Umtali to
Salisbury, leaving at 6am with a tin of biscuits and some cheese
to sustain him. There were no stations on the way and he arrived

two hours late at 8pm. Having examined the carriages at Salisbury and effected adjustments, Bailey returned to Umtali. He noted:

> We had to ride in a covered wagon with the mailbags—thirteen of us. It was bitterly cold, with a white frost when we left at 6am. Next to our van was a flat wagon with no sides. On this we had a fire in an old tin and then the boys made tea. It was a real picnic to be having breakfast on a wagon going at 20 miles per hour, through lovely country extending for miles and miles, but the dust and sparks were terrible, and the shaking made it rather difficult to stand in the middle of the wagon and drink tea. We had lunch in the same way and I nearly fell off the wagon over the fire. Saw one large baboon quite near. As the sun got up it became scorching hot. We arrived at Umtali at 4.30pm, one-and-a-half hours before time. A very enjoyable day, if only for the novelty of the thing.

These four carriages became MR nos 1 to 4; two were first class and cost £1,841 each, placed in service, and two were second class and cost £1,428. The first class had four four-berth compartments and a two-berth coupé with a toilet at each end of the corridor. End balconies with small tip-up seats and brass railed gates were provided. Oil lamps were fitted in the roof, which was of the clerestory type. Two class indicator boards and 'MR' in scroll on the centre panel were placed on the carriage sides below the waist, all the lettering being in gilt. After several years of service as carriages, they were converted to various types of service vehicles, one eventually going to the Mozambique Railways in 1950 as a postal van, while two others' frames and bogies were still running in 1967.

By August 1899 the first passenger train services was advertised:

MASHONALAND RAILWAY

Mileage	Stations	Up Trains Tuesday/Saturday	
			no 2 Up
222	UMTALI		6.00am
284	Rusapi	10. 5	10.25am
306	Siding (Headlands)	12. 0	12.10pm
347	Marandellas	2.45	3.00pm
372	Siding	4.45	
392	SALISBURY	6. 6pm	

			Down Trains Mondays/Fridays
392	SALISBURY		6.00am
372	Siding	7.20	
347	Marandellas	9. 5	9.25am
306	Siding	12. 5	12.12pm
284	Rusapi	1.50	2.00pm
222	UMTALI	6.00pm	

Goods trains run daily as required. Passengers allowed to travel in such trains at their own risk.

Fare: Umtali—Salisbury – 1st Class   £4 10s 0d

Further details from Traffic Manager, A. H. Martin, Umtali.
Chas Buchan, Manager.

The railway was still under the control of Pauling & Co, Charles Buchan being on the staff of Lawley. It will be seen that the distances were based on the narrow-gauge mileage from Beira, but when the gauge widening was completed the distance from Beira was shortened to 204 miles.

Small station buildings, not much more than wood-and-iron huts, had by now been erected at the two stations between Umtali and Salisbury, while at the capital a much larger wood-and-iron structure on a low-level platform served as station and parcels offices with several smaller buildings close by. Its position in the vicinity of the Makabusi river had aroused some complaint, though the site had been chosen by Rhodes so that the railway buildings would fill up space between the kopje and the causeway and so make a united township. The fact that the station was of wood and iron also raised protests, which were ignored by the contractors, and this 'temporary' structure was to serve Salisbury for many years as a monument to the economy practised by the railway company. In fairness, it must be said that a high proportion of the buildings in Salisbury at the turn of the century were of wood and iron, such form of construction continuing for very many years throughout Rhodesia.

In the meantime the railway link from Cape Town to Bulawayo, which had reached that town in October 1897, was now to be extended via Gwelo to the Globe & Phoenix Gold Mine, at what is now known as Que Que. This extension was under the

aegis of Rhodesia Railways, and so closely related to the Mashonaland Railway with which it was soon to be linked both physically
and in administration. Pauling & Co had been given the contract
by Rhodes for the line to Globe & Phoenix, which was being
carried out under the charge of Harold Pauling, cousin of George,
and the first sod was cut at Bulawayo on 30 May 1899. It was
well understood that this line would be carried through to Salisbury to provide a through connection from the Cape, but in
October the plans were upset by the outbreak of the war in South
Africa, which soon brought construction to a halt.

In London the MR board decided on the appointment of Charles
Alfred Lowe as the general superintendent to take charge of the
Beira & Mashonaland Railways from the contractors. Lowe had
had experience with the Great Western Railway and in South
America and on 1 January 1900 he took over from Paulings with
his headquarters as manager at Umtali. Unfortunately in February he was taken seriously ill and succumbed after a brief
illness, having only been in charge a few weeks. On his death Sir
Charles Metcalfe, then in Salisbury, took over the temporary
management of the line until Col R. Beal, CMG, who had the
previous year left the British South Africa Company's public works
department to become assistant general manager of the Beira Railway, was appointed acting manager of the BMR.

A permanent successor had to be found and at a board meeting
in October 1900 Charles Wibberley was appointed for three years
from 1 November as superintendent general, the post later to be
designated as manager. Wibberley had started in 1866 at the age
of fifteen as an office boy on the Midland Railway at Derby
and after holding various positions he was appointed assistant
manager of the Buenos Aires & Rosario Railway in 1888, where
he remained until, while on leave in London, he accepted the
offer to go to Rhodesia. It was therefore upon Wibberley that the
work devolved of organising the railway headquarters at Umtali
and taking over control of the Beira & Mashonaland Railways.
Wibberley was hastily sent out from England and, on reaching
Bulawayo from the Cape, he found a four-day journey of 300 miles
by Zeederberg's stage coach ahead of him. This coach trip, behind

constantly changed mule teams, ten in a span, was a good introduction for the new railway manager, since it would impress upon
him the need for the early completion of the line between Bulawayo and Salisbury. This had been started in 1899 but with the
Cape line cut north and south of Mafeking from October 1899
until the siege was lifted in May 1900, construction work had
petered out for lack of material. A start had, however, been
made from the Salisbury end towards Bulawayo with permanent
way material imported through Beira, and Paulings were making
progress with this extension.

On 17 December 1900 Charles Wibberley took over at Umtali.
His staff then included Owen Griffen as traffic manager, N. Gibbons,
locomotive superintendent, Guthrie in charge of the mechanical
workshops, A. Soley as maintenance engineer and Frank Buchan
of Paulings as the accountant. Umtali also boasted a stationmaster, George Reynolds, who had recently replaced George
Elcombe; he had been transferred to Salisbury, where later he
was to resign and build up a very successful town cartage business. Thomas P. Gilbert was goods clerk and checker, Joe Ward
was locomotive foreman and Bob Edney and A. E. Wainwright
were locomotive inspectors, with George Harris and Allan Bowes
among the drivers.

For motive power there were two six-coupled tender engines
used mainly for goods trains, two four-coupled passenger engines
and two 4–6–2 tank engines used for shunting and to help on the
section to Salisbury. The Beira Railway had *Jack Tar* for shunting
at the port, such as it was in those days, and three of the subsequently ubiquitous 7th class 4–8–0 tender engines, which had
been landed at Beira and erected at Bamboo Creek to work on the
recently widened line to Umtali. Trains were run as and when a
locomotive became available, and since wood fuel was still being
used the loads were light.

Sparks from the wood-burning engines falling on the wooden
bridges led during the dry season to fires and the MR board sanctioned the spending of £70,684 on substituting steel girder spans.
Efforts were also made to obtain coal for the locomotives as it
was soon obvious that it would not be possible to go on cutting

timber from convenient areas along the line. A shipment of 1,590 tons of Merthyr steam coal from Cardiff was the first trial; this cost 24s per ton less 2½ per cent, plus sea freight at 32s 6d per ton. Later on a shipment of Australian coal was tried but this was found unsuitable, and by then the locomotive superintendent must have been hoping that the rumoured coal deposit in the Wankie area would prove to be the answer for his engines.

During 1900 the changes in manager and the preoccuption of the limited staff in moving General Carrington's forces and equipment between Beira and Marandellas had resulted in the completion of monthly returns and accounts being sacrificed in order to move the rush of traffic. Returns to the head office in London were delayed unavoidably but it is evident that the position deteriorated, as late in 1901 a chartered accountant was sent out from London to examine the books of accounts. His report to the board of the MR stated that he found the labour of correcting the books would be far greater than that of entirely re-writing the accounts for the previous two years into new books. Two accountants were sent out to Umtali by Cooper Brothers, a firm of accountants long to be connected with the railways of Rhodesia, and these two with the local staff grappled with the revision of two years' accounts as well as the current work.

As a sideline to running the railway system the MR directors, on learning of the scarcity of slaughter cattle in Rhodesia and the consequent high price of meat, decided to have cold-storage plants constructed at Umtali, Marandellas and Salisbury so as to receive frozen meat from Australia via Beira, where already cold-store facilities had been erected. Cold-storage 'boxes' for use in railway trucks were provided and it was anticipated that a considerable revenue would derive from the traffic. In the event only at Salisbury was the building erected and plant installed, and soon this and the Beira plant were leased to the Rhodesian Cold Storage & Trading Co. Doubtless Wibberley was glad to be freed of this sideline.

Several years later the cold-storage building at Salisbury reverted to the railways and as it was sited close to the east end of the station it was put to good use as single quarters and rest rooms. Many railwaymen fifty years later have somewhat gloomy recollections of being 'billeted' in this old double-storey brick building and welcomed its later demolition to make room for extra sidings and platforms.

So with worries over shortage of staff, insufficient engines and fuel, the books of accounts, and starting a cold-storage business, the railway manager saw the end of 1901 and hoped for brighter days to come.

The 3ft 6in-gauge lines to Selukwe and Gwanda, opened in 1903, were not, in fact, the first branches to be completed in Rhodesia, being preceded by a 2ft-gauge line from Salisbury which enjoyed the imposing title of the Ayrshire Gold Mine & Lomagunda Railway. This line was built by Pauling & Co for the mining company as a private venture but in the terms of the agreement with the British South Africa Company it was stipulated that the Mashonaland Railway had the right to purchase it at cost when desired.

Work was put in hand early in 1902 and the line was built with second-hand material recovered from the original Beira Railway. The Ayrshire had proved to be a lucrative goldmine but it had become practically cut off from Salisbury owing to cattle disease, which had killed most of the oxen used for the transport of vital stores. The railway was also of great importance for the carriage of firewood for the mine plant, and an assured supply of fuel was obtained from two large wooded areas, 160 square miles in extent and containing some 150,000 cords of timber, set aside by the British South Africa Company for the sole use of the mine. This timber also provided fuel for the locomotives.

The railway reached the mine on 13 August 1902, and so eliminated the constant delays caused by irregular ox-waggon transport. On completion of work on the eighty-three miles of line, it was handed over by Paulings and opened to public traffic on 1 November 1902. Locomotives, wagons and even a passenger coach had been transferred from a dump in Bamboo Creek where all the disused narrow-gauge rolling stock had been stored, and the line was staffed and operated by the MR for the mining company.

At Salisbury a separate station known as 'Salisbury A' was laid out as the terminus at the Umtali end of the main-line station. A small shed for two engines was also provided. The line ran out round the north-east side of the town across the present university grounds through Avondale and past Mount Hampden. In the early days there was only the one intermediate siding at Gwebi, where the river of that name was crossed near the future village of Darwendale, but there were three other watering points and a wood siding twelve miles from Ayrshire. A mixed train with a passenger carriage ran twice weekly, taking eight hours for the journey in either direction, the train crew spending the night at Ayrshire. In addition, goods trains were run on other days when required, while a cross-trip service was run for firewood between the timber cutting areas and Ayrshire.

The locomotives used were the 4-4-0 tender engines built by the Falcon Engine & Car Works, Loughborough, for the original Beira Railway in 1895-7. (Picture, p 66.) They weighed only 18 tons and with a tractive effort of 3,987lb hauled a gross load of 42 tons, which represented some eight small bogie trucks. The railway possessed both open and covered wagons, guards' vans and initially the one passenger coach, all bearing 'MR' to denote ownership. The carriage, classified as first class, had open balcony ends with iron gates, while the longitudinal seats inside were like those in tramcars, the passengers having their backs to the drop windows. With its hard wooden seats it was a source of many complaints from the passengers of those days despite their being inured to rough living. However, the train did at least stop at tea time so that a fire could be kindled at the trackside and a kettle boiled. No doubt the third-class native passengers riding on the open trucks assisted with the tea-making. Later a carriage was provided to serve as a 'pay coach' once a month; it had a strong box for the paymaster's cash, with which he paid the various gangs, pumpers and station masters at Banket and Ayrshire.

It is related by a policeman that when travelling into Salisbury one day, a revolver fell from the luggage rack out of the window. At the next stop the driver agreed to set back to find the weapon which was an exhibit in a murder case. Timekeeping was not of much moment and if a buck was seen the train stopped for the driver or the passengers to have a shot at it. On another occasion a locomotive hauling a train of empty wagons lost steam on the bank from Mount Hampden approaching Avondale. As no fuel was handy the guard and others on the train uncoupled the wagons and pushed them after the engine to the summit. From this point the engine and wagons were able to coast the rest of the way into Salisbury.

The Ayrshire mine at this time was crushing some 8,000 tons a month with sixty stamps and was one of the three largest gold-mines in the country. However, in 1905 a new reef was discovered at Eldorado and Paulings were called upon to construct a spur line 12 miles long from a point at 67 miles, later named Banket Junction, to Eldorado to enable the rock to be taken to Ayrshire for crushing. It is probable that it was for this extra rail traffic that the Ayrshire Mining Co ordered their own locomotive from Hunslet Engine Co, Leeds. An 0–6–0 side tank engine, with cylinders $9\frac{1}{2}$in by 12in, driving wheels of 2ft and a total weight of 12 tons 13cwt, Hunslet no 867 was named *Hans Sauer* in honour of Dr Sauer, chairman of the Ayrshire company. On arrival, the locomotive came into the charge of the MR staff and it soon became apparent that it would be much more use if converted from a side tank to a tender engine. The tanks, which only held 300 gallons of water, were removed and a tender carrying 650 gallons was provided. The nameplate *Hans Sauer* was placed on the tender sides, the cab was modified and a polished brass dome improved the appearance of this useful machine. It had outside Walschaerts valve gear, an inside frame and the circular sandbox on the boiler top behind the chimney gave an unusual appearance. *Hans Sauer* was more powerful than the Falcon 4–4–0s and could haul a load of 72 tons. It was, in consequence, very popular and between 1905 and 1912 it clocked up some 92,000 miles in service.

THE LOMAGUNDA RAILWAY.

UP

DISTANCES.	STATIONS AND SIDINGS.	2 MIXED.
From Salisbury "A."		Tuesdays and Fridays.
Ml. Ch.	SALISBURY "A" dep.	9.0
41 56	Gwebi Siding ... ,,	12|45
83 16	AYRSHIRE .. arr.	5|0

DOWN.

DISTANCES.	STATIONS AND SIDINGS.	1 MIXED.
From Ayrshire.		Thursdays and Saturdays.
Ml. Ch.	AYRSHIRE ... dep.	9.0
41 40	Gwebi Siding ... ,,	1|0
83 16	SALISBURY "A" arr.	4|30

LENGTHSMEN'S COTTAGES are situated
at the following mileages :—

$4\frac{1}{2}$	15	23	39
48	56	$72\frac{1}{2}$	$82\frac{1}{2}$

WATER TANKS.

SALISBURY "A"
23 miles.
$41\frac{1}{2}$,,
56   ,,
74   ,,
AYRSHIRE.

Page from 1904 working timetable of the Lomagunda, or Ayrshire
2ft-gauge railway

It was about this time that F. G. Williams, then a fireman, was at Eldorado where two Falcon locomotives were stabled to run the twice-daily round trips to various wood-loading points to bring in firewood for the mine plant. For these trips, Williams recalls, the Falcons hauled three bogie wagons stacked high with firewood, but at times *Hans Sauer* was available and this engine hauled an extra wagon. Williams states that *Hans Sauer* was a bit top-heavy and inclined to roll badly at slacks in the track, which were many. By 1911 there was a small hotel at Darwendale where the Eldorado passenger train stopped for half an hour for lunch, but it was at Banket on the return trip at monthends that trouble occurred. The train was usually filled with miners bound for Salisbury with their monthly pay and the Banket hotel was the scene of a rush for liquor by the thirsty passengers. A roaring trade led to much delay to the train.

For this narrow-gauge line expense was kept to a minimum and wayside sidings were not usually installed. Firewood was cut and stacked at convenient points on the line and then loaded direct into the waiting train. A few farms had cattle to despatch by train and a primitive ramp would be put up beside the line. On one occasion when a cattle train was loading, the oxen became jammed in the race from ramp to truck and the beasts could not move. After all efforts had failed to free the oxen and get them loaded, the engine driver told Williams to heat up the 'pricker' in the firebox and when red hot the driver took it and touched the ox jamming up the job. The poor animal took a great leap when it felt the burn and rushed into the truck, so clearing the way. Such improvisation was needed as battery-operated electric cattle prodders formed no part of railway equipment in those days.

In 1908 the Ayrshire reef petered out and the centre of activity moved to Eldorado, resulting in the line between Banket and Ayrshire gradually falling into disuse. Several goldmines had been opened in the Lomagundi area near the present town of Sinoia and thought was being given to the widening of the gauge and further extension of the line to Sinoia. In the meantime the Jumbo mine, twenty-three miles north of Mount Hampden, had come to the fore and the MR decided to construct a 3ft 6in-gauge

Page 83 (*above*) Rosher's party leaving to survey the Bulawayo
—Gwelo line, 1899; (*below*) first passenger train from Umtali
on opening of Mashonaland Railway to Salisbury in May 1899.
Locomotive MR no 1 named *Cecil J. Rhodes*

Page 84 (*above*) Train crossing the Shashi river, Bechuanaland, before Paulings built the bridge, 1897; (*below*) Rosher's inspection trolley, with De Dion Bouton car engine, on Gwanda branch, 1903

line from Mount Hampden to serve it, a line which eventually became the Shamva branch. The MR arranged to widen the narrow-gauge Salisbury—Mount Hampden section to standard in conjunction with the construction of the line to Jumbo and this was completed in August 1911, after which the section to Jumbo was built and opened to traffic in December 1911.

The natural consequence of the construction of the 3ft 6in-gauge line between Salisbury and Jumbo was the widening of the 2ft gauge line from Mount Hampden to Eldorado, especially as the track and equipment were rapidly deteriorating. This was put in hand and then as valuable goldmines had been discovered in the Bindura and Shamva areas the line was extended by fifty-two miles from Jumbo to Shamva. Paulings completed these various works by April 1913. Because the Ayrshire mine had closed down in 1908, the narrow-gauge section between Banket and Ayrshire was never widened to standard gauge.

It was not until 1915 that it was decided to lift the old rails and sleepers and the ballast train on this duty was hauled by *Hans Sauer*, the last 2ft-gauge locomotive to remain at Banket Junction. The stationmaster there at the time of the lifting of these sixteen miles of track was E. W. Alderson. He lived in Banket's first station, a wood-and-iron three-room structure, with a shelter behind as kitchen; there was no bathroom, no water supply and, of course, no electric light. Alderson recalls that one Sunday the rest of the staff called on him early and suggested that they ran a special train out towards the Ayrshire to do some shooting. There being nothing about 'Shooting Specials' in the regulations Alderson, after some thought, decided not only to turn a blind eye to the scheme but to join in himself. So the 'Shooting Special' was made up with two covered trucks, two open bogies and a van, the little *Hans Sauer* providing the power. The party had a wonderful day's shooting and was never in any danger of collision as this was the only narrow-gauge train left.

A final story of the line in its heyday is that of the passenger who was so absorbed by the passing scenery from the carriage window that he dropped his false teeth on the track. At the next halt the sympathetic driver and fireman enlisted the help of most of the passengers and the train slowly backed while everyone looked for the missing dentures.

During the dismantling of the narrow gauge, a good many iron sleepers were 'picked up' by the local farmers for various purposes and eventually, after the track had gone, the culverts were filled in and an enterprising farmer turned the formation into a good road from his farm to both Eldorado and Banket.

Before the gauge was widened a halt had been established at Avondale, a growing suburb ·of Salisbury, six miles out by the winding rail route. This was in 1911 and later when the 3ft 6in track was laid, a short loop with a goods shed provided public facilities for the area.

That the narrow-gauge railway served a useful purpose over the years between 1902 and 1913 is clear from the mileage run by the locomotives. The three Falcon 4–4–0s on the line when it opened, nos 30, 40 and 42, are recorded as having run 103,031, 105,745 and 118,499 miles respectively to the end of 1912. BR no 41 joined them in 1904 and clocked up over 110,000 miles, while nos 43 and 44 were brought in to help in 1911. These gallant little engines were all sold when the line was closed and ended their days on various industrial light railways in Rhodesia.

As the widening of the gauge approached Eldorado much agitation was roused for the extension of the line across the Hunyani river to Sinoia. The mining and farming development in this Lomagundi area had been rapid and the British South Africa Company realised that the five miles of track from Eldorado to Sinoia, despite the expensive bridge over the Hunyani, were justified and soon the first train, carrying George Pauling among others, ran into Sinoia station on 22 June 1914.

CHAPTER FOUR

On to the Victoria Falls

UPON completion of the main line from Bulawayo to Salisbury, 'through' accounting arrangements were brought into operation for all traffic between the RR, the MR, the CGR and other South African railway administrations. It had already been agreed in 1900, when Wibberley became manager at Umtali, that the interests of the Mashonaland and the Beira and Beira Junction Railways were so close that it was desirable to place them under one management for control, as well as for the pooling of revenue and expenditure, and the subsequent division of net earnings. Meanwhile the CGR was still in charge of operations over the lines from Bulawayo to Gwelo, Bulawayo to Mambanje and the Vryburg —Mafeking—Bulawayo section. So far as the lines in Rhodesia were concerned, this had been regarded as a temporary expedient and on 1 May 1903 the administration of the RR lines north and east of Bulawayo were placed in the hands of the Mashonaland Railway Co with Charles Wibberley as manager for the whole railway system. The line south from Bulawayo to Vryburg was left in charge of the CGR under a working agreement. The position of general manager at Bulawayo, held by J. L. Bissett since 1897, was abolished and this gentleman left RR. Bissett had represented RR at the first conference of managers and senior railway officers to be held in South Africa, that at Cape Town under the chairmanship of C. B. Elliott, CMG, general manager of the CGR in 1898

The headquarters for the whole system was at Umtali, which

with the extension of the main line already going further north via Wankie, placed Wibberley a long way from the scene of new developments. Bulawayo had become an important railway junction and was already growing into a 'railway town', though gold-mining was probably its chief interest. Staff were being recruited for the RR sections taken over from the CGR, many coming from the United Kingdom while others forsook railways in South Africa to chance their luck in Rhodesia. Under the supervision of the RR chief resident engineer, S. F. Townsend, a railway village, Raylton, had been created near Bulawayo station and a number of wood-and-iron and brick cottages had been built. A few more substantial houses were erected for the senior staff while a row of brick cottages appeared a few hundred yards across the road from the station entrance. To provide for the social needs of the staff a railway institute was begun, the foundation stone of which was laid by Mrs S. F. Townsend on 18 March 1902, when the walls had almost reached roof height. A photograph of this event shows cattle grazing in the background on a wide stretch of bare veld, very different from the tree-lined roads in the Raylton of today.

The Beira & Mashonaland Railways issued for the price of 6d a combined timetable, regulations, and rates and fares booklet, effective from March 1901, and this was enlarged to include the train service between Salisbury and Bulawayo in a new booklet costing only 3d from September 1903. The 1901 timetable showed a mail train from Beira on Friday night at 10pm reaching Umtali at 6.2pm on Saturday. Here passengers spent the night in the train presumably, if bound for Salisbury, as the connection left at 4am on Sunday morning and arrived at the capital at 6.22pm that evening. Much the same times applied for the down train to the port. A goods train ran on the six non-mail days and a conditional goods train was scheduled to run when required in both directions.

By 1903 two mail trains a week were running between Beira and Salisbury, and by cutting out the overnight wait at Umtali the journey time had been reduced from 44hr 52min to 32hr 25min for the inland run and from 36hr 57min to 28hr 30min for the down train to Beira. Refreshment rooms were open at Mandegos, Umtali and Salisbury, as well as at Gwelo and Bulawayo. On the Salisbury—Bulawayo line there were four mixed trains each way weekly, carrying passengers, the trip taking about twenty-five hours. The noon train from Salisbury on Fridays gave connection at Bulawayo with the Cape Town Train de Luxe as did the 10am train on Saturdays from Bulawayo to Salisbury.

Passenger fares differed between the Beira—Umtali and Umtali—Bulawayo sections, as the first class was 4½d and 3d per mile respectively. Natives in batches of not less than twenty were carried at ½d per mile each. A concession to parties of not less than ten members of cricket, football and other sporting teams allowed travel at single fare and a quarter for return journeys; it would seem that teams of eleven were sometimes difficult to raise.

The work of the rates clerk in goods offices was not over-difficult as the goods classification listed only 119 commodities in three classes, with 'sundries' in class one to cover anything else. Goods traffic carried towards the coast enjoyed half rates, indicative that imports much exceeded export goods, a position that was to reverse itself completely in the course of some ten years or so.

But timetables and tariff books were all very well when it came to the problem of running a railway during record rains in the territory between Umtali and the sea. Paulings in the narrow-gauge days had had their troubles and now it was the turn of the BMR manager and his engineers to cope with floods that inundated the line, washed away embankments and upset bridges. The Pungwe flats were to be the bugbear of railwaymen for many years to come. In the 1900–1 wet season traffic had been interfered with for ten weeks and the following rainy season caused a six weeks' stoppage of traffic. It was quite usual for Beira to have a rainfall of up to ten inches in twenty-four hours when cyclones swept down the Mozambique Channel; inland the catchment area of the Pungwe and Muda rivers gathered such enormous volumes of water that the floods could not escape and inundations followed.

To counter the flooding, heavy works were undertaken over the three years 1901–3, which included raising the main line between mileposts 28 and 42 to such a height that the rails were placed above the highest recorded flood level and a number of large openings were provided for the escape of water. Actually, in these three years, no less than 84 additional girder and masonry culverts and 147 pipe culverts were installed, while the Pungwe bridge was lengthened by three new spans totalling 152ft in length. The London board optimistically announced that it had every reason to believe that future floods would leave the railway unharmed and its traffic unimpeded. For a while their hopes were realised but this was only due to lighter rains and the Pungwe lulled the administration into a false sense of security.

While these troubles were being met there were other developments necessary for the BMR to become a railway. The story goes that Wibberley once received a cable from London complaining that his predecessor had made profits, to which Wibberley's reply was that he was 'making the railway'. At Umtali for example, waterworks had to be constructed at the joint expense of the British South Africa Company and the BMR for the use of the railway and the township. The working of the water supply was in the hands of the railway but private consumers' requirements were met on equitable terms, which was an immense boon to the town. The importance of Umtali as a railway centre had been increased by the transfer of the workshops and machinery formerly standing at Beira, and centralising the work saved much expense. Many houses were built for the railway staff and a recreation club was provided, with sports fields on which railway teams did battle with the townsfolk and visiting teams. An aptitude for cricket or football was a great advantage to the young man seeking a job on the BMR.

The long line of rail from Mafeking to Bulawayo ran through completely undeveloped country and the scattered gangers, pumpers and station staff had no facilities at all for the education of their children. In very primitive buildings, mainly huts, a small private school was started at Plumtree, sixty-three miles south of Bulawayo, for the sons and daughters of the pioneer railwaymen.

In 1902 Sir Charles Metcalfe had discussions with the South African Church Railway Mission, as a result of which Plumtree School was founded and boarding facilities provided for railway children. For some years both girls and boys were educated there. Later, this was to become one of the finest boys' schools in Rhodesia and its railway connection is symbolised by the old railway engine incorporated in the school badge.

Metcalfe and S. F. Townsend were very fully engaged in the further extension of the railway to the north, Pauling having been given the contract for the next section, between the colliery 'town' of Wankie and Victoria Falls. Work on this was begun in September 1903, financed by RR which was also responsible for the bridge over the Zambesi and the stretch of line from the river into the then North-Western Rhodesia as far as Kalomo, which was the administrative centre.

The sixty-eight miles of line from Wankie to Victoria Falls included forty-seven miles of very heavy work through difficult country and the line was constructed to the stiff grade of 1 in 50, uncompensated, with 7-chain curves, equivalent to 1 in 37 over the curves. Two severe banks were encountered, one from Deka siding up the Katuna valley and the other from Matetsi to a point later named Fuller. These climbs were both on maximum grade against northbound trains and the Katuna bank was aggravated by a horseshoe bend, which was to cause endless trouble to enginemen over the years to come. Two major river crossings were involved, one over the Deka, nine miles from Wankie, with a water tank sited not far away to top up supplies before tackling the Katuna bank, and the other was the Matetsi, about half way to Victoria Falls. For the latter a temporary trestle bridge, 260ft long and 43ft high, was built to carry the line forward. It was probably the biggest trestle bridge to be built by Paulings and was later replaced by a steel girder structure.

Harold Pauling was once more in charge of this contract and, as usual, the work was speedily pushed ahead to reach Victoria Falls, where the site for the famous bridge had already been selected. On 24 April 1904, only seven months after work began, the first construction train pulled in at the site of Victoria Falls station, then to be a dead end. The train was hauled by RR 7th class no 22 and for the last lap was driven by Harold Pauling's daughter, Blanche, with the locomotive flying a Union Jack and bearing a board below the headlamp reading 'We've got a long way to go'. This referred to Cairo, as the target of Cecil Rhodes was still very present in men's minds. Blanche Pauling had already travelled on the first engine to reach Bulawayo in 1897, so she could well claim to be a pioneer engine driver. In wide-brimmed felt hat, high collared white blouse and dark skirt down to her ankles, she made an unusual figure on the footplate. (Picture, p 133.)

As soon as the last sleeper was laid and the train came to rest, celebrations began, with native sports, mock battles by the tribesmen, and a feast for all the staff, white and black, engaged on the work. Percy Clark, who had reached the falls in May 1903, in his book *An Old Drifter*, tells of his success in taking photographs of the occasion and selling them at five shillings each to all the engineers, contractors and railway staff present.

Paulings started public traffic between Wankie and Victoria Falls on 10 May 1904, by running two trains a week each way for people anxious to visit this 'Wonder of the World'. The railway company had quickly despatched material for the early erection of a hotel, the forerunner of the famous hotel of today. The original building opened in June 1904 was of wood-and-iron, well raised from ground level to give ventilation and freedom from damp and pests. Twelve single and four double rooms in a long block, with a nearby cottage for honeymoon couples, comprised the first accommodation, to which was added soon after a dining-room block which had originally served as locomotive shed at Mandegos on the Beira narrow-gauge line. (Picture, p 66.) The hotel tariff was from 12s 6d a day upwards and the first lessee-manager was M Pierre Gavuzzi, who had had experience at the Carlton and Savoy Hotels in London. Before coming to Victoria Falls he had had a spell at the Grand Hotel in Bulawayo and so had acquired some knowledge of Rhodesian clientele, but he had to withstand many troubled days and nights coping with the uproarious workmen employed on the bridge construction. Whenever he came in sight of these workmen, he was chased round the hotel and, if caught, had to stand them all drinks. On one occasion when the whole gang was having a very hilarious night of it in the hotel bar Gavuzzi, who was small in stature, was hoisted up on to the mantelpiece and obliged to sing a song.

The hotel soon achieved popularity with visitors and more bedrooms, some with bathrooms for the wealthy, were added. For the younger Rhodesians it soon became a Mecca for honeymooners, a custom that has continued through the decades. The couples of those days can hardly have visualised the fine buildings of today with swimming pools, attractive gardens and motor-launch trips up the Zambesi, though Percy Clark started river excursions with a small launch and nine canoes as early as 1908.

When the hotel was first built the railway line passed in front of it on its way to the bridge site and this continued for some years. Later the main line was diverted to pass behind the hotel and in the present brick building to sit over a drink in the cool of evening on the open verandah, with its unobstructed view of the gorge and the bridge, is one of the features of a visit.

The line to Victoria Falls was officially taken over for traffic on 20 June 1904 and it was a Cape Town businessman who organised the first train tour to the beauty spot, which left Cape Town on 22 June with Mr Arderne and thirty-seven of his friends. This enterprising gentleman had hired the RR Train de Luxe with a refrigerator van attached and the dining-saloon bore the legend 'First Through Train—Cape Town to Victoria Falls'. The party spent six days at the Falls and three at Bulawayo, with a trip to Matopos, on the return journey. A descriptive and illustrated account of this inaugural tour was privately published in Cape Town as a souvenir. Another special train later in the year brought HRH Princess Christian on a visit, the first royal visitor.

The ordinary public did not, of course, enjoy the luxury of a special train in which to travel and sleep, but in July 1904 RR offered reduced fare tickets from Bulawayo at £5 5s first class and £3 10s second class. In advertisements it was baldly stated that passengers must provide their own meals and blankets and they were warned that there were no intermediate stations where refreshments could be obtained. The trains took 22 hours on the Bulawayo—Falls journey and 24 hours on the return trip, so that quite a large hamper of food was needed for the expedition.

However, by 1905, the train service was much improved by the introduction of the Zambesi Express, a through train from Kimberley to Victoria Falls, covering the 278 miles from Bulawayo in 17½ hours. This was a fully equipped train with dining-car and bedding services. All passengers were handed an *Annotated Time Table of the Zambesi Express on the Rhodesia Railways*, which gave details of the times at the stops en route in both directions, interesting information on the places passed, with illustrations, and pages for autographs, photographic notes and appointments. This must have been one of the first attempts at railway publicity by RR.

In contrast to the hampers passengers had to carry on the first excursion service to the falls, those who enjoyed the comforts of the Zambesi Express could lunch in the dining-saloon. It is interesting to see what one obtained for a half-crown in 1905. The menu consisted of:

Tomato soup; Boiled Kabaljoe with parsley sauce; Haricot Mutton; Roast Ribs of Beef; Assorted Vegetables; Cold York Ham and Roast Beef; Chicken and Tongue; Dressed Salad; Tapioca Pudding; Stewed Fruit; Cheese and Biscuits; and Black Coffee.

Not bad fare in a country which fifteen years before had been under the yoke of Lobengula and the nearest railway at Vryburg, some 600 miles south of Bulawayo.

THE VICTORIA FALLS BRIDGE AND BEYOND

Cecil Rhodes, who had never visited Victoria Falls, always visualised *his* railway on the Cape-to-Cairo route crossing the Zambesi river by a bridge over the gorge, yet close enough for the passengers to feel the spray as it fell on the carriages. That this wish was fulfilled is due to Sir Charles Metcalfe, who was such a true friend to Rhodes that, despite there being a much easier crossing of the river some six miles farther up beyond Kandahar

Island, he fixed the bridge site as we know it. Thus the Victoria Falls bridge became famous for its beautiful setting to visitors from all over the world. Built in one magnificent arched span, its design blended perfectly with the grandeur of the scene and provided a vantage point unequalled elsewhere for surveying such an awe-inspiring waterfall and the gorge through which the river swirled.

About October 1903, after the site had been settled, the two cliffs of the gorge were linked. First a rocket with a fine string was fired and on the third attempt the string reached the other side. This enabled a cord to be pulled across, then a wire, and finally a $\frac{3}{8}$th-in steel cable, carried on supports and strained tight. Then by means of a bosun's chair one person at a time was able to travel from side to side. Later, a much stronger steel rope was secured to carry the Blondin overhead carrier, which was powered by an electrically-driven winch. This Blondin had a capacity of fifteen tons and by this was conveyed much of the heavy material for bridgework and for the extension of the railway on the farther bank to Livingstone and beyond towards Kalomo. Thus the Blondin, named after the famous tightrope walker Charles Blondin, played an important part in railway expansion as well as in the construction of the bridge itself. One of the biggest jobs was the transfer of a locomotive from the south bank to work on the line on the north side of the river. This engine was dismantled, the boiler and lighter parts going over first; then the frame with cylinders attached and weighing over twelve tons followed. H. F. Varian has described how the cable sagged under this load and the carrier stopped at the centre where the dip was over forty feet, until after the boosting of the power in the electrical plant and by other means the carrier slowly managed to move again and reach the other side. The driver sitting in his little seat with a drop of 350 feet below him is said to have coolly smoked throughout his ordeal.

George Pauling, who had accompanied Metcalfe on his journey to pick the site for the bridge, tendered for its construction but to his disappointment his tender was beaten by that of the Cleveland Bridge & Engineering Co Ltd of Darlington, England, whose price was £72,000. Pauling consoled himself over losing the honour by the belief that the winning tenderer was involved in considerable loss!

The bridge was designed by G. A. Hobson and the preliminary calculations were made by Mr (later Sir) Ralph Freeman, who later designed the Sydney harbour bridge and the Birchenough bridge over the Sabi river in Rhodesia. A Frenchman, Georges C. Imbault, was the contractor's agent in charge of the erection and he promised that all traces of the construction camp would be removed and the beauty spot restored. This promise was duly observed as he burned down the huts used by his workers and had the ground cleared of all rubble, so that nature soon covered any traces of the camp.

The bridge itself has a graceful main arch of 500ft with two approach spans of 62ft 6in and 87ft 6in, and now contains a total of 1,868 tons of steel. It was first assembled in sections at the works at Darlington and then taken to pieces for shipment to Beira. These methodical preparations resulted in the actual erection of the steelwork taking only nine weeks, while the whole job extended over fourteen months. Some difficulty was experienced on the southern side as suitable rock for the foundations was not reached at the expected level and it became necessary to lower the whole structure in plan by some twenty feet, with the result that the bridge was not built on the intended level with the lip of the falls. This accounts for the rock cutting approach at the northern end of the bridge, on to which trains suddenly emerge and give passengers a wonderful view. (Picture, p 202.)

Once the work was started there was no hitch in its smooth progress. In the whole period there was only one death by accident and the net spread beneath the work across the centre part of the gorge was never needed. By the end of March 1905 the steelwork was advanced enough for the linking of the lower boom of the arch and this was completed on 1 April 1905. Connecting up the upper boom soon followed and at once a temporary track was laid on the open girders and a lightly loaded railway truck was run over, after which the shunting engine *Jack Tar* slowly propelled two trucks over. All went well and a regular flow of loaded trucks, two at a time, were passed over the bridge to enable Paulings to continue with the railway to Kalomo.

Already thirty miles of this line had been completed with material brought across the gorge by the Blondin. Paulings had established a depot with a small engine shed, coaling and watering facilities and a storage dump for the permanent way material. This was sited close to the south end of the Livingstone station of today and a small village of houses for their staff was erected, including a guest house for the use of George Pauling and his friends when on tour of the railway works. With traffic being passed over the Victoria Falls bridge, construction of the line, again under the direction of A. L. Lawley, was pushed ahead quickly to Kalomo. Although it climbed fairly continuously most of the way the country was easy for track-laying, the only obstacle being the Kalomo river which needed a bridge with three 100ft spans. The then administrative capital was reached in May and the line from Victoria Falls to Kalomo was opened to traffic in July 1905.

In the meantime the Victoria Falls bridge was being completed and the surroundings tidied up for the official opening ceremony on 12 September. The opening was performed by Professor G. Darwin, who was leader of the British Association party touring South Africa and Rhodesia after their congress. In his speech he quoted a remarkable poetical prophecy made by his great-grandfather, Erasmus Darwin, in 1785:

'Soon shall thy arm unconquered steam, afar
Urge the slow barge and draw the flying car'.

The professor then touched a button which fused a cord stretched across the width of the bridge, after which the first train, which had halted in the middle of the bridge for passengers to alight for the ceremony, slowly drew forward amid cheers. One of the new 8th class engines, no 54, gaily decorated with flags, palm leaves and other foliage, was at the head of the train, the driver being Allan Bowes. The event was also celebrated by the issue of a special set of postage stamps depicting the Victoria Falls.

This party of learned scientists formed part of the large crowd

BULAWAYO TO VICTORIA FALLS.   MONDAY, SEPTEMBER 11TH.   [DOWN

	1		2		3		4		5		6	
	arr.	dep.	arr.	dep.	arr.	dep.	arr.	dep.	arr.	dep.	arr.	dep.
Bulawayo	...	9.0	...	9.30	...	10.0	...	10.30	...	11.30	...	12.0
Pasipas Siding	9.48	9.50	10.18	10.20	10.48	10.50	11.18	11.20	12.18	12.20	12.48	12.50
Redbank Siding	10.14	10.19	10.44	10.49	11.14	11.19	11.44	11.49	12.44	12.49	1.14	1.19
NYAMANDHLOVU	10.56	11.0	11.26	11.30	11.56	12.0	12.26	12.30	1.26	1.30	1.56	2.0
Igusi Siding	12.8	12.10	12.38	12.40	1.8	1.10	1.38	1.40	2.38	2.40	3.8	3.10
Sawmills Tank	12.30	12.35	1.0	1.5	1.30	1.35	2.0	2.5	3.0	3.5	3.30	3.35
GWAAI	2.15	2.22	2.45	2.52	3.15	3.22	3.45	3.52	4.15	4.52	5.15	5.22
Ngamo Tank	3.29	3.37	3.59	4.7	4.29	4.37	4.59	5.7	5.59	6.7	6.29	6.37
Ngamo Siding	3.42	3.44	4.12	4.14	4.42	4.44	5.12	5.14	6.12	6.14	6.42	6.44
Intundhla Siding	4.24	4.26	4.54	4.56	5.24	5.26	5.54	5.56	6.54	6.56	7.24	7.26
MALINDI	5.36	5.46	6.6	6.16	6.36	6.46	7.6	7.16	8.6	8.16	8.36	8.46
Dett Siding	6.32	6.34	7.2	7.4	7.32	7.34	8.2	8.4	9.2	9.4	9.32	9.34
INYANTUE	7.42	7.45 ×38	8.12	8.15 ×38	8.42	8.45 ×38	9.12	9.15 ×38	10.12	10.15 ×38	10.42	10.45 ×38
Temporary Siding	8.0	8.2	8.30	8.32	9.0	9.2	9.30	9.32	10.30	10.32	11.0	11.2
Lukosi Siding	8.53	9.0	9.23	9.30	9.53	10.0	10.23	10.30	11.23	11.30	11.53	12.0 (Tuesday)
WANKIE	10.5	10.35	10.36	11.5	11.6	11.35	11.36	12.5	12.35	1.5	1.6	1.35 (Tuesday)
Deka Tank	10.59	11.4	11.29	11.34	11.59	12.4	12.29	12.34	1.29	1.34	1.59	2.4 (Tues.)
Deka Siding	11.18	11.20	11.48	11.50	12.18	12.20	12.48	12.50	1.48	1.50	2.18	2.20 (Tuesday)
Katuna Siding	12.17	12.19	12.47	12.49	.1.17	1.19	1.47	1.49	2.47	2.49	3.17	3.19
MATETSI	1.32	1.38	2.2	2.8	2.32	2.38	3.2	3.8	4.2	4.8	4.32	4.38
Kesi Siding	2.58	3.3	3.28	3.33	3.58	4.3	4.28	4.33	5.28	5.33	5.58	6.3
Masuie Tank	3.36	3.40	4.6	4.10	4.36	4.40	5.6	5.10	6.6	6.10	6.36	6.40
Victoria Falls	4.0	...	4.30	...	5.0	...	5.30	...	6.30	...	7.0	...

Goods Trains No. 39 Monday, September 11th, and Wednesday 13th, are hereby cancelled.
Goods Trains No. 42 Sunday, September 10th, and Tuesday 12th, are hereby cancelled.
Mixed Train No. 38 Monday, September 11th, must be detained at Inyantue to cross the six specials as above shown.

Working timetable of six special passenger trains from Bulawayo to Victoria Falls for opening of the bridge on 12 September 1905

98

assembled on the bridge for the occasion and the story goes that there was some speculation as to how far down was the flowing river. One professor is said to have held a stone and his watch, one in each hand, with the idea that he would drop the stone and time its fall. Unfortunately he dropped the watch instead of the stone. Actually, the lower boom of the span is about 350ft above the swirling water.

For the conveyance of the British Association party and others for the opening the BMR performed a feat of some magnitude in running six passenger trains at half-hour intervals over the main line between Bulawayo and Victoria Falls and back. In those days there were only six intermediate staffed stations over the whole 278 miles of forest and sparsely inhabited country with very unreliable telegraphic communication. The CGR gave help with carriages for the extra passengers but otherwise the Rhodesians were responsible for the whole operation.

As part of the celebrations for the opening of the bridge a programme was arranged to include a one-day regatta on the Zambesi, a day's racing, and a day of athletic sports. For the regatta, Metcalfe had sent to Oxford for clinker-built fours for the Rhodesian crews, two of which were made up from the railway and contractors' staff, while other crews came up from South Africa to compete. To take the boats to the river and to carry spectators, a siding 1½ miles long was constructed from the main line to the river bank, for which old 45lb rails were used. This became known as Regatta Spur and for long after it was used for shunting wagons of coal to the railway pumping station until electric power became available and the old siding was lifted.

When finally completed the bridge had two railway tracks, the idea being that the main line would be switched from one to the other from time to time to ease the strain on the bridge and this is believed to have been done for a few years. In 1930, however, the bridge was widened to permit road traffic and one of the two rail tracks was removed. This modification involved a widening by 13ft to carry the road and sidewalks, and the bridge floor was raised 4ft 6in in height, the work being done by the Cleveland Bridge Co, which had built the structure in 1905. On completion of this job the first motorcar to cross the bridge by road was driven by Charles K. Thompson, one of the railway engineers associated with the work.

The falls and the bridge were soon favourite tourist attractions and to augment revenue the railways imposed a toll on all who wished to walk on the bridge. For this a bridge guard was installed in a small toll house close to the southern approach, from which tickets at 1s each were issued. For some years Jack Soper was the guard and he had made a 'tube', similar to those in ticket offices, to hold the card tickets supplied for the toll by the accountant's office. All went well until Soper went on leave and stationmaster W. T. Breach enlisted a local resident to cover the duty. Very soon a trainload of excursionists arrived and their wish to walk over the bridge was to result in disaster behind the scenes. For, on seeing the relief guard in the evening to find out how the trippers had fared, Tommy Breach was told that all went well but that great difficulty had been experienced in issuing so many tickets as the guard could not get them out of the tube except by using a pin. The guard thought the tube idea was stupid—or words to that effect! To Breach's horror he found that all the tickets had been issued out of sequence, having been lifted out of the top of the tube with a pin instead of being drawn out at the bottom by finger in the usual way. The whole affair needed special explanation to the accountant and 'much binding' ensued.

As Livingstone grew in size and population some diversion was needed at weekends, and what better than a picnic on the river bank with an exploration of the rain forest and views of the gorge, ending up with a visit to the Falls Hotel. Not only was there no real road from Livingstone to the river but the bridge then only provided for the railway. To meet the desires of the residents, a local train service was started and this was operated from about 1910 for many years on Saturdays and Sundays. The train usually consisted of one first-second class composite carriage and a goods guard's van hauled in the early days by one of the Nasmyth Wilson 4–4–0 tender locomotives and later by a 7th class 4–8–0.

The train was colloquially known as The Weekender and the

Saturday night dances at the Falls Hotel brought good patronage from the young people, especially as the railway detached one or two carriages at Victoria Falls station into which in the small hours the tired dancers would retire for a few hours rest before the carriages were coupled to a northbound train back to Livingstone. (Picture, p 202.)

For a time in 1916 the steam train was replaced by the first Rhodesian railcar. This 'rail motor coach', as it was officially described, was propelled by a 70hp petrol engine; it was 24ft in length and seated twenty passengers with a little space at one end for light packages. Built by the Drewry Car Co in England it did not remain in service for very long but it was tried out on short local trips elsewhere on the system.

When war broke out in 1914 a military guard was at once provided on the bridge. German South-West Africa was not far away and sabotage could be attempted. A blockhouse commanding a view of the bridge was erected and S. A. Tomalin, then loco foreman at Livingstone, gave assistance when a mobile searchlight was used as part of the security measures. This was mounted on a truck which was shunted from one position to another on and close to the bridge, until it was finally parked on the south bank from which the light could command almost the entire bridge. Again in 1939 the bridge was at once placed under guard on the outbreak of World War II.

During 1905 the newly-discovered lead deposit at Broken Hill was being developed to the stage where rail transport was essential, as it was expected that production would call for a train a day. This was the magnet for the extension of the line from Kalomo. From Bulawayo the line had been financed by Rhodesia Railways, but for the next stretch it was the Mashonaland Railway that provided the funds. Once more the job was given to Pauling.

Harold Pauling, who had been chief agent, had died soon after the line reached Victoria Falls and A. L. Lawley had taken charge at Livingstone with P. St G. Mansergh doing the preliminary survey. A contract had been accepted by George Pauling for the 281 miles from Kalomo to Broken Hill to be built at the rate of a mile a day, so that once again Lawley was faced with a target only a man with unbounding enthusiasm and inspiration could achieve. For the railways, H. F. Varian was the local resident engineer under S. F. Townsend, who was still chief resident engineer with headquarters at Bulawayo.

Between Kalomo and the Kafue river the country was not difficult, though the Magoye, Kaleya, Mazabuka and Nega Nega rivers required steel girder bridges with 100ft spans. The main problem was bridging the Kafue—that steady flowing mass of water that has given railway engineers many a headache with its floating islands of sudd. For this crossing Lawley and Varian chose a site and decided that a bridge of thirteen 100ft spans was needed, this becoming the longest bridge on the whole system, indeed in Southern Africa, for many years to come. The order for material was placed in England, the overhead braced girder work being fabricated for erection in situ on the river bank. As construction of the bridge was to be carried out from both ends, Lawley designed a prefabricated pontoon 95ft long, 45ft wide and 5ft deep, large enough to carry a locomotive or two loaded trucks across the river at a time. The pontoon was suitable for the bridge spans themselves when the time came to float them into position.

In the meantime platelaying was proceeding apace across the Batoka plateau and while some delay was caused by the temporary bridging of the four rivers south of the Kafue, the arrival by ox-waggon from railhead of material for bridge piers and for the pontoon enabled work to be started. Such was Lawley's drive that the rails actually reached the Kafue three months ahead of the contract time.

At the bridge site most of the ground near the river was marsh land but a suitable piece of high ground on the south bank served as the depot for offloading and assembling the thirteen 100ft spans. These spans were erected in echelon alongside a railway track and were slid on rails and winched on to the pontoon, one at a time, thence being floated into position between the piers, after which the pontoon was moved away leaving the span in its final site. On one day as many as three spans were launched and placed into position.

By means of the pontoon, permanent-way material was being ferried over the Kafue and work went ahead on the north side. At first, due to the swampy ground, only lightly loaded trucks could be run on the new track and haulage was by a span of oxen known as 'engine no 32', but soon the formation was raised and the first steam locomotive, CGR 4–6–0 no 75 hired by Pauling, was floated over and placed on line. (Picture, p 151.) Beyond Kafue the country was broken and hilly with heavier work for the contractor to surmount the 1 in 64 rising grade to the vicinity of where Lusaka now stands.

Despite this, earthworks and platelaying went ahead without delay and Broken Hill was reached on 11 January 1906 within the specified contract time. As a final display of their skill the platelaying gangs, who had been with Pauling for many years, laid the last half-mile into Broken Hill with materials being offloaded from the train as it slowly passed over the newly laid track just placed on the formation. This last dash was filmed by Pathé, the first news-reel to be made in Northern Rhodesia.

The 106 miles of line, bridges and culverts were built entirely with material taken over the river on the pontoon before the Kafue bridge was completed and opened by the first train to cross. This first train comprised Pauling's private saloon, Lawley's coach with guests and Varian's coach, with an open bogie truck at the rear next to Pauling's coach. This open truck carried the construction gangs and was stacked with hams and other foodstuffs, while drinks were dispensed from his saloon balcony by George Pauling to his men. As no hard liquor had been allowed during the work on the bridge it was soon a very convivial party of wide-hatted roughly clad bridgemen, standing in the open wagon as the train slowly rumbled across the river. The bridge gang undertook to push the truck back to their camp on the south bank, and when Pauling returned a couple of days later it was clear from the black eyes and other casualties that the gangs had well and truly celebrated the opening in a very informal manner.

On 20 June 1906 a special train reached Broken Hill for the official opening of this new extension of the BMR. T. G. Davey, who had discovered the lead and zinc in 1902, was now general superintendent of the Broken Hill Development Co and welcomed the guests at the ceremony. In his speech of welcome Davey paid tribute to George Pauling and his men and told of how on one occasion 5¾ miles of rails were laid in eleven hours near Pemba. There is no doubt that Pauling and Lawley had imbued their pioneer railway construction gangs with a marvellous spirit of enthusiasm, but a salient point was that they always kept their African labour force well fed with plenty of meat.

The Kalomo—Broken Hill section was worked under construction conditions until it was handed over for full traffic on 1 September 1906 and at once the mine began despatching lead and zinc ores to Beira for shipment. At this stage all trains were worked on the caboose system from Livingstone, where a loco depot had been established on the site of Pauling's camp. There was no shed for engines at the railhead and Broken Hill station was a small wood-and-iron building with a few thatched mud huts near the kopje well to the south of the present station and yard. The few railway cottages were small wood-and-iron shacks with an outside convenience at the bottom of the garden, which could only be made when the high grass had been cleared and a stockade erected. It was quite usual for a lion to prowl through the housing area and the station undisturbed by the occasional train, and the men and their families had many a fright and narrow escape.

The train service consisted of two mixed trains each way weekly taking 30½ hours from Livingstone to Broken Hill and 32 hours on the southward trip, while a special goods train was run when required. The trains were hauled by 7th or 8th class engines with two crews working the round trip of 740 miles on the caboose system.

Unfortunately, after moving 13,428 tons of ore from Broken Hill, this traffic suddenly ceased in May 1907 owing to difficulties in the treatment and separation of the lead and zinc ores at the refinery in Wales. So the expected daily train did not materialise and the service was cut to one train a week. This was a great disappointment and, coupled with the depression which prevailed in Rhodesia, led to considerable retrenchment of staff throughout the system. Railway expansion ceased and for over two years no new construction was contemplated.

However, although finance did not at once permit the continued extension of the railway northwards, the project was kept well to the fore by confirmation of rich mineral deposits in the Katanga Province of the Congo and of copper at Bwana M'kubwa, some 120 miles north of Broken Hill. The Katanga mines were discovered by Robert Williams, mining engineer to Cecil Rhodes in the early Kimberley days, but the Belgians had forestalled Rhodes by their occupation of Katanga. Williams had, however, obtained a concession from the Portuguese to build a line from the west coast port of Lobito through Angola to the Congo, which would involve some 1,300 miles of new railway, a work of great magnitude in undeveloped country. For the extension from Broken Hill to Katanga, only some 300 miles of line were needed to the mining area.

As a first step Sir Charles Metcalfe, Townsend and Varian made a reconnaissance of the route from Broken Hill to the Congo border, which was then not properly defined but lay some miles north of where the town of Ndola was later established. It was some time before Robert Williams, who was intimately connected with the development of the Katanga copper mines, was able to persuade financial backers that it was of primary importance to link Katanga with the Rhodesian railway system rather than wait for the line from Lobito Bay. The supply of coke and coal from the Wankie colliery had a strong influence on the decision and in 1908 the Rhodesia—Katanga Junction Railway & Minerals Co Ltd was formed by Williams and the British South Africa Company to construct a line from Broken Hill to the Congo border. Debentures for £800,000 were issued to pay for the line, the British South Africa Company having an option of purchase, which was exercised twenty years later.

Once more George Pauling was called on to carry out the work of this, the last section of the main line to the north so far as the BMR were concerned. Pauling also carried on with the line into Katanga to Elisabethville, 165 miles from the Northern Rhodesia border, for the Chemin de Fer du Katanga, a Belgian company, and was later associated with further railway extensions in that territory.

Platelaying was begun from Broken Hill in May 1909 and no undue difficulty was experienced with construction through the 132 miles of forest country interspersed with the occasional river or stream. The Mulungushi needed a bridge with a 150ft span and the vlei at the Itawa on the approach to Ndola required a girder bridge of 100ft, but no serious obstacle affected the easily graded line, a feature of which is the sweeping curves dipping to streams in marshy vleis. By November the border was reached and on 11 December 1909 the railway crossing of the Congo frontier was celebrated by a gathering of British and Belgian notables, at which the rail lengths on the border were connected with specially made copper fishplates, placed by the governor of Katanga.

The depot set up by Pauling was used for the continuation of the line to Elisabethville and material for this formed a large part of the traffic over the newly-opened line. It is recalled by one driver that owing to the shortage of guards' vans it was the practice to use a covered truck as brake van, but of course no brake was fitted for the guard to apply when needed. As these box wagons had end ventilators it was customary to carry a piece of hemp rope, one end of which was passed out through the ventilator and tied to the lug of the vacuum pipe, so that when the guard wished to stop the train he pulled the pipe off the stopper and the vacuum brake was applied. This Heath Robinson fitting worked well as an expedient, but on one occasion on a night train from Broken Hill the guard forgot his rope and at the first stop he got some natives to make a substitute out of bark from trees and attached this to the vacuum pipe. Nearing Bwana M'kubwa a covered wagon next to the 'guard's van' became derailed and the guard made a lunge, as his van rocked, and grabbed his bark rope, which with the jerk immediately broke. Fortunately the driver soon felt the drag and stopped his train. On going back he found one axle box broken as well as other damage to the trailing bogie of the truck, which incidentally carried several passengers, including Pauling's Irish locomotive superintendent, whose language at this mishap in the middle of a wet night was choice.

Driver Miller had to improvise and he remembered that at Bwana M'kubwa, a few miles on, the station 'building' was a covered truck of similar design. So with half his train he went on and, reaching the station, he jacked up the 'office' and removed one of the bogies. Then he called out the ganger who, with his gang, trolleyed the bogie back to the scene of the derailment, where Miller with his help changed the bogie and re-railed the passenger boxcar.

Running through thick forest for much of the way, this was one of the loneliest sections on the whole system and in the early days the isolated gangers and pumpers had no amenities at all. Shooting for the pot provided meat, but the monthly pay and stores train brought the essential supplies of provisions to these men, some with families, who lived with little contact with the outside world. Heavy rain in the lonely forest, with lions, leopards, elephants and other wild life as neighbours and only a momentary glimpse of the infrequent train, induced nerves and depression. Some took to the bottle while malaria and blackwater fever ended the lives of many. One can still see the occasional lonely grave near pump houses or platelayers' cottages. Even in recent years the Broken Hill—Ndola section of the line was the most isolated as the modern main road is miles from the railway in many places. But despite the discomfort and loneliness the men of the BMR kept the railway running.

CHAPTER FIVE

Bulawayo Becomes Headquarters

WHILE Pauling had been busy on the rapid extension of the BMR towards the Congo, consolidation of the railway system was quietly going on in Southern Rhodesia. The country was develop- ing as more mineral discoveries were made; goldmines were open- ing and needed plant and machinery; copper and chrome deposits were being mined, while coal from Wankie was already a useful traffic. Agricultural produce, such as maize, was offering and ranches were now able to sell cattle on the hoof for slaughter. The greater proportion of traffic, however, was still imports from the ports to the interior, which necessitated long trains of empty trucks being worked back to Beira or handed over to the Cape railway at Bulawayo.

Efforts were being made to build up a settled staff at Umtali, where Henry Chapman had become accountant in 1904. The railway workshops at this centre were being enlarged and the introduction of two Kitson-Meyer locomotives had led to the need to strengthen certain small bridges on the Umtali—Salisbury section.

Goldmines discovered beyond Gwanda brought a demand for the extension of the branch from Heany (first known as Gwanda Junction) and on 1 March 1905 the section from Gwanda to West Nicholson was opened with mixed trains running twice a week to the terminus and once weekly to Gwanda. The chrome mined at Selukwe was growing and a train ran from Gwelo six days a week. The track was only 45lb and had been previously in use on the Vryburg—Mafeking line. Loads were light with the small engines used—from 170 to 360 tons gross, equal to six to twelve bogie wagons—while passengers could not expect a fast trip over the 23-mile branch line. When driver Ted Cornish took his train out of Gwelo it depended on his whim when passengers got to Selukwe. At Surprise siding, fifteen miles out, it was his frequent practice to stop for a game of billiards at the Napier-Rogers hotel; 50-up was normal but if the passengers protested too much Cornish and his fireman would make it 100. On one occasion they arrived at Selukwe on Christmas Eve and celebrated to such an extent that the train remained there for three days, with the local stationmaster keeping the fire going in the engine. Guinea Fowl siding was another popular stop as the game birds were very prevalent and a brace of guinea fowl was usually shot for the driver's pot.

Coupled with the sudden cessation of the zinc ore traffic from Broken Hill in 1907 there was a depression generally in Rhodesia and staff had to be retrenched as traffic dropped off considerably. Fortunately the rains were not so destructive this year and the newly completed bridge at Pungwe ensured freedom from traffic interruption.

During August 1907 the crown prince of Portugal visited Mozambique and consented to the Pungwe bridge being named Dom Luiz Phillippe Bridge. The prince and his father, the king of Portugal, were soon afterwards to die tragically by assassination in Portugal.

The discovery of gold and copper in the Umvuma district led to the Blinkwater Railway Co, the capital of which was subscribed by the Beit Railway Trustees, giving George Pauling the construction of a 50-mile branch to Umvuma. Begun in August 1908, this line ran from Lyndhurst siding, eight miles from Gwelo on the Selukwe branch, and apart from the mines served a new farming area. It was opened to traffic on 19 June 1909, and then in 1914 was extended a further seventy miles from Umvuma to Fort Victoria, where the Pioneer Column in its march into Rhodesia in

1890 had established a fort. Here gold and chrome mines were a source of traffic and some thirty years later asbestos and lithium ores were discovered in the district.

By 1909 traffic was picking up and the prospects looked much brighter. Many of the staff who had been laid off were re-employed to handle rising traffic, which included heavy tonnages of construction material for the CFK and mining machinery for the Union Minière du Haut Katanga. In the year 1908–9 the railway carried 11,733 tons of general goods and 2,363 more tons of minerals than in 1907–8, while net revenue rose by more than 58 per cent from £120,297 to £190,162. The best feature was that the tonnage of minerals, mainly Selukwe chrome, had practically doubled and almost equalled imported general traffic, so reducing empty truck haulage. The colliery at Wankie was supplying loco coal at 13s 6d per ton and mines and other consumers were switching from firewood to coal, so creating more traffic.

While the extension to Sakania, the handover point with the CFK, was bringing improved traffic returns the fact that railway headquarters were still at Umtali, 1,263 miles from Sakania, was proving a great inconvenience to the manager and his officers. When the line only ran between Beira and Salisbury the head office had been central, but now it was too far away and a move to Bulawayo was decided upon. New brick houses had to be built in Raylton but by October 1910 the move was scheduled. All work more or less ceased as in the spirit of economy the offices—wood-and-iron—were dismantled and loaded into trucks to accompany the staff to the new HQ. Married employees were busy stowing their household effects into a covered truck each and the train-load of staff, wives and children, personal belongings and furniture, office buildings, files and equipment set off for Bulawayo. Each member of the staff had been given £5 in glittering sovereigns for their expenses on the journey.

The trip was a memorable one as everyone relaxed in one big family until arrival at Bulawayo meant offloading and settling into their new homes. Sixteen houses had been built in Raylton while a two-storey mansion had been erected in the suburbs of the town for the manager, Charles Wibberley. This house, set in delightful grounds, became the home of successive general managers and the scene of many functions.

The old wood-and-iron offices from Umtali were soon erected and the staff moved in to pick up the threads of work. At that time it was the manager, the traffic manager and the accountant and staff who were involved, while the locomotive superintendent and the stores remained at Umtali. So Bulawayo, already an important railway junction, became the hub of the system, a factor which was to have a large bearing on the growth and development of this fine city in years to come.

About this time Thomas A. Mallett, who was managing the Victoria Falls Hotel for the railways, was called upon to inaugurate a catering department to control dining-cars, refreshment-rooms and hotels. Initially the department was operated from Victoria Falls but this soon proved inconvenient and Mallett was found offices at Bulawayo.

It was in November 1910 that Rhodesia welcomed its first royal train when the Duke and Duchess of Connaught and Princess Patricia included a visit to Victoria Falls and Livingstone in their tour of the newly-formed Union of South Africa. The South African Railways—also just formed—provided a train of eleven vehicles, including special saloons for the royal guests. Over the BMR the train came in the charge of local staff and 8th class engine no 54 was specially prepared for the journeys. A pilot train ran ahead of the royal train and an emergency train followed at an interval of 30 minutes, this being deemed necessary in case of breakdown between widely separated stations. A feature of the tour was the haulage of a bogie truck carrying four cows to supply fresh milk each day. These survived the three weeks' tour and must have achieved a record journey for cows.

The royal party stayed four days at Livingstone, living in their train, which made short trips to the Falls for sightseeing from the bridge and elsewhere. The tour also included visits to Salisbury and Bulawayo and, in all, the royal train spent twelve days on BMR lines. At the conclusion of the visit the duke conferred the MVO on Charles Wibberley, the manager, as a tribute to the efficient manner in which the tour had been carried out by the

BMR, as well as for his personal attention while travelling on the train. This honour was particularly appropriate as Wibberley was retiring in the following year.

The upsurge of traffic was continuing with the expansion of the system and the development of the territories. That the extensions were sound business was shown by an increase in revenue from £345,000 in 1902 to £970,000 in 1910. The tons carried had risen from 74,000 to 480,000 and passengers from 29,000 to 254,000 over the same years, while the mileage of line open—374 in 1900 under Rhodesian administration—had grown to 1,743.

To meet the rise in traffic Wibberley persuaded the London board to buy additional locomotives and rolling stock. Another batch of 8th class 4–8–0s came into use late in 1910 and 600 wagons were being delivered, while a new running shed and a start on workshops had been put in hand at Bulawayo. Increased goods shed and siding accommodation was being constructed at Salisbury and Bulawayo and extra housing and additions to workshops at Umtali had been provided.

From the staff angle the establishment of a non-contributory pension fund for all permanent employees was a very welcome move and Wibberley could feel that not only was he leaving a large increase in staff to meet business offering, but that they were more settled and contented, with an incentive to remain in the service.

In 1911 Charles Wibberley retired after forty-five years of railway work and was succeeded as general manager by Edward R. Ross, who had previously been in charge of the Natal Government Railway, now absorbed into the SAR. Before coming to Natal in 1906 Ross had had eighteen years with the GIP and Madras Railways in India.

Another change was Lewis Thomas as traffic manager in place of Owen Griffin, who had retired. Thomas was one of the 'characters' among the BMR senior staff and, like several others, came from South Wales. Always very carefully dressed, he was insistent on his uniformed staff being smart and properly attired on duty. Looking out of his office window one day he saw a man in shirt-sleeves and knee breeches turning over packages in the van of an incoming train. Out stormed Thomas shouting, 'You're sacked, man, you're sacked', only to discover it was a passenger searching for his luggage.

Working conditions at many places were still of a pioneering nature as finance was tight. Loco sheds were small and leaky with primitive drainage; in fact, at Livingstone after a heavy storm the water would rush through the shed like a river, flooding the pits and stopping work. Caboose working was still in vogue in 1912 over the whole line from Livingstone to Sakania, trains being worked chiefly by 7th and 8th class locomotives, though a few 9th class were coming on the north run. During the rains the train service often became disrupted by frequent minor washaways and derailments so that single crews would have to work right through the 500 miles to Sakania and back again. With the resultant shortage of enginemen, an engine crew would be booked out again from Livingstone within a few hours, merely having time to clean up, fill their food boxes and have their loco coaled before undertaking another 1,000-mile round trip.

It was probably after one of these occasions that a driver and fireman did not hit it off too well when working an old 7th class engine from Livingstone. Bob Emerson recalled that this crew had to feed their firebox by hand. Apparently the fireman was reprimanded by his driver for not keeping the footplate clean. 'I suppose the handbroom is no use to you,' said the driver sarcastically. 'No', came the answer, 'it isn't', whereupon the driver flung the broom into the firebox. 'And I suppose the shovel is no use either', he continued. Again an abrupt reply and the shovel followed the brush. Too late they realised what the argument had led to. The train still had to run and the engine be fired, so it was hands to coal until they could borrow a shovel from a ganger's cottage many miles further on.

On another occasion a loco crew feeling a little thirsty helped themselves to a case of whisky from the guard's van while the guard was busy at a stop. They had a fine time and are reported to have got through at least three bottles before they decided to call it a day. Though intoxicated by then they realised they must not be caught with the case and threw it into the firebox. 'Let's see how she runs on whisky', said the exuberant fireman. But they did not escape detection and both were dismissed.

In 1911 the first step was taken to convert the 2ft line from Salisbury to Mount Hampden to the 3ft 6in gauge as the condition of the narrow-gauge track and rolling stock was deteriorating badly. This permitted the construction of the Mount Hampden—Jumbo section of the eventual Shamva Branch in the wider gauge, and this was opened in December 1911. Another short branch, 2¾ miles long, was opened on 16 May 1912 from a junction a mile north of Gatooma to serve the Cam & Motor goldmine at Eiffel Flats. This mine was then developing and in 1914 became one of the most valuable Rhodesian gold discoveries.

The new general manager, after a survey of the track, soon submitted proposals to London for considerable expenditure over two years for improving the road, ballasting, and easing grades and curves. The old round-top 60lb rail was replaced by new flat-top rail, though north of Kalomo the latter type was used from the start, and the relaying gave better running conditions for the heavier locomotives then being provided.

The Katanga copper mines had imported coke through Beira so far, but in 1911 the Wankie colliery began to produce suitable coke and 4,600 tons were railed. The coal was of fine coking quality and as the Wankie output rose so the imported coke dropped, until in 1912 a contract for 100,000 tons a year was concluded between Wankie and the UMHK bringing lucrative traffic for many decades to the BMR.

In the meantime, at Beira, work had been going ahead with a new wharf to cope with the increasing import and export traffic, this being a lighterage wharf at the entrance to Chiveve creek. Plans drawn for further additions were discussed by the Mozambique and Beira Railway authorities at much length and were not finalised before war broke out in 1914. It was not until 1920 that a 400ft extension on the Chiveve was completed for an expansion of the lighterage facilities.

The old wood-and-iron headquarters offices from Umtali evidently did not impress the new general manager, who had been used to better things in Natal, and in 1912 Ross was able to secure sanction for new brick headquarters and station offices for Bulawayo. The first to be completed was the administrative block, single storey with two wings, set at right angles to the new station which faced an open space with a row of trees screening the backs of railway cottages built in the CGR days. Many years later this area was improved by the demolition of the cottages and the laying out of gardens to form Metcalfe Square in memory of the famous railway engineer, Sir Charles Metcalfe.

The new offices cost £12,000 and, though single storey, had foundations and walls to carry an upper floor when the need arose—as it did in 1925. The brick building with tiled roof compared well with others in Bulawayo then and provided offices for the accountants in one wing and the civil engineers in the other, while the general manager and staff occupied the centre portion. Opened by Mrs E. R. Ross on 9 June 1913, the new offices were a boon to the staff whose inadequate facilities had been recognised by Mr (later Sir) Henry Birchenough during his visit as a board member the year before. His influence had also led to the new station building, the foundation stone of which was laid in April 1913 by Mrs Rochfort Maguire, wife of the BMR chairman.

The new station was also erected originally as a single storey and was placed a little to the east of the 1898 building. Constructed at a cost of £18,000, it was on the site of the kraal of one of Lobengula's crack regiments and underground storage bins for their grain were found when the foundations were being excavated.

The traffic manager and his staff were housed in a portion of the station, which also provided much improved public facilities. It was set well back from the main platform, so providing a very spacious open concourse, on which was to appear a wooden book-stall with six display windows, which was rented by the *Chronicle* and remained a feature of the station for very many years.

The main platform, with a crossover track in the centre, was very long and could accommodate two trains with ease. The longest in Africa, this platform was for many years the second longest in the world. All trains to Gwelo and Salisbury left from the east end and proceeded slowly through the Bulawayo suburbs passing over five level crossings, a permanent speed restriction of 10mph applying to all trains. At the western end trains left for South Africa and for Victoria Falls and Northern Rhodesia, the junction of the two lines being close to the station. Here trains to Mafeking took a wide curve and ran south-west past the loco shed and workshops on an easy grade which enabled speed to be attained for the rise to Bellevue, a small outlying suburb. Northbound trains took a falling grade curving round the western outskirts of the town passing the explosives siding and native locations on the way. Many changes were to be made in the years ahead.

The Rhodesia Katanga Junction Railway from Broken Hill to the Congo border was from the start operated as part of the Mashonaland Railway, though separate working costs were kept. This through connection to the rich copper discoveries made in Katanga brought to the BMR an increasing tonnage of railway construction and mining materials, the CFK having been opened as far as Elisabethville to link up with the RKJR. An extension of the CFK to Kambove, farther north, was in hand by Pauling and soon rolling stock was arriving from Belgium for these lines opening up the copper areas. This in turn affected the BMR train service and some of the new 9th class engines were placed on the Livingstone—Sakania run, as by 1911 the Union Minière was calling for more and more coke and coal for its plant.

With the issue of the June 1914 timetable the BMR made an innovation by adopting the 24-hour system in order to avoid irritating errors between 'am' and 'pm'. This was not followed by the SAR and, while public timetables later reverted to the 12-hour practice, the working timetables have adhered to 24 hours ever since on Rhodesian railways. Its value was particularly apparent for the correct compilation of the paper orders issued to train crews as their authorities to proceed, in which accurate timing was vital and mistakes could be fatal.

Three types of train proceeding orders were in use. The 'Station to Station' order on green paper gave trains a clear run from one station to the next without effecting a crossing with an opposing train. The 'Crossing' order, on pink paper with a yellow cross, detailed the intermediate sidings at which trains had to meet and pass one another in opposite directions, while the third was a 'Ballast' order on yellow paper with a large orange 'B', which served for a train working in a section but required to clear it at a certain station for the passage of a through train. All these orders were compiled and issued to train crews after the exchange of messages by morse telegraph between stations at the ends of the particular sections, and they gave all essential information as to the trains which had left for or arrived from the station ahead.

This method of working with simple train orders served the BMR well and irregularities were comparatively infrequent, until more recently when the train service increased to the stage when crossings in section became very complicated with late running. Station officials arranging crossings in long sections then really needed a crystal ball to help their train arranging, but this was a problem of the future.

In 1914 the passenger service ran four times weekly in each direction between Bulawayo and Salisbury, the journey taking 18 hours, while two trains a week ran on the Bulawayo—Victoria Falls—Congo line, the run to the Falls taking $16\frac{1}{4}$ hours, to Broken Hill 47 hours and to Elisabethville 71 hours. The BMR trains terminated at Sakania, a joint station then manned by British and Belgian railway staff, and here passengers changed to a CFK train with wood-burning locomotive for the journey to the Katanga capital.

Three trains a week connected Bulawayo and Cape Town, those connecting with the weekly Union-Castle mail steamer being titled 'Southern Limited' and 'Northern Limited', while Johannesburg and Durban were also served thrice weekly. The trains between Bulawayo and Mafeking included carriages for both the Cape and Transvaal and were divided at Mafeking.

Dining-cars were provided on BMR long-distance trains with meals costing 2s 6d for breakfast, 3s for lunch and 3s 6d for dinner, while a bed could be hired for 2s 6d, this latter consisting of two pillows, sheets and three blankets. The meals were varied and lengthy, giving good value for money. Rhodesian dining-cars were always well stocked with liquid refreshments and it was often difficult for the stewards to close down the convivial parties of celebrating miners, farmers or holidaymakers intent on making a night of it. At stops at wayside stations residents often slipped into the diner for a drink or some tobacco, and to collect any interesting news during the short stay.

A daily suburban service was run in the 'wet' season to Salisbury from the suburb of Avondale to enable residents to get to work or to shop in the capital and home again. Avondale in the rains became almost isolated by the vlei which flooded and became a haven for wild duck, the road becoming a quagmire and impassable for the few motorcars, while buses were unknown. This train trip of six miles took twenty minutes, the first-class return fare being 2s 6d. Usually one carriage and a van sufficed, no strain on the Nasmyth Wilson 4-4-0 locomotives, MR nos 3 and 4.

Another unusual service was the 'railmotor coach' run from Bulawayo to Plumtree and back thrice weekly. This was a journey of 4hr 10min each way and the single fares were 13s 9d first and 9s 4d second class. This experimental service does not appear to have lasted long, owing to lack of patronage. Doubtless the few farmers and missionaries did not have time or inclination to visit town very often.

On 10 July 1914 the extension of the Blinkwater Railway to Fort Victoria was opened to give access to a fertile farming area, later the source of much mineral traffic. At this time the Umvuma line diverged from the Selukwe branch some six miles from Gwelo station but it had been found that trains converging from the two branches at a distant unattended junction was a complication. A new line was constructed from the north end of Gwelo station curving round the edge of the township and running on straight to link up 10½ miles out, saving about 2¼ miles compared with the old route via Lyndhurst. This separate Fort Victoria line was opened in September 1915. Many years later the Selukwe branch in its turn was deviated to join the Fort Victoria line two miles from Gwelo.

In August 1914 World War I broke out and there was an immediate rush by railway employees to volunteer for the Rhodesian forces or to join up in Britain. While the sudden loss of experienced staff was to some extent an embarrassment to the administration, it was not long before a serious drop in traffic was felt. Imported goods showed a substantial decline and this was particularly apparent over the Beira—Salisbury line as war restrictions diverted shipping from Beira to South African ports. While the loss of high-rated general goods continued during the war years, revenue later improved by war demands for copper, lead, chrome and other minerals.

Copper ingots from the Congo and the Falcon mine at Umvuma, which had totalled 5,890 tons in 1913, rose to over 32,000 tons in 1917–18, chrome from 54,600 to 98,300 tons, and lead from Broken Hill began at 232 tons in 1915 and shot up to 11,000 in 1918. Coal and coke were also in demand, jumping from 261,000 in 1914 to 398,000 tons in 1918, a fair proportion going to Beira for bunkerage when shipping resumed calling at the port.

Apart from the boost to mineral exports, the war led to the establishment on a small scale of local industries in Rhodesia. Factories were started to produce bacon, oil and oil cake, cattle feed, butter and cream, while a cement industry was started eleven miles out of Bulawayo at Cement siding and soon produced much useful traffic. At that time the factory obtained its limestone from hills some fourteen miles distant, the cement company operating their own 2ft-gauge light railway. Several years later when local supplies were exhausted, limestone was quarried from a large hill at Colleen Bawn and provided heavy traffic over the West Nicholson branch.

Altogether 398 railwaymen were on active service during the war and of these twenty-nine were killed or died on service. The total European staff in 1918 numbered 2,316 with 6,803 natives. Umtali workshops undertook a variety of jobs for the military forces, including the preparation of armoured wagons for the mounting of guns, as early in the war it was feared the main line in Bechuanaland might be attacked by rebels from the Transvaal, but this did not eventuate. Maxim gun tripods and shields were made for troops operating in German East Africa, while castings and machinery were supplied to many mines which were unable to import from overseas.

Railway services were severely crippled in 1918 by two unexpected troubles. A very heavy rainfall was experienced over Southern Rhodesia and Mozambique and by the end of January the line between Salisbury and Beira had been completely cut in two places. The rain had swelled the Odzi river to the extent that the pier on one side of the bridge settled and on 26 January three 100ft spans collapsed. A pontoon was placed across the river and by shuttle trains from Umtali and Salisbury to the bridge site passengers, mails and urgent packages were ferried over. This continued until 21 April when the bridge was brought back into use by the sterling efforts of the engineering staff.

Two days after the Odzi bridge collapsed the floodwaters of the Pungwe river, fed by the torrential rain in the highlands, had risen so high that at several points on the line across the Pungwe flats embankments fell in and culverts were washed out, while the Pungwe bridge itself was threatened by the river scouring the banks. A gale occurred as the floodwater built up and the pressure washed out sections of embankment on each side of the bridge, and so from 28 January to 4 April 1918 the train service between Beira and Umtali was cut. One mixed train was badly derailed crossing the flats and was soon surrounded by water. Efforts were made to maintain an irregular connection by motor-boat for urgent needs, but such long stretches of line were so isloated that little success could be achieved. Boulder stone and fill for the washed-out track had to be brought from many miles up country and the permanent way and telegraph repair staff were faced with continual difficulties in effecting repairs in this malarial and swampy area.

Rochfort Maguire, chairman of the Beira Railway, said at a meeting in London that 'in 1902 a good deal of money was spent in raising the level of the line across Pungwe flats and the then chairman had told shareholders that he believed the line was safe against floods. For sixteen years with the exception of small washouts he had been right.' The exceptional rains coupled with high winds had once again conspired with the Pungwe to upset all previous calculations by railway engineers.

With Beira cut off, the BMR was faced with a heavy diversion of traffic to and from South African ports over the Mafeking line, and revenue suffered. Then in October 1918 came a second calamity in the outbreak of the 'Spanish' influenza epidemic which was sweeping the world. A high proportion of the Rhodesian population was affected and at Bulawayo the railway institute was converted into a hospital for seventy-eight patients, mainly railway men and their families. At wayside stations most—quite often all—of the staff were ill in bed. Altogether forty-six railwaymen died. Offices were closed so that the few fit men could help in the hospitals, while the train service was reduced to a minimum or cancelled altogether. No train ran from Bulawayo to Victoria Falls and beyond for two weeks as all the train crews were either ill or nursing their families.

While in Britain and other countries this flu had serious effects and a high deathroll, it was in the small communities of Rhodesia that it caused almost total cessation of normal activities among the sparse population. Mining production was severely reduced and many local industries ceased work during the epidemic as the Africans went down with the disease in large numbers or fled to their kraals.

For some time there had been a good deal of public agitation concerning the high rates charged for rail transport in Rhodesia and eventually Mr (later Sir) William Acworth, a British authority, was entrusted with an investigation. In his report in 1918 Acworth stated that he could find no other railway system capitalised at so low a figure as the BMR. Regarding rates, his considered view was that the complainants of high rates at the hearings had wholly failed to prove their case. His report found that the railway companies were soundly managed and the system well operated. So for a time public criticism was stilled over fares and charges.

The Victoria Falls Hotel was originally built by a separate company as an offshoot of the BMR. This was leased to private individuals until, in 1917, the lease was taken over by the recently formed catering department of the railways. By this time the first section of the brick hotel had been constructed, though the old wood-and-iron section was retained for many years as an annexe at a lower tariff. The main line ran in front of the original hotel until in 1909 a violent storm, during which seven inches of rain fell in five hours, washed away the sand formation of the track, and the opportunity was then taken to relay the main line at the back of the hotel as it is now. This was an improvement as it gave an uninterrupted view from the hotel verandah of the famous bridge and the gorge behind which spray from the mighty Zambesi constantly rises.

Many of the tourists visiting Victoria Falls were elderly people who found the walk or a rickshaw ride to the river and the rain forest in the heat very trying; so in 1920 a trolley service was started. A 2ft-gauge track was laid down partly on the old main-line formation from close by the hotel to near the Southern Rhodesia end of the bridge, with a separate section on the other side of the main line to a point near the rain forest and Devil's Cataract. Trolleys with garden seats and striped canvas awnings were propelled by Africans, two to a trolley. This service became very popular with visitors, apart from one who was well known on the stage. George Graves, the famous London comedian, was injured in an accident when his trolley derailed, resulting in a claim for £2,000 being met. Trolleys continued in service until December 1957 when buses were introduced, but one has been preserved as a relic in the grounds of the hotel.

With the greater traffic originating from the northern part of the system, engine depots with more adequate facilities became necessary at Livingstone and Broken Hill. The workshops at Umtali were so far away for general repairs to locomotives and for the supply of replacement parts that the locomotive superintendent had for some time been planning mechanical workshops at Bulawayo as being more central. When the war ended it became possible to implement 'Togo' Hosgood's aim and a start was made in 1919 with the erection of the first section. This was a brick building, 240ft by 126ft with a height of 45ft to 76ft, providing for erecting, machine, boiler, blacksmiths, coppersmiths and electricians shops. The main erecting shop had three tracks with pits and provision for two 60-ton overhead travelling cranes for lifting locomotives. Ample space for nine engines at a time was made available.

Concurrently with the workshops, a water supply had to be provided and this had to be met by constructing a dam on a railway-owned farm on the Khami river, close to the siding of that name eleven miles south of Bulawayo. This dam had a capacity of 175 million gallons and a 6in pipeline brought the water to the new workshops, for which a power station was erected to give electricity for the pumping plant and workshop equipment.

Over the next two years this project was developed until a foundry and a carriage and wagon shop had been erected, while an engine weighbridge of 160 tons capacity and several overhead electric cranes were installed.

These new workshops were to make a striking difference to the area south-west of the Raylton 'Camp', by which the village was known. The new buildings were constructed with service sidings leading from the running shed into the shops, and the large structures and tall power station chimney became a feature of the skyline for trains approaching Bulawayo from the south. Roads through Raylton gave access for the artisan staff, most of whom cycled to work in those days over the Fort Street crossing at the east end of the station. Recruiting the growing number of artisans needed set a problem for the loco superintendent but advertising in Britain and South Africa brought many recruits, some from the Rand mines and Natal and others from industrial towns in the United Kingdom. Those with sporting ability were very welcome and it was not long before the railway soccer, rugby and cricket teams became formidable in the local leagues and the Raylton sports field was the scene of many stirring games, including some with overseas and South African sides. Bulawayo as a town benefited from the increased population spending its wages in local stores, bars and places of amusement and soon justified its cognomen as a 'railway town'.

During this building-up process the loco superintendent was still at Umtali but he made regular visits with some of his staff, until in 1921 his office was transferred and he moved into rooms in the station area at Bulawayo close to the traffic manager. In those days enginemen were in the Locomotive Department while guards belonged to the Traffic, a practice that led to arguments and disputes not conducive to harmonious working.

About this time caboose working of trains from Bulawayo to Dett and Livingstone was discontinued as the erection of single and married quarters, mainly in wood-and-iron, at these two stations and at Wankie permitted the increase of staff to enable single crew working to be introduced. Re-crewing of Bulawayo engines for the round trip to Wankie by men living at Dett gave the Bulawayo men resting time, while cross-trips with Wankie crews up to Dett provided the extra tonnage for the 1,200-ton loads over the easier graded line as far as Sawmills. Dett was not then a popular depot for married men as there was no schooling or amenities, while lions and leopards abounded in the area and were often seen in the village.

It was about 1920 that a section of thirty miles of 60lb track was relaid with the first 80lb rails to be used on the BMR. These rails were wartime stocks in 33ft lengths of what was known as 'American Railway Standards B Section' and as there were no steel sleepers of a design suited to these bigger rails use had to be made of hardwood sleepers. It seems probable that as the wooden sleepers were cut at the sawmills of the Rhodesian Native Timber Concessions alongside the line near Malindi and Intundhla, it was decided to lay this stretch of 80lb on the 'long straight' between Gwaai and Intundhla, so that easy replacement could be effected of the sleepers, of which engineers had had little experience under Rhodesian conditions. A few wood sleepers of various timbers had been previously tried out but not in long lengths of track.

The RNTC sleepers were only roughly treated with arsenic and were not tarred, as was the practice later, while as no 80lb sole-plates were available and no adzing was done, coupled with the absence of any stone ballast, the sleepers suffered severe punishment in use. White ants also attacked the wood, which was of several kinds of timber and not restricted to the redwood (Baikea

Plurijuga), which became standard in later years. As a result the sleepers had a life of only about eight years, or less than half what was achieved when proper treatment was given and stone ballast put down in later years.

At the port end of the system the erection of a further 400ft of wharfage on the Chiveve creek had been completed in 1920 and this gave the long overdue addition to the lighterage wharves at Beira. It was in this year that Pauling & Co was given the contract to construct the Trans-Zambesia Railway from Dondo, a station on the Beira Railway eighteen miles from the port. This new line was to run to Sena on the south bank of the Zambesi and so give rail connection with Nyasaland. This British protectorate had a railway between Port Herald, on the Shire river, and Blantyre, opened in 1908 and known as the Shire Highlands Railway. This had been extended in 1913–15 by the building by Paulings of the Central African Railway between Port Herald and Chindio, lying on the north bank of the Zambesi and in Portuguese territory. The TZR was constructed to replace the river steamer service on the Zambesi which had provided Nyasaland with her connection with the Indian Ocean at Chinde, and with its completion in 1922 Beira derived much benefit from import/ export traffic, the goods being ferried across the Zambesi until a bridge was built years later. By agreement with the Beira Railway running powers were given for TZR trains over the line between Beira and Dondo.

As for the Vryburg—Bulawayo section little of note occurred at this time. It was increasingly busy during the war years when traffic was diverted from Beira to South African ports due to shipping control, but little local business was dealt with through Bechuanaland. However, in 1916 the RR account from the SAR Kimberley, for work done included an amusing item: 'To cost of fencing Paradise . . . £10 4s 6d.' It is not known whether Eve was enclosed or whether she moved off north to Figtree, where the clothing was cheaper.

CHAPTER SIX

Pungwe Floods—and Other Troubles

THE shortage of trained staff during the later war years, as the result of men having joined the forces, reacted very much on those remaining in railway service. They worked excessive hours in the national interest and as the war dragged on the strain began to be felt, particularly by enginemen and guards. No overtime was paid nor was there extra pay for Sunday or public holiday work, and it was only following upon a petition by the enginemen at Umtali that a war bonus was granted in June 1916 and later a small overtime allowance was introduced. By then a trade union had been formed by the railwaymen and in 1918 a court of enquiry was held into conditions of service, followed by arbitration under a high court judge. The men did not accept the first offer by the railway company and a strike resulted; this led to an agreed 25 per cent increase in basic salaries and wages.

In May 1919 E. R. Ross, who had been general manager since 1911, retired and was succeeded in November by Col C. F. Birney, DSO, RE, who had had considerable experience as an engineer in India and, after war service in France, had been in charge of railway arrangements for a large area of the army of occupation in Germany. During the interval between Ross's departure and Birney's arrival in Rhodesia, G. R. Holgate was acting as general manager. Holgate was the chief engineer, the first to hold this title as previously there had been a chief resident engineer (S. F. Townsend) with a resident engineer and a maintenance engineer under him. 'Togo' Hosgood was still locomotive superintendent, T. Beach Smith was the traffic manager, Frank Key the chief accountant and the redoubtable Dan Livingstone was the stores superintendent, his office still being at Umtali.

Birney took charge of the BMR at a time when the after-effects of World War I were being felt. Trade had dropped off with the reduced demand for strategic minerals, while the staff was in an unsettled state with rising living costs and ex-servicemen finding it difficult to resume peacetime activities and normal work. Higher working costs had led to a general increase in rates and fares, to the extent of a 10 per cent surcharge on fares and 25 per cent on parcels, goods, minerals and livestock, effective from 1 April 1920. This was not popular with the users, whose relations with the railway had been strained by the recent 13-day strike. The pay award quelled the agitation among the staff, while the railway medical service improved relations by the creation of a medical fund advisory board, with six elected staff members and six senior officers. At the same time a new dispensary was provided at Bulawayo with adequate accommodation for the principal medical officer, his staff and for doctors' consulting rooms.

The postwar trade depression in 1920–1 was having its effect on Rhodesia and passenger fares again had to be increased; the 10 per cent surcharge was raised to 16 per cent, while the goods tariff surcharge was lifted from 25 to 33 per cent. This increase in fares did not, however, deter the Africans from travelling by train and the numbers carried continued to rise. The standard of carriages, if they could be called such, for the native fare passengers was poor, most of them being bell-buffered covered wagons with seats placed along the sides, a few small windows high up to give a little light, and a central sliding door on each side. In 1921 the first improved native coaches came into service with the delivery of six built by the Gloucester Carriage & Wagon Co, these having better seating, normal drop windows, four lavatories, and electric lighting instead of small oil roof lamps.

The introduction of composite guards' vans with second and native-class compartments placed at the ends, and a central space for parcels, cans of cream and similar traffic under the guards' eyes, was a great improvement for short distance passengers on branch lines and on main-line 'pick-up' trains.

Until 1920 all first- and second-class carriages were fitted with four bunks in compartments and two in coupés. The upper bunks were formed by lifting up the backs of the daytime seats and securing them in position with straps and metal supports. It was decided to differentiate between the two classes by rebuilding the internal fittings of second-class stock to provide six bunks in compartments and three in coupés, and the change was started in 1920. All second-class coaches were changed over the next two years and from then on this higher sleeping capacity was maintained. While six people, with their hand luggage, made rather a crowd in a compartment, it was necessary to take this action in order to retain a lower fare for second-class passengers and to meet the demand for travel by the growing population.

The Canadian-built 11th class locomotives, now thirty in number, were all in service by 1921, and it was found essential to lay two extra steel sleepers per rail as a strengthening measure for the track to withstand the heavier engines. This was done over the main line from Que Que to Bulawayo, and then as far as Kafue in the north, as the 11th class was employed over all these sections.

In order to reduce the long turns of duty and overtime, new re-crewing depots for enginemen and guards were opened at Gondola and Inyazura, after quarters and rest rooms had been erected. This enabled the Umtali men to rest at Gondola, local men taking the engines to Vila Machado and back, while Salisbury crews who booked off at Inyazura likewise rested as their reliefs worked on to Umtali and back.

Salisbury at this period was lagging behind the development of Bulawayo, which had a large distributive trade with the north as well as local mining and ranching to bring it prosperity. Most of Salisbury's original station building had been burnt down in a disastrous fire on Christmas morning 1917, but it was considered adequate to replace the station with another wood-and-iron structure sited close to the demolished buildings. These station offices were then nearly opposite the foot of Wynne Street, with a number of small shacks, store rooms and latrines backing on to Railway Avenue—not a very impressive sight. There was only a low-level platform, which was merely a gravelled slope from the station offices to the trackside, with a low face wall. A short spur served for the Shamva and Sinoia branch trains, while traffic for the goods shed and sidings was back-shunted from the Umtali main line down to the lower yard over level crossings with the Fourth Street extension. These crossings soon became a menace as road traffic between goods yard and town increased, this being a much shorter route to the business area than by the Hatfield Road, then a dusty track.

At this time the locomotive running shed, coal dumps, loco office and quarters were still sited in line with the station, with tracks coming to a dead-end near the present-day west end signal cabin. The main line to Gwelo curved away to the left from the station, leaving the loco area with the triangle taking off to the right of the line. There was a level crossing over Hatfield Road and the line then crossed the ground subsequently occupied by the new steam running shed built in 1930.

The original railway housing was in the space between the main line and the goods yard and comprised two blocks of semi-detached cottages and nine small houses, while nearer the station the district traffic superintendent and the railway medical officer shared two small wood-and-iron office blocks. Other railway houses had been built on the eastern side of the town and a recreation club with playing fields was established later between these houses and the station, the whole being skirted by the Shamva line on its way to Avondale.

By 1921 goods traffic had developed to the extent that a brick goods shed and new offices were needed to augment the existing wood-and-iron sheds in the lower yard, and gradually in the next few years the goods depot was enlarged and more tracks added to the station yard.

About this time a general improvement was the installation of electric coaling cranes at most of the busier loco depots where power was readily available. Hitherto all coaling of engines had

129

been by native labour, shovelling coal into the tenders direct or filling buckets which were lifted by hand crane and tipped. Labour was cheap and easily obtained but coaling by hand was a slow process and badly needed speeding up.

Funds available for bettering facilities were not ample but the management was making an effort to improve methods. Unfortunately the world depression continued to affect Rhodesia and, despite tariff increases, revenue dropped in 1922 by over £117,000. It became essential to reduce staff and 184 Europeans and 1,500 natives were laid off, while salaries and wages were cut on a temporary percentage basis, a serious blow to the already hard-hit economy of the country.

But still more trouble was in store for the BMR. Since 1918 the Pungwe had not flooded and indeed at Beira there had been a shortage of water suitable for the boilers of the steam cranes on the wharf. This occurred before the onset of the 1921–2 rains and it seems ironic that water from the Busi river had to be pumped into tanks on barges and brought across to the Chiveve wharf. The position was eased later by the opening at milepost 6 of a new storage lagoon from which water was pumped, but throughout this period intensive use was made of water tank wagons on the Vila Machado—Beira line. This proved to be a lull before more serious trouble appeared early in 1923, when an exceptionally heavy rainy season developed in Mashonaland and the Manica area and before long the rivers draining into the lowlands of Mozambique were rising rapidly. First of all the Munene river flooded and cut the main line for five days from 21 January, this river being crossed by the line some ten miles east of Umtali.

By March the continued rain inland had swelled the rivers draining the escarpment and had reached the Pungwe flats, where water banked up until the embankment and bridge abutments at 34 miles collapsed under the pressure. A gap of 100ft with a 25ft deep channel was gouged out below rail level, through which a new river was created, and so once more, on 15 March, the Beira railway was cut and the through train service suspended. It was, however, possible to bring trains fairly close to the gap and to ferry passengers and light articles by boat across the inundated area. Filling a gap this size with boulder stone and rock was no easy task and involved the running of frequent work trains from quarries and elsewhere up the main line. Fortunately no further serious washaways occurred and by 12 April 1923 the line was reopened to Beira. That the rains were exceptional is borne out by the recording of 86.87 inches of rain at Amatongas station in the year, with falls approaching this high figure at other stations on the Beira line. Most of this rain fell in four or five months.

This heavy rainy season had also brought difficulties to the new Trans-Zambesia Railway, which had been opened to Murraca, on the south bank of the Zambesi near Caia on 1 July 1922, so link-ing Beira closer to Nyasaland. This newly-built line suffered con-siderable damage to the formation from the torrential rain. To assist the new railway in its early days the BMR had loaned two 7th class locomotives and sold two 1st–2nd composite carriages to it. By agreement, the TZR shared the use of Beira station and its locomotives were serviced at the running shed, while at Dondo, the junction station, the BMR stationmaster and foremen undertook the issue of proceeding orders for TZR trains en route to Murraca. Thus there was friendly collaboration from the start between the two railways linking the port of Beira with the inland territories.

Apart from his worries over the Pungwe flats, the chief engineer was faced with the need to strengthen many main-line bridges, which had been built in the construction days to cater for the 9½ton axleload of the 7th class locomotives as compared with the 13ton axleload of the new 11th class Mountain type. As a start, in 1923, bridges between Que Que and Wankie were scheduled for replacement with girders to carry a 17.3ton axleload and work was put in hand. In many instances the rebuilding of bridges was an opportunity to deviate the line and give better approaches, easing grades and curvature. One of the first was the 3½ mile deviation west of Shangani, with a new bridge over the river; this was part of the programme of deviations carried out on the main line between Bulawayo and Salisbury to improve the 1 in 60 (or 66) uncompensated grade to a new standard of 1 in 80 com-pensated.

The stage had been reached when the traffic carried and the heavier engines had outgrown the 'pioneer railway' track conditions, with old rail and so-called 'muck' ballast, and track defects were now the cause of frequent derailments to the detriment of train operating. In 1922 there had been 207 main and branch line derailments—94 due to track—but in the following year derailments rose to 419, of which no less than 270 were attributed to to track defects. Broken rails had risen from 154 in 1922 to 230 in 1923, much of this increase being in Northern Rhodesia where the older 11th class were responsible to a large degree. It was clear that drastic measures would be needed to restore the track to a more reliable condition and remove the hazard of serious accidents.

The war, shortage of experienced staff, rising traffic and difficulty in obtaining permanent way materials had all contributed to the unhappy state of the road. However, the original round-top, and later flat-top, 60lb rail had not been left entirely unreplaced. Much had been relaid with stretches of 60lb OBSS and RBSS rail, but there were still hundreds of miles of the early track still in use. As an example, it was not until 1923 that the 45lb rail of the Gwelo—Selukwe branch line built in 1903 was relaid with second-hand 60lb rail recovered from released main-line track. This 45lb wrought iron rail had originally been used on the Cape Town—Worcester line in 1870 and was bought from the CGR for the Vryburg—Mafeking section of the Bechuanaland Railway in 1893. Ten years later it was replaced and brought up to Rhodesia. Some of this 45lb rail in 24ft lengths had been used in 1903 for the Matopos branch and for the Gwelo—Umvuma line in 1909, but even when it was discarded from the Selukwe line its life had not ended. The BMR sold it to the Zambesi Saw Mills in 1924 in order that its forest railway from Livingstone might be converted from its wooden rails to more modern track!

To improve the track bed extensive ballasting was undertaken on long sections of the main line but the use of stone ballast was still in the rather distant future. On the Gwelo—Bulawayo line where much trouble was experienced there was almost a complete absence of suitable material for ballast and gangers had a constant

Page 133 (*above*) Victoria Falls bridge nearing completion with *Jack Tar* 0–6–0 tank at work, 1905; (*below*) RR 7th class no 22 with first train to arrive at Victoria Falls, 24 April 1904. Group includes Harold Pauling (standing 3rd from right) and his daughter, Blanche, (in white blouse)

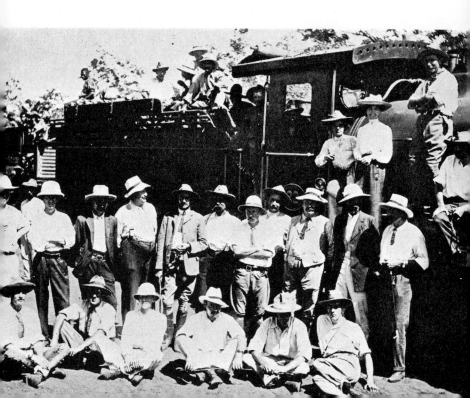

Page 134 (*above*) Victoria Falls station in 1906; (*below*) the Victoria Falls Hotel in the same year

task in maintaining the formation. A journey by train here was a dusty experience.

The Umtali—Vila Machado line through the mountains was given special attention as frequent derailments were occurring due to track defects resulting from the heavy rains, while across the flats at two or three points where culverts had failed with collapse of the embankment, the erection of released 100ft span girders from up country, as bridges to help clear the flood waters, was a pious attempt to alleviate the danger to the line. In actual fact it was found in the next season that these new bridges merely caused deep scour holes and the amount of water passed was literally 'a drop in the ocean' of the flooded Pungwe flats.

The heavy rains in the 1922–3 season cheered the Rhodesian farmers and the maize crop was a good one. In those days the surplus maize was exported overseas and the line from Salisbury to Beira was kept very busy with maize specials. In the Congo, the Union Minière was expanding the copper mines with consequent development of hydroelectric schemes to provide power for the mines and the growing towns of Katanga. To the BMR this brought much extra traffic with imports of machinery, plant and equipment, while increased coke and coal orders boosted the flow of traffic from Wankie northwards. Chrome ore for export was again doing well and a useful new traffic was an SAR contract for 400,000 wooden sleepers cut in the forests outside Livingstone and along the Sawmills—Dett line.

A new re-crewing depot was opened at Kafue in 1923, with single quarters and a few houses, and this enabled the caboose working by trainmen from Livingstone to turn round at Kafue instead of going beyond. Local traffic over the main line through Northern Rhodesia was relatively sparse at this time, being chiefly farm produce and trade goods at the wayside stations, the European settlement on farms being very scattered. A start was made about this time in the development of the copper deposits discovered at Bwana M'kubwa, on the main line seventeen miles south of the Congo border. This was to be the forerunner of the vast copper mining industry which was to play so important a part in the prosperity of the northern territory and of the

Rhodesian railway system, though the Bwana M'kubwa mine was not to prove a great success itself.

Up to the end of 1923 the policing and security of railway areas in Southern Rhodesia had been carried out by 'constables' employed by the BMR and while such a practice was accepted without question in the pioneering days it had a defect. These constables had never been attested and, having no statutory powers, they were unable to effect an arrest with any legal backing. Arrangements were made with the government for the British South Africa Police on 1 January 1924 to take over the policing of the main railway centres, including housing in the 'camps', at Bulawayo, Gwelo, Salisbury and Umtali. For this the railways provided housing and office accommodation for the police. Thus began a long, close and happy association between the British South Africa Police and the railways, which footed the bill for this official protection.

Native watchmen continued to be employed at the workshops, goods sheds and in native compounds, not only in the main centres but at the outside small stations. In addition, for claims prevention work European investigation inspectors were attached to the head office of the traffic manager and were responsible for enquiries into claims for goods lost or pilfered in transit. In many cases of this nature close liaison was maintained, to mutual benefit, with the British South Africa Police and their assistance obtained when crime was detected.

In later years the British South Africa Police was asked to extend its supervision to other stations, while in Northern Rhodesia the NRP undertook patrolling at large railway depots. Nearly forty years later, however, due to the disturbed conditions and the attempts at sabotage along the line by African nationalists, Rhodesia Railways was asked to provide its own security force for the protection of railway property and so ease the burden on the police forces.

Not only was the Beira Railway a constant headache to the civil engineers in combating floods but with the rise in traffic to and from the port the demand was for more powerful locomotives to cope with the business offering without running too many extra trains. E. H. Gray succeeded 'Togo' Hosgood as chief locomotive engineer in 1924, the position being re-designated as chief mechanical engineer the following year, and it was he who, in order to ease the situation, introduced the articulated Garratt locomotive to the BMR.

Before his retirement Hosgood had ensured that the mechanical workshops were in good fettle for their task and one of his last moves was the transfer from Umtali to Bulawayo of heavy repairs and re-varnishing of coaching stock. This had been made possible by the completion of a carriage shop in the layout at Bulawayo. Since this was at the central point of the system, the withdrawal of coaches from service for periodical repair was easier to arrange with the traffic department and, as it was an entirely new shop, it was soon possible to achieve considerable savings in costs.

This transfer of carriage maintenance relieved Umtali and gave the works manager there more room for wagon repairs and the erection of new trucks landed at Beira. A high proportion of the wagons, both open and covered, then had wooden bodies and the replacement of worn and damaged timbers was a constant and costly process. It was only the open bogie wagons with high sides that were of all-steel construction; these were of $33\frac{1}{2}$ and 37 tons carrying capacity and many dated back to the original orders of 1901. They were all fitted with the bell buffer with pin and link coupling and, while coaching stock was largely equipped with automatic couplers, it was only in 1925 that a start was made on converting wagons from bell buffers to modern couplers.

Umtali was being kept very busy with wagon maintenance, as apart from the age of many vehicles the defective track was causing damage to frames, springs and buffers. In addition, accident repairs imposed a burden on the wagon shop. An extremely bad year for derailments on main and branch lines was 1925, the total being 1,277 compared with only 216 in 1924. Of the 1,277 no less than 948 derailments were attributed to the defective state of the road and track, while 200 were due to rolling-stock defects. Never before or since has there been such a bad record and the incoming chief engineer, M. N. Varvill, who took over in

1925, was at once faced with the very serious state of the track.

Heavy rains began soon after Christmas 1924 and severe storms were experienced daily in many parts of the line until the end of April 1925. While the Beira line was, as usual, the worst affected, much trouble also occurred on the main line north of Livingstone. When derailments were reported the Livingstone breakdown train would be despatched to the scene and it has been recalled by the men concerned how on its way the 'breakdown' would encounter other derailments and would even come off the road itself. As the rains continued, washaways became more frequent and there were several periods when all traffic was brought to a standstill for some days while gangs feverishly struggled to restore the line to a passable condition. The crew of the 'breakdown' never knew when they would get home to depot and had to stock up with food bought at wayside stores to tide them over their trips, which often lasted several days. With all the roads reduced to a quagmire it was impossible to send out help by car or lorry even if one was available.

The track had reached a deplorable state from the incessant rain; most of it was unballasted or had poor gravel ballast, which was perhaps good enough for infrequent traffic in a dry climate but could not stand up to heavy rain and traffic. The roadbed became water-logged, steel sleepers were crippled and rails bent. As a result, speed restrictions were in force at periods practically throughout the whole line, resulting in excessive delays to trains, and only by keeping every available engine in traffic and letting maintenance slide was some sort of a service kept running. The position of the track was so acute that night running of trains had to be abandoned at times on the Beira line, as being unsafe.

Flooding on the Pungwe flats led to the line being breached by gaps of 70 and 160ft at $33\frac{3}{4}$ and 34 miles, while the embankments at the Pungwe bridge were scoured out by the rush of water. The line was closed for through working from 4 February to 2 March 1925 and it seemed clear that the five-year spell between 1918 and 1923, when the line had been free from serious interruptions, had lulled railwaymen into false hopes of the weather cycle having changed for the better. This was not to be and it was clear that very heavy remedial work, providing additional waterways for the floodwaters to escape and raising embankments, was vital to ensure the safety of the line in future years. The ingenuity of the engineers was to be greatly taxed in devising a solution to this periodic flooding of the main route between Rhodesia and the sea.

At this time the railway wharf on the Chiveve creek was 905ft long and handled practically all cargo landed and shipped, lighters being used to carry the goods from ship to shore and vice versa. By this method a record of 50,864 tons was handled in September 1924 but the wharf frontage was inadequate and the time was arriving when ships would wish to come alongside and achieve a quicker turn-round than was possible with lighterage. Time, too, was lost when lighters were grounded on the mud as the tide receded, the rise and fall of the Pungwe being prodigious, and more dredging was vital. Plans for an extension of 380ft to the wharf had been prepared but the approval of the Mozambique Company was awaited. In 1925 the Beira Junction Railway had proposed the sale of its rights, properties and possessions in the port area, including the lighterage wharves, to a new company, Beira Works Ltd, which would henceforth undertake developments at the port on behalf of the Mozambique Co and the Compagnia do Porto da Beira. This sale was not to include the passenger station, certain goods sheds, and tracks and equipment for railway working. After considerable negotiation between the railways and the Portuguese the new port company was sanctioned and the sale for £350,000 was effected in 1927. The actual shore working of the port facilities was continued under the direct control of the BMR district superintendent, while Beira Works Ltd was responsible for new wharves, cranage, sheds and allied plant.

While the staff at Beira had a number of well experienced railway men from Rhodesia, an increasing number of Portuguese nationals were being employed and with training were proving very competent. The staff was, however, very cosmopolitan and included Goanese tally clerks, Greek and Italian artisans and crane-drivers, and Chinese carpenters, as well as men from various parts of the British Empire. As a social and sporting centre a railway institute was erected in 1924 near the station and soon a soccer field and tennis courts were established and Beira railway teams had encounters with visiting teams from Umtali, Salisbury and elsewhere. Hard drinking sessions ensued with wild parties to round off the visits and the local police occasionally had to cool off hot heads in the 'calaboose' until their friends bailed them out next morning.

In the construction days of the Beira Railway little thought had been given to export traffic, the main concern had been the best possible location of the line to meet the essential imports. Now Rhodesia was selling its minerals and surplus maize overseas and attention was needed to re-grade certain sections to gain a better load in the down direction, namely coastwards. Deviations were opened in 1925 between Almada and Gondola to give a 1 in 70 compensated grade, so stepping up the load from 360 to 600 tons, while farther on deviations near the Siluvu hills made it possible to eliminate splitting loads in half to surmount the bank against down trains.

A brighter traffic position with better revenue enabled all rates and fares raised in 1920 to be reduced. Native passengers benefited by an average cut of 15 per cent in their fare scale, while the surcharge on first- and second-class tickets was also reduced. Encouragement was given to visitors to the Zimbabwe ruins by improving the passenger train service over the Fort Victoria branch and running through carriages from Bulawayo with a quick connection at Gwelo, so enabling tourists to spend twenty-four hours in the Fort Victoria area.

A highlight in 1925 was the visit of the Prince of Wales (the future King Edward VIII) to the Rhodesias during June–July in the course of his extensive tour of Southern Africa. The South African Railways provided two special trains, one of which was specially built for the royal visit and comprised several luxurious saloons for the prince and his party. This train was painted white with gold lining and lettering and became known as the 'White Train', afterwards being used by the governor-general of the Union of South Africa. This train and the pilot train were used throughout the Rhodesian visit. The prince arrived at Bulawayo on 29 June and his itinerary included Fort Victoria, Salisbury, Livingstone and Victoria Falls, and Broken Hill, the tour covering 3,000 miles on BMR lines. Everything went off without a hitch, thanks to close co-operation between the officials of the SAR and BMR. For much of the tour 10th class 4–8–2 no 158 hauled the royal train with selected drivers and firemen, while the BMR general manager, Col Birney, accompanied the trains in his private saloon, also painted white, along with senior officials.

The Prince of Wales was greeted at the various towns by distinguished representatives of the population, including the principal tribal leaders of the indigenous peoples; prominent among those at Livingstone were the Paramount Chief (Lewanika) of the Barotses and his sister, Morena Mukwae, whose status as 'princess' was very high in this extensive protectorate. This lady, who was of exceptional size and weight, resided at Nalolo on the banks of the Zambesi some three hundred miles north-west of Livingstone. Most of this journey was undertaken by barge, the traditional means of transport on the river, but near Katombora the Barotse royal party transferred to the Zambesi Saw Mills Railway for the last stretch into Livingstone. Due to her girth, it was found impossible for the royal lady to pass through the doorway of the ZSMR carriage and her rail journey became almost unique. A specially-made large armchair was securely fixed to the wooden floor of an open drop-sided timber wagon, a carpet was laid, and surrounded by her retainers sitting in smaller chairs the noble lady was solemnly conveyed in this open wagon to Livingstone.

This year also saw the first extensive tour of the famous Pagel's Circus, which was to become an annual feature and the forerunner of rival circus tours. Pagel himself was a lion tamer but Madame Pagel was capable of taming any human, as well as animals, and many were the occasions when railwaymen had stormy disputes with this famous character. The planning of a circus tour had to be very precise, as the tent, animals, both caged and walking, and all other equipment had to be loaded by the artistes and others on to the special train, after the evening show ended at one place, to be moved in the night hours to the next town. All hands made a mad rush to strike the big tent, load up and then seize the chance of a sleep before the train reached their next stop, when offloading and erecting the big top was the first chore.

In several places the circus had permission to use a site in a corner of the railway reserve and to tap water supplies for which a charge was made. The collection of these fees was generally a matter of some difficulty as Madame Pagel was not only dominating but very tight-fisted. She lived in a private coach during the tour and one inspector sent to collect payment for railway services found her sitting in her compartment with two young lions; however, by maintaining a calm he did not feel, he managed after some argument to get the money.

Operating through many areas of completely undeveloped country brought unusual incidents with wild life. From the early days of the Beira line, when lions were a constant menace and claimed several victims among the construction workers, these animals were a source of much anxiety to the lonely stationmaster or platelayer at his isolated station or cottage along the line. This was specially so in the Amatongas forest and on the Pungwe flats and when a passenger train came through in the night the stationmaster had to turn out to signal the train in with a hand lamp. To do this was a test of nerves at times when the roar of a lion had been heard nearby, and an escort with a rifle was sometimes summoned.

Elephant and giraffe had a happy knack of becoming entangled with telegraph wires and the poles were very attractive as scratching posts. Telegraph mechanicians were often called out to restore communications by re-erecting poles and sorting out tangled wires. In more recent years, in the section of line running through the Wankie Game Park, heightened poles were erected to combat the nuisance of broken wires, while still later, when CTC signal wires, which are normally strung on posts, began to suffer, it was considered expedient to place cables underground at two or three isolated sidings to foil the animals. Termites however seized on the cable wrapping as a tasty meal and that experiment failed.

However, it was when a herd, or a lone elephant, decided to

142

argue the right of way with a train that real trouble ensued. A 7th class engine on a goods train near Dett was probably the first to have such an argument, leading to a serious derailment and the death of the elephant. This huge beast had to be cut up to clear the track and the gangs of natives on the job relished plenty of roast elephant meat while re-railing the locomotive. The skull of the animal was cleaned and for many years was a feature outside Dett station office.

Later the line between Dett and Lukosi was realigned for easier grading and curvature and this involved high embankments and deep cuttings in several places. Unfortunately, in crossing the line elephants sometimes turned into the cuttings when meeting the glaring headlights of an approaching train and as they were un-able to scale the sides to get out of the way a collision followed. Then the engine or a vehicle would occasionally be derailed while the unfortunate animal was usually fatally injured.

On a more recent occasion the northbound passenger train was nearing Wankie and after it had taken first a left and then a right-hand bend the powerful headlight picked out straight ahead a herd of elephants crossing the track. There was no time for the driver to bring his train to a standstill and a collision occurred. Two of the beasts, a fully-grown bull and a half-grown cow, were hit and killed on the spot. Unfortunately the bull was in the entrance to a steep cutting and although thrown aside it was bounced between the leading saloons and the side of the cutting. Some of the carriage steps were ripped off and the train stopped with a dead elephant wedged firmly between the cutting and a saloon. As the carcase weighed some tons it took several hours to cut the train free, while the passengers busied themselves with their cameras.

On a flat open section in 1928 a goods train slowed to avoid a small herd crossing the line on the 'long straight', but a mother elephant was hit slightly and made off into the bush leaving her infant bellowing to attract attention. Little bigger than a large Alsatian dog, this squealing baby aroused the sympathy of the train crew and after a wait to see if mother returned the forsaken child was picked up and brought into Bulawayo in the guards' van. The guard took it home to his quarters in Raylton, where it was the centre of attraction for several days while frantic efforts were made to keep it alive with milk. An attempt was made to sell the baby to Pagel's Circus but to no avail and the Raylton baby died.

It was not unusual for wild animals to be trapped and railed to zoos and a curious sight was that of the head and long neck of a giraffe peering out of the roof opening of a cattle truck. Captured leopards, lions, monkeys and snakes were crated for their long journeys and were occasionally seen in a baggage van destined for South Africa or even to a port for export to an overseas zoo. An unusual consignment from Livingstone once was two crocodiles caught in the Zambesi and railed to the Pretoria zoo. When the truck arrived at Bulawayo with two large crates on the floor, it was found that one of the reptiles had died, allegedly from laryngitis!

Animals and game birds were often seen from the train in the early days but now are not often spotted except near the Wankie Reserve. There was one water buffalo with its home in the veld near the Fort Victoria line not far out of Gwelo, which often ran alongside a train. An Irish inspector, coaching new guards in their duties, used to tell his pupils as the train neared Gwelo to keep a lookout for this buffalo; when he was seen it was time to complete the return of ticket issues and so be ready for arrival at the terminus. As recently as 1963 a disturbance was caused at Mazabuka station when a hippopotamus from a nearby river marched down the platform and had to be shot by the stationmaster, as it was a menace to passengers and staff. An angry hippo can be a real danger to humans.

Fencing the railway strip to prevent animals straying on to the line was of some avail with cattle but in the earlier years this was only undertaken in collaboration with the more wealthy farmers. Elephant and giraffe were however not unduly worried by fencing, while goats and other small animals managed to scramble through when tempted by a ganger's vegetable plot or his gang's mealie stand. Under legislation, the railways had a limited compensation scale laid down to recompense farmers whose cattle or

sheep were killed by a passing train in daylight; at night the straying animals was the farmer's own responsibility as the engine
driver could not be expected to avoid the beast, which in any case
should have been kraaled. If a ganger found a dead ox at the
lineside in the morning it was a case of quickly skinning the
animal and salvaging the meat. If the owner could be traced he
was entitled to the sum realised from the sale of the skin, but the
meat was more often than not a feast for the ganger's labourers.
In daylight the engine driver had to report a mishap with cattle
on the line and notify the nearest ganger. It was often a source of
wonder to the claims clerk at railway headquarters that what,
according to the driver, was a trek ox became a pedigree cow,
generally in calf, when a claim was received from the farmer.

Over the years the main line has gradually been fenced and the
slowing down of trains to avoid cattle has decreased, though there
is always the herdsman or motorist who forgets to close a farm
level-crossing gate. But gates and fences do not stop locusts. In
1924 in particular, vast swarms of these insects were on the move
in Bechuanaland and Matabeleland and inevitably they came to
the railway. In May they were coming north and crossed the line
at points near Wankie and despite the gangers using pumps spray-
ing poison the line was covered with locusts, causing engines to
slip and come to a stand, as their wheels crushed thousands on
the metals. The line between Vryburg and Mafeking and between
Gwelo and Heany was also 'attacked' and much trouble resulted
from the swarms.

A few swarms were also seen in Northern Rhodesia, but it was
mainly from Bechuanaland that the migrant locusts emanated.
This was again the case in 1933 when large swarms delayed many
trains on the Wankie—Victoria Falls line. One swarm near
Matetsi was reported to be eight miles long and six inches deep
on the ground, which impeded traffic for several days owing to
locomotives slipping on the up grades. Odd swarms were seen in
later years but not to the extent of previous invasions. Fortunately, nowadays, science with modern methods has largely eradi-
cated the locust nuisance and the remark on guards' journals
'Train delayed . . . mins, by locusts' would be a curiosity.

Just as the oil from the crushed locusts brought trains to a stand so did oil on the rails from another source. For many years the Congo produced large quantities of palm oil which was railed in tank wagons to soap manufacturers in South Africa. Over the years the condition of these wagons deteriorated and the attention given by the BCK was inadequate, with the result that leakage of oil occurred in transit and when this fell on to the rails on a heavy grade the next train climbing the grade soon met trouble. Sand was used but the thick oil was the cause of many train delays on hilly sections of line; representations to the BCK eventually brought more effective attention to the old tank wagons—until the next time.

The second storey of the administrative offices was begun in 1925 and on completion it became possible for the chief mechanical engineer and his staff to be housed on the upper floor and so leave the old offices they had occupied since the move to Bulawayo from Umtali in 1921. An upper floor had also been provided in the brick station building to give more room for the traffic manager and his clerks and so free the ground floor for better passenger facilities in the busy station. It was when this upper storey was nearing completion that a senior official, having climbed a ladder, was looking things over. He complimented one of the carpenters on the good job he was doing when this man said quite calmly, 'But how is the staff going to get up here?' Only then was it realised that the architect had forgotten to provide a staircase, and this explains the unusual half-moon window lighting the stairs to the top floor, which puzzled so many people.

The floods in the 1925 rainy season had been bad enough and it was hoped that after these extraordinary rains the following season would be more normal and so give the new chief engineer time to decide what further measures were necessary to safeguard the Beira line for the future. This hope was not to be fulfilled. As a start it had been decided to raise the height of the railway embankment over the flats by 18 to 24 inches for some nine miles in the worst area for flooding and to provide more openings for the water to pass under the line. Owing to the heavy pressure of other work little raising had been carried out by the end of the 1925

146

dry season, but two extra bridges had been started. One at 37 miles was finished but the other at 38 miles only had the abutments ready and one girder placed when the worst floods ever stopped all work.

Accounts of these floods might appear somewhat repetitious but emphasis must be given to the enormous problem the men of the BMR had to meet in trying to cope with the forces of nature. Early in 1926 far heavier rains occurred between Umtali and Beira than elsewhere on the system and these were at their worst in the nine days from 12 to 20 January. Falls ranged from 25in at Beira and 28in at Vila Machado to as high as 42in at Gondola, while Umtali had 16in in those nine days and nights when the rain practically never ceased. The area affected was quite different from in other years and several washaways occurred on steep hillsides where the drainage was quite unable to meet the flow. The Amatongas forest was struck with great intensity and along the escarpment new torrents joined normal rivers, carrying destruction in their path. At $93\frac{1}{4}$ miles an embankment was undermined and collapsed under a train, the engine of which overturned killing driver Fryer.

With these torrential rains it was not difficult to foresee that floods lower down on the Pungwe flats were inevitable, as the excessive rainfall found its way down towards the sea. The vast volume of water had to cross the line of rail in some way or other and as the water rose whole stretches of country gradually disappeared in the deluge. The Muda river broke the railway bank near 48 miles, while on 16 January the Pungwe had risen 18ft in four days and the bottom of the girders were under water at the bridge. This level was $2\frac{1}{2}$ft higher than the previous record floods in 1925.

The plains were now under water for many miles and 14 miles of the line were submerged, over much of the distance to a depth of 5ft. Many breaches were made and deep pot-holes were scoured out by the flow. The Pungwe bridge was in danger from excessive scour and, after all available rock was used up, resort was made to loading some Rhodesian chrome ore from the dumps at Beira and this, with local gravel, was used as fill. At 38 miles the incomplete new bridge, around which a low level deviation of the main line had been laid, had flood water half way up the main girder, about 3ft higher than what was to be the future rail level! The bridge gang on this job just managed to escape to Muda siding before they were cut off.

B. H. Johnson, then an assistant bridge engineer, recalls meeting Varvill, the chief engineer, who had come down by motor trolley to inspect the floods but could not proceed beyond 42½ miles. After much endeavour a telephone message was relayed from station to station to the engineer at Beira to send a launch to take Varvill forward. It was indeed a memorable trip, chugging along back and forth across the totally submerged line all the way to Inyati (28 miles), with the tops of telegraph poles and palm trees only a few feet above water. In many places where big breaches had been cut in the embankment, usually at the sites of culverts, the torrent was very strong and the launch passed a lot of unfortunate game being swept seawards in the swirling waters. Standing in the launch, Johnson hooked the portable telephone on to the telegraph line quite easily to pass reports, while at the top of the palm trees crowded all manner of 'crawlers' from large snakes to masses of ants which formed themselves into black swarms like bees at the very tip of the tree. The party returned safely that night to Vila Machado and by then the line was closed for over twenty-six miles.

Washouts had now cut the line to Muda, where the bridge gang had been left, when Johnson had a message to say that one of the bridgemen was dying of blackwater fever. No doctor was at hand so it was decided to try and fetch the unfortunate man to Vila Machado and get him moved up to Umtali. Johnson set off by trolley to within a couple of miles of Muda, where he was met by some natives in a dug-out canoe and somehow the rescuers navigated their way to Muda, only to find that the man had just died. He could not be buried there so Johnson set off once more in the dug-out with the corpse, aided by a solitary and eerie swinging hurricane lamp, and eventually found the motor trolley, which conveyed the sad party back to Vila Machado.

An early committal of the remains in the cemetery at this little station then had to be arranged and, to enable Johnson to make the daily launch inspection trip with the chief engineer, the role of padre for the funeral service was undertaken by senior traffic inspector J. Miller, a versatile and trusted railwayman of the old school, who was in charge of the traffic arrangements at the scene.

By the end of January the rain had abated and trainloads of rock and boulders were run out to the railhead, as many as four trains a day being loaded and offloaded by the 1,800 native labourers on the job. The gap was gradually diminished and had been reduced to four miles on 10 March when heavy rain again caused trouble and widened the gap to nine miles. This was fortunately the last setback, the railheads being linked on 27 March; the running of through traffic between Beira and Rhodesia resumed on 29 March, after a break of well over two months.

Such incidents as these exemplify the very trying conditions under which the men of the BMR worked during their service in Mozambique, or PEA (Portuguese East Africa), as it was usually termed. Practically all buildings and housing were of wood and iron, raised from the ground for ventilation, and this was a saving grace in times of flood, as one could bring a canoe to the front door. There were very few rest rooms for travelling staff, who had to make do with a sleep on the floor or on a table in an office or in a covered truck. Hot water for making tea or coffee often had to be taken from the locomotives—scale and all! Fortunately whisky was cheap.

After the experience of these record floods it was vital that the line be safeguarded for future years and the BMR engaged James McKenzie, a distinguished bridge engineer recently retired from the South African Railways, as consultant for the problem of the Pungwe flats. Bertram Johnson was his aide from the BMR and throughout much of 1926 they spent months on the flats and in Beira compiling a report on the remedial measures. This report formed the basis of the comprehensive protection works, which included a new bridge over the Pungwe with a deviation of line to it, the substitution of 7,500ft of viaducts (in a series of eight) for the existing embankment where flooding was usually most severe, the raising of the bank for 15 miles to 3ft above flood level, and the raising of the 100ft span bridge at 34 miles. The cost of these works was to exceed £400,000 but it was to be money well spent. (Picture, p 152.)

The Beira line had scarcely been re-opened before the position at Kafue bridge, on the main line in Northern Rhodesia, gave considerable anxiety due to the steady rise in the level of the river as a result of heavy rain in the Kafue catchment. By 13 April the river was within three inches of the bridge girders and was six inches over the rails at the south approach to the bridge. While the track was immediately raised on the south bank, and no interruption to traffic occurred, the real danger was to the bridge. It is a feature of the Kafue that the rising river collects large masses of sudd which knit together en route and float down the stream as large islands. With the clearance beneath the girders reduced to a minimum the sudd banked up against the bridge abutments and piers and caused damage, which if allowed to continue would have endangered the whole bridge. Staging, with scoops of corrugated iron sheets, was quickly erected under the eight central spans and large gangs of labourers were employed to cut away the sudd, which then floated away clear of the girders. This was a temporary solution and as the river subsided the decision was taken that for the future safety of the line the bridge should be raised by five feet to ensure better clearance beneath the girders. This work was speedily put in hand and completed during the dry season of 1926.

Although beset by the flood problems, Varvill had had time to review the condition of the entire main line and in order to meet the increasing traffic and heavier engines he drew up a programme for the stone ballasting of the 1,400 miles of track. It was essential to provide proper ballast as a good roadbed for the permanent way and so eliminate the cause of so many derailments and interruptions to traffic. The plan proposed that the whole line from Beira to Ndola be stone-ballasted over the next five years at a cost of some £900,000. It was estimated that the continuous use of seven or eight engines and 150 drop-sided trucks would be required. Several quarries were opened and contractors found, and a start was made in 1927.

Page 151 (*above*) CGR 4th class no 75, hired by Paulings, on pontoon crossing the Kafue river, 1906; (*below*) MR 0–6–0ST no 7 *Jack Tar* at Bulawayo workshops, 1930

Page 152 (*above*) Kitson-Meyer 0–6–6–0, RR no 52—tender not visible, c 1908 (*below*) goods train crossing one of the new viaducts on Pungwe river flats, 1930

With heavy expenses on the Beira line and for the stone-ballasting it was fortunate that the operating revenue of £4¼ million in 1925–6 was a record for the BMR, this despite rates reductions and the dislocation of traffic by washaways. There was a building boom in the two Rhodesias, where housing was notoriously inadequate, while in the north continued mining development, especially at Bwana M'kubwa copper mine, was creating new traffic. The scientific prospecting of very large areas by both ground and air surveys already showed favourable indications for extensive mineral discoveries in what became the Copperbelt.

The asbestos mines at Shabani were stepping up their output to meet the growing overseas demand and it was obvious that animal-drawn road transport over bad roads between the mines and Selukwe for onward rail haul was outmoded. The Shabani Railway Co was formed for the construction of a branch line from Somabula, 20 miles south of Gwelo, running in a south-easterly direction for 62½ miles. Financed by the asbestos interests, work was begun late in 1926 and this new line, costing £315,000, was opened on 11 May 1928, operating under the control of the BMR.

Efforts were being made to foster the tourist trade and in 1926, in conjunction with the SAR, two special trains carrying 350 American tourists from a world-cruise liner included visits to Bulawayo and Victoria Falls, the parties staying at the Falls Hotel for a couple of nights. The success of this tour, to be the forerunner of many more, led to the enlarging of the hotel. Another fifty bedrooms were built, with bathrooms and other facilities, along with modern station offices in a style to harmonise with the hotel.

At Salisbury, where a wood-and-iron station building had served the capital since the pioneer days, a new brick structure more in keeping with the dignity of the city was started, the foundation stone being laid on 17 November 1925. This two-storey block provided offices for the district officers and their staff on the upper floor, with passenger facilities at platform level, though it was to be a few years before a high-level platform was provided. At Bulawayo, the catering superintendent had been housed in

153

small wood-and-iron structures, quite inadequate for the growing department, and opportunity was taken to acquire a disused tobacco factory for conversion into offices and storerooms. This building was close to the station and administrative offices, and was served by a rail spur where dining-cars and private saloons could be placed for replenishment. With additions, this has served as the catering headquarters ever since.

The arrival of the Beyer-Garratt locomotives on the Umtali—Vila Machado section released 9th class 4–8–0s for the rising fuel traffic north from Wankie to the Congo, while Gray's newly designed Mountain type, the renowned 12th class, began to come into service on the main line between Salisbury and Bulawayo, so freeing some 10th class 4–8–2s for the extra trains required by the growing traffic through Mafeking. While some imports came through South African ports Southern Rhodesia was beginning to draw more freely on manufactures and supplies from South Africa itself, a trade that was to develop extensively over the years and to provide very lucrative traffic for the BMR.

A serious accident occurred at Sawmills on 22 April 1926, when due to defective points no 12 Up passenger train was badly derailed, the dining-car, five carriages and a goods wagon leaving the rails. Several passengers were injured, as were some of the train staff, but next morning as attempts were made to rerail the vehicles, fire broke out in the wreckage of the dining-car and the flames quickly spread, resulting in the diner, three SAR coaches and a truck being completely burnt out. Fortunately no one was injured.

The use of SAR carriages on a Bulawayo—Livingstone passenger train was indicative of the shortage of coaching stock owned by the BMR. That this had been realised was clear from the order for ten first-class coaches and four baggage vans placed with the Metropolitan Carriage & Wagon Co, and a year later four dining-cars and six native-class carriages were ordered from other British builders.

When the carriage shop was first established in the Bulawayo workshops, it was under the control of a carriage and wagon foreman, whose truckfitters attended to the running gear of coaching stock, but for steel structural work the boiler shop foreman and his men were called in. Gray soon decided that this was not a good arrangement and he secured additional land for new wagon repair sidings and split the work by appointing a separate carriage foreman with knowledge of steelwork and running gear, as well as having charge of coachbuilders, trimmers and carpenters. Eventually, in 1928, a modern wagon shop was built and the carriage and wagon sections were completely separated. It was not long after that new coaching vehicles were being designed, constructed and erected in the case of special requirements, while carriage bodies were rebuilt to modernise the stock. Some very fine examples of carriage stock were to appear in later years from Bulawayo shops, though large orders for new stock were still placed with overseas builders.

Meanwhile the wagon shop was busy with the replacement of bell buffers by automatic couplers on the older stock and with the substitution of steel wheels for the cast-iron chilled wheels of a large number of 37-ton open bogies and four-wheeled cattle wagons. These cast-iron wheels had been the cause of a high preponderance of hot boxes.

Tree-planting is not usually a railway activity but Col Birney decided in 1926 that it would be advantageous to plant trees alongside the line near gangers' cottages in Matabeleland with the object of growing timber for railway needs. This planting was done by Pat Judson, who was the son of the pioneer, Col Dan Judson, and was later to make his name as an early Rhodesian pilot of light passenger planes. The clumps of trees, mainly eucalyptus, were soon to become a pleasing break in the monotonous sand veld with its low scrub, between Heany and Gwelo, and some of these trees still survive.

Although the Acworth Report on the railways in 1919 had stilled public comment on rates and fares, after responsible government had been granted to Southern Rhodesia in 1923, agitation in the Legislative Assembly led to the Railway Enquiry Act. Under this Brigadier-General F. D. Hammond was appointed in 1924 to review the working and finances of the railway companies. Hammond came to the same conclusion as Acworth and reported that the system had been soundly financed and was efficiently managed and worked, but he recommended that there should be a measure of control over the rates and charges. Designed to give legislative effect to a scheme of rates control, the Railways Act, 1926, was passed to vest control in an independent commission representing the three territories—Southern Rhodesia, Northern Rhodesia and Bechuanaland Protectorate. This commission was given the task of so adjusting rates and fares as to produce a certain revenue after payment of all working expenses.

Mr E. H. Hiley, a retired New Zealand railway officer, was appointed chairman in 1927, with three commissioners, one nominated by each of the three territories. The Beira Railway, being in Portuguese territory, was excluded from the commission's jurisdiction. Mr Hiley served as chairman until Sir William Hoy, who had been general manager of the SAR, took over the position on retirement in 1928.

In the meantime Rochfort Maguire, chairman of the railway companies, had died in 1925 and had been succeeded by Sir Henry Birchenough. Maguire had been one of the original members of the board, taking over the chairmanship on the death of Cecil Rhodes in 1902, and with constant visits to the country had devoted great energy and time to the development of the Rhodesias and their transport system. In Sir Henry Birchenough the railways and the British South Africa Company gained another very astute and farsighted leader. With the London manager, R. J. Hackshaw, Sir Henry made an extensive tour of the railway system in 1927 to survey future potentialities in the rapidly expanding Rhodesias.

Birney introduced an interesting change in the departmental organisation in April 1927. This was the 'Transportation' system, which expanded the old traffic department to include the entire responsibility for all running staff concerned with the movement of traffic and for the repair of locomotives in running sheds and of vehicles in repair sidings. In the past, engine drivers and firemen had been under the control of the mechanical department, which with guards as traffic staff, had led to some lack of co-operation between the men at the 'head and tail' of a train and to friction between departmental officials. The traffic manager, T. Beach Smith, became chief superintendent of transportation, with mechanical officers to assist him and his district superintendents, while the chief mechanical engineer retained responsibility for heavy repairs of all stock in the workshops, for electrical installa- tions, weighbridges, pump plant, and so forth, and as the principal mechanical adviser to the management was concerned with the design and production of rolling stock. After a short settling-down period there was soon no doubt that smoother working and closer co-operation between the old traffic and loco staffs were achieved, with benefit to the running, which manifested itself in the easy flow of the rapidly rising traffic.

Bwana M'kubwa copper mine had come into production, while in 1927 the UMHK mines in Katanga were railing more copper to Beira, which led to a sharp rise in coal and coke north from Wankie. A record of 749,000 tons was railed from the colliery, including 307,000 tons for the Congo. This demand had caused the Wankie Colliery Co to open its no 2 colliery at Thomson Junction and enabled the despatch of coal trains direct from Thomson with Livingstone-crewed engines running round trips.

Chrome ore exported through Beira made a new record at over 247,000 tons, 80,000 tons more than the previous year, while the tobacco farmers in Southern Rhodesia had doubled their acreage and so realised a bumper crop of 19 million pounds weight, which created over 6,000 tons for export. However, it was to prove diffi- cult to sell such a greatly increased crop and overproduction was unfortunately to be the downfall of many farmers in the next two years. For this new business one hundred covered wagons were ordered, these being the standard 30-ton type. Later on, as the tobacco export trade increased and the use of hogsheads was adopted by the trade for packing, the covered truck bodies were heightened by about fifteen inches to accommodate more hogs- heads and get a better pay load. Many years of ups and downs in the tobacco business were to pass before Southern Rhodesia became one of the leading producers of Virginian tobacco leaf and secured a high place in the world markets.

With the greater settlement in outlying farming and mining areas remote from the railway line, and in order to avoid costly branch lines, the BMR introduced in June 1927 its first road motor service. This was run from Sinoia to Miami, seventy-two miles away, the centre of the mica mining district. Within two years no less than fifteen road services to feed the railway had been started, of which eight were subsidised by the government to serve developing areas. Motor lorry services were a completely new feature of life in Rhodesia and quickly proved of immense value in helping farmers to market their produce and obtain their supplies. In the early days light six-wheeled Morris and Thornycroft petrol-engined vehicles were used, all the roads being gravel and the river drifts rough and ready, until low-level bridges were constructed—often with funds from the Beit Trust—over the most troublesome rivers. The Road Motor Services came under the new transportation department and Beach Smith selected W. T. Breach, who had been stationmaster at Que Que, to take charge as road transport officer. He was soon assisted by an enterprising and loyal team of drivers and mechanics who battled to keep the services running through all weathers and over very bad roads.

The Road Motor Services played a very important role in opening up promising farming country and in providing cheap transport for both agricultural and mining produce, so bringing extra traffic to the rail system. A very close relationship existed between the lorry drivers and the farmers along their routes and often the driver would do a little shopping or carry a message for a farmer, and in turn when a lorry broke down or was held up by a flooded river the farmer rendered help to the stranded driver.

At the time of the introduction of the Road Motor Services, mechanical transport was almost a rarity; the two cartage contractors at Bulawayo and Salisbury, handling traffic from the goods sheds, were still using four- and six-span mule teams for their waggons, while teams of donkeys slowly hauled ox waggons along the wide Bulawayo streets, delivering loads of timber, iron sheeting and the like. For parcels traffic a light motor van was the contractor's only acknowledgement of progress, and it was many years before lorries began to replace mule and donkey transport.

Sinoia saw the first two Road Motor Services routes, the no 1 driver being one, Jim Parks, who saw many years of service and ended up as an inspector. From Umtali, services were opened to the mountainous districts of Chipinga and Melsetter, while soon there were routes from many other stations, the mileage rising from 266 in 1927 to 1,626 in 1937. Two services were tried from Lusaka in Northern Rhodesia without much success and all others were in Southern Rhodesia, where the government continued its subsidy for four years on certain routes, after which the Beit Trustees took over liability until 1935. Apart from regular services, a number of special seasonal trips were run for the maize and other crops in Mashonaland and elsewhere.

CHAPTER SEVEN

New Branch Lines—Faster Trains

IN the 1920s when an increasing flow of new settlers was arriving in Rhodesia the country could only be reached by rail, generally from the Cape or Beira, and so newcomers' first impressions were influenced by comparisons with train travel in Europe. The narrower gauge of 3ft 6in was at once striking, and then as one stood on a low-level platform the size of the locomotives seemed so much more massive than those in Britain and raised some anxiety that their overhang of the rails would lead to a derailment. After climbing the two or three steps at the end of the carriage on to the open balcony with its little flap seats, one was surprised as one went down the corridor at the width of the compartments. All first- and second-class carriages then had clerestory roofs with ventilators and luggage racks above the folded-back upper bunks, a washbasin against the windows, with lower bunks—seats in daytime—on either side. As all long distance journeys involved night travel, one's compartment was a 'home' for a day or two and one soon settled down with one's 'stable companions'. Families were booked together but individuals were placed with others of the same sex, unlike the casual manner of continental rail travel. With the hired bedding laid by an African attendant, passengers went comfortably to bed at night, an unusual experience for most from overseas. Day would be ushered in with a steaming cup of coffee from the dining-car.

From the window at crossing loops a goods train might be seen with a long string of trucks. Here, too, the contrast between the 18-ton open steel bogie wagons, carrying over forty tons of chrome or bagged maize, and the small four-wheeled trucks in Britain was another surprise. Most BMR goods rolling stock was carried on two bogies and 'shorts' (or four-wheelers) were relatively few in number. Clearly this railway system in Central Africa was geared for the bulk transport needs of the territories served.

Made up as it was of several separately financed companies, the BMR had always been 'operated' by the Mashonaland Railway Co, but from 1 October 1927 Rhodesia Railways Ltd, became the 'operating company' and its title 'RR' gradually replaced the old BMR. In 1928 the Rhodesia Katanga Junction Railway, 132 miles of which linked Broken Hill with the Congo border, was purchased by the Mashonaland Railway Co for £1,001,227, and it was the latter company that negotiated with the copper mining groups for the construction of branch lines from Ndola to Roan Antelope (later named Luanshya) and to Nkana.

Surveys had now confirmed the existence of vast copper deposits west and north-west of Ndola on the Northern Rhodesian side of the Belgian Congo border and branch lines were urgently needed to carry enormous quantities of construction material and plant, and later the output of the mines. Work began on the Roan Antelope line in 1928 and this 23-mile branch was opened on 22 January 1929, while the Nkana branch, forty-one miles in length, was completed on 21 May 1930. In the meantime the Rhodesian Selection Trust was so anxious to go ahead with its Mufulira mine that it had a 15-mile branch line built from Mokambo, on the BCK main line from Sakania to Elisabethville, and this was opened in September 1929. These lines to the copper mines were all constructed by Pauling & Co.

The development of the Copperbelt was to be of tremendous importance to the RR system and Ndola, which had been a wayside station, soon became a junction of great activity. The Roan Antelope branch ran south from Ndola station for half a mile before swinging away to the west and was of relatively easy construction. The Nkana branch, on the other hand, ran north from

Ndola and, in order to avoid a junction at this isolated spot, was laid down beside the main line to the Congo for two miles until it swung away to the west along the border. Many years later it was found that a short section of this line was actually constructed on the Congo side of the international border due to an error in survey and in 1961 a deviation was carried out to rectify the position.

The main engineering feature of the Nkana line was the Kafue river bridge, which was of five spans of 75ft. This second crossing of the Kafue by the railway was soon to be followed by another crossing, on the Chambishi—Mufulira line. Many years later the Kafue was again bridged when the Bancroft branch line was constructed in 1956 to serve yet another copper mine. All these new lines on the Copperbelt were provided under agreements with the various mining companies, which guaranteed operating losses initially, and also that they would direct their imported plant and machinery, and later their mineral output for export, over the RR via Beira. Such contracts were to prove of immense value to the RR system in future years.

While developments were going ahead in the far north, railway extensions were also being made in Mashonaland. Beyond Sinoia settlers were opening up the country for farming and with a guarantee by the Beit Trustees the branch line was pushed out into the Umboe Valley for twenty-one miles through Lions Den to Zawi. In the Umvukwe hills along the Great Dyke chrome ore deposits were being exploited and from Maryland, on the Sinoia line, a branch twenty-four miles long was constructed to Kildonan to tap the chrome workings. This line was guaranteed for ten years by the Chrome Corporation Ltd, which anticipated railing 50,000 to 70,000 tons of ore each year, but this optimism was unfortunately proved unfounded by the world depression soon to break. Both these rail extensions were constructed departmentally with the aid of subcontractors, the Kildonan line being opened on 2 July 1930 and the Sinoia—Zawi section the following month.

From mid-1927 work had been going on over the Pungwe flats with the extensive scheme for safeguarding the main line against future floods and, while good progress had been made, nature decided to intervene once more and in January 1929 exceptionally heavy rains caused interruption to traffic. This time a cyclone in the Mozambique Channel brought torrential rains across the flats which led to a flood, which was the second highest on record, submerging the line between 31 and $42\frac{1}{2}$ miles and stopping traffic for three weeks. It was satisfactory to see the new viaducts standing up well, as did the new Pungwe bridge, but serious damage to the newly raised embankments and the approach banks was caused by waves created by the cyclonic winds. The heavy rain spread up country and led to the collapse of the abutment of the Revue bridge on 3 February 1929, the river level being only nine inches from the bridge girders. It was decided that the quickest way to restore through working was to construct a deviation and a new bridge, and it was while a special train with bridge material from Umtali to Revue was en route that the embankment near 203 miles caved in and plunged the engine and tender into a 50ft cavity. Driver de Beer and fireman Wadsworth were killed and a second fireman badly injured, while 8th class loco no 54 was so badly damaged it had to be scrapped. Despite this mishap, however, the line was restored and traffic resumed to the port on 12 February.

The last viaduct and the embankments of the new Pungwe bridge were completed by mid-1929 and these extensive—and expensive—works were to prove the salvation of the Beira Railway from its frequent flooding troubles; the route via Beira was no longer a constant anxiety to Rhodesia.

Hardly had the line to Beira been re-opened after the floods when traffic was again disrupted, this time by a strike of railway employees. For some time the Rhodesia Railway Workers Union, led by J. W. Keller MP, who after some years as a guard had become general secretary of the union, had been agitating for a consolidation of the war allowance into the basic pay and for other improvements in the conditions of service. Negotiations with Col Birney reached an impasse and for three weeks from 16 February to 8 March 1929 a large proportion of railwaymen went on strike. A skeleton service was maintained until settlement of the dispute was reached and the strikers returned to work.

Rapid development and the growing population in the two Rhodesias called for the expansion of train services and from 1928 much attention was given to improving passenger timetables. A fourth weekly train in each direction was introduced between South Africa and Bulawayo; as each of these trains conveyed both Cape and Transvaal portions over the Mafeking—Bulawayo section, which resulted in heavy loads of up to sixteen or seventeen vehicles, they were a hard duty for the 10th class locomotives. A fifth train soon followed but until the track could be stone-ballasted and relaid the overall time for the 484 mile run remained at between 23 and 24 hours.

Stone-ballasting north and east of Bulawayo had been making good progress and over a thousand of the 1,400 miles had been finished by 1930. Completion from Bulawayo to Salisbury and up to Livingstone had permitted Beach Smith to introduce in 1928 the long-desired acceleration of passenger trains. To Salisbury the run was cut by 3 hours to 13½ hours and to Livingstone by 2½ hours to 14 hours, this being achieved by running twelve bogie trains with first- and second-class passengers only, so providing the fastest regular schedules over the RR. The third and native-class passengers were catered for by mixed trains stopping at all stations and sidings throughout the main line, these trains running daily.

These faster trains were enthusiastically welcomed by the public and soon the Bulawayo—Salisbury section had six passenger trains a week, three each way being to fast times, while between Livingstone and Sakania two extra trains were introduced in connection with the service from Bulawayo, to meet the much increased traffic to and from Northern Rhodesia and the Congo. Late in 1929 the SAR, after representations from RR, introduced a new fast train from Cape Town docks carrying passengers and mail off the weekly Union Castle mail steamer. This express, no 105 Down, left Cape Town at 11.40am on Mondays and arrived at Bulawayo, 1,354 miles away, at 7.20pm on Wednesdays where RR provided fast connections east and north. A similar but quicker service was also given with Wednesday's train from Bulawayo at 8.15am, reaching Cape Town at 1.9pm on Fridays to connect with the mail ship sailing to England. Over the following years the SAR Rhodesia Express and Rhodesia Limited trains were to be progressively accelerated until in December 1932 the express from Cape Town arrived at Bulawayo at 10am on Wednesdays giving an average speed of 29.2mph. This enabled the connecting RR Rhodesia Express to leave at 10.45am, and by smart running it covered the 296 miles in $10\frac{3}{4}$ hours (27.5mph) pulling into Salisbury at 9.30pm. For the first time passengers from Cape Town enjoyed the journey of 1,650 miles with only two nights on the train, while Beira was reached at 8pm on Thursday, a very substantial speed-up.

No 7 Down Rhodesia Express became the crack train in Rhodesia; its first stop for passengers was at Gwelo, though a stop was made at Lochard for water, and the run of 72.9 miles from Lochard to Gwelo was then a record non-stop engine trip. To the north, the Northern Express left at 12.10pm arriving at Victoria Falls the same evening and at Ndola the following night, with a BCK connection reaching Elisabethville early on Friday morning. This, too, was a great step forward in train times on the subcontinent—the journey from Cape Town to the centre of Katanga now needed only four nights on the train—and it influenced a number of Belgians to travel by the route.

About this time Bulawayo station was improved by the lengthening of the platforms. The main platform—nos 1 and 2—was now 2,316ft long and so became the second longest in the world, only exceeded by Sonepure in India, which was 134ft longer. A scissors crossover in the centre of the platform facilitated train arrivals and departures and it was the custom to have the north express ready on no 2 platform, the Salisbury train in the dock platform, no 3, and for the Cape Mail to be brought in over the crossover to no 1 platform. This placed the baggage vans near to each other, while the van carrying several hundred packages of mail and periodicals off the mail steamer was shunted by the arriving train engine, to which it was coupled ahead of the coaches, and placed via the crossover on to the platform behind the northbound express. The speedy offloading, checking and reloading of mails and baggage became a point of honour among the checkers and labourers, to avoid delay to the outgoing RR expresses, especially when the SAR train came in late. On one occasion the author saw the tranship job done in 32 minutes, while on another occasion when 105 Down came in $3\frac{1}{2}$ hours late due to loco trouble the two RR connecting expresses were despatched complete with passengers, luggage and mails in 35 minutes. The scene, with crowds of passengers and their friends, porters with luggage, mailbags and newspaper bundles flying out of the van to be rushed on barrows to the outgoing connections, and a harassed stationmaster overseeing the mêlée, was a sight to be remembered. The esprit de corps was high and everyone pulled their weight in giving service to the public.

To those accustomed to large stations, fully equipped with signals and interlocked points controlled from a cabin, the apparently casual working at Bulawayo must have been a shock. The scissors crossover points were hand-thrown after unlocking in the presence of an inspector, and engine moves were signalled by hand. There were no departure signals and the so-called home signals controlling the admittance of trains from the east, north and south lines were operated by levers near the facing points at the ends of the station. A station inspector co-ordinated arrivals and departures by telephone with the foreman shunter at each end. It was remarkable how seldom any incident occurred to upset the working.

The home signals were of the lower quadrant type on steel masts, as was RR practice, until in 1932 remodelling at the west end of Bulawayo station led to mechanically interlocked homes for the Mafeking and Falls lines and a two-arm bracket signal for outgoing trains. These new signals were the first RR upper quadrants and conformed to SAR standards. With these signals the points were interlocked and all were worked from a small ground frame in a shelter.

While the telegraph order system was in use from Bulawayo northwards, Webb & Thompson electric train staffs had been introduced on the east line between Bulawayo and Heany Junction. This eased the burden of the station foreman at Bulawayo, who had to be proficient in the SAR paper order system for trains working on the south line; the latter system was very much more complicated in the preparation of train orders than the RR method. Station foremen working at this inter-system junction had much to contend with, especially as the train services increased over the years, and they fully earned their special allowance. Their tempers were sorely tried by the constant enquiries about train arrivals and many other matters, particularly at weekends when other railway offices were closed. The British South Africa Company guest house was named 'Sunrising' and the caretaker telephoning the station early one morning said, 'Sunrising here', to be greeted with the acid response, 'Well, what do you expect it to do here?'

Top hats and morning dress were seldom seen at Bulawayo station, except when worn by the local undertakers. One harassed station foreman on a Saturday afternoon, after countless enquiries, snapped at a small gentleman in a topper and frock coat, 'No, the corpse hasn't arrived yet'. He did not realise that he was addressing his general manager, whose daughter had just been married and was leaving on the Cape train.

Another amusing incident at Bulawayo station was when a special train for delegates to the British Association for the Advancement of Science came through from South Africa en route to Victoria Falls. Half an hour before it was due to leave an African appeared on the platform pulling a trolley on which were displayed three oversize specimens of black beetles and ants, advertising some insecticide. Their legs waggled jerkily as the trolley was hauled alongside the trainful of learned professors, with the native grinning widely as he proceeded up and down.

Although many improvements were being made to the track with relaying and ballasting, one section giving constant trouble was that carrying the increasingly heavy fuel traffic north from Wankie. The line from the colliery centre to Victoria Falls was on a 1 in 50 uncompensated grade with 7-chain curves, equivalent to a true grade of 1 in 37 over the curves. Two particularly severe sections were both of maximum grade for six or seven miles in length, one being the Katuna bank from Deka siding up the Katuna valley and the other the Fuller bank from Matetsi. Of these the Katuna bank was far the worst as it included a horseshoe about half-way up from Deka, much of which was on a high curved embankment.

While up trains were mainly of coal and coke, in the opposite direction traffic included a fair number of BCK trucks with Isothermos axleboxes, many carrying palm oil in drums from the Congo to South African soap factories. Not only were the drums in poor and leaky condition but the axleboxes spread a trail of lubricant along the rails with unfortunate consequences for the opposing trains coming up the banks. The 11th class locomotives handled goods trains and double-heading was the order of the day, the load being only eight bogies for a single engine. Coping with slippery rails, as well as break-aways due to faulty drawgear, caused heavy delays and dislocation of the train service, and it was decided to try 'combined' trains, that is one-third of the load was placed between the leading and second engine with two-thirds behind the latter. It was thought that the drawgear and the foreign wagons in poor condition would respond more readily than to the double-headers, but experience with combined trains on this heavily graded line was most unhappy.

The horseshoe on the Katuna bank was the scene of frequent derailments due to slipping by the engines and to the snatching of loads on the poor soft track in the rains, which were usually heavy in this area. A derailment in the leading section of a combined train on the bank often resulted in the second engine pushing the trucks ahead and spreadeagling them across the line on the high embankment, so making re-railing operations no easy matter. After some months of this it was decided to revert to normal double-heading but it had long become clear that a more permanent solution was needed if traffic continued to rise.

The possibility of building a major deviation of the entire main line from Deka, eight miles north of Thomson Junction, to Victoria Falls was then explored, and this resulted in a very fine new line being planned by A. M. Close, the location engineer. So was born the Deka—Falls deviation, seventy-four miles long and costing over £440,000. This increased the gross load of up trains hauled by 12th class engines from 390 to 1,100 tons and thus effected a large saving in train mileage and working costs. The deviation was the most extensive ever undertaken on the BMR and involved over seventy miles of track, ten major bridges, twenty-nine box culverts, new watering points and new stations with housing. Though it was almost twelve miles longer than the old main line, the grades were much easier, being 1 in 120 for up trains and 1 in 80, compensated, for down, with 22-chain curves, and overall much running time was saved.

This stretch of hilly wooded country, threaded with valleys holding rivers and streams flowing towards the Zambesi, was described as very difficult by the early railway surveyors in 1903 and it is a tribute to Close's ingenuity that he found such a vastly improved location for the new line. In places the deviation was four to six miles from the old line. One section of fifteen miles was placed on a continuous ruling grade from the Katuna bridge all the way up to Zanguja siding and included a complete horse-shoe where it crossed the Zanguja river in two places about half a mile apart, providing a spectacular scene seldom seen by passengers, as it is usually traversed at night. Matetsi river, farther on, was crossed by a bridge of four 100ft spans near the new station of that name and this river provided one of the main watering supplies.

The opportunity was taken to lay the deviation with 80lb rails of 33ft lengths on hardwood sleepers and when the line was opened in September 1932 the smooth running was at once evident. Drivers found that the 12th class 4-8-2s responded magnificently to the easier well-aligned track and the schedules of fast passenger trains were cut by 2hr 25min. When the material had been lifted from the abandoned line the formation was handed over to the government for conversion into a main road between Wankie and Victoria Falls and it served as such until very recently.

Stone-ballasting of the entire main line was making rapid strides and by early 1932, except for two short sections where deviations were proposed, the ballast had been laid all the way between Beira and the Congo border. Apart from eliminating the dust raised by trains passing over sand ballast, which was unpleasant for passengers and bad for rolling stock, the track was vastly improved as is borne out by the reduction in derailments attributed to 'defective road' from 240 in 1929 to 55 in 1931. Another benefit was the modification of speed restrictions on the sharper curves, as cant was increased with stone ballast, so giving smoother riding and reduced wear. The general speed limit of 35mph was maintained over the main line and remained in force until 80lb rail was laid, when the maximum speed was advanced to 40mph over some sections.

Col Birney's term as general manager was to expire before the Deka—Falls deviation was actually put in hand but he had had the satisfaction of helping the BMR develop into a more up-to-date concern with modern locomotives, a much improved permanent way and better facilities in every respect for its users. He was succeeded in 1930 by Mr (later Sir) Henry Chapman, who had been assistant general manager, and whose service with the BMR had started as far back as 1905 when he came to Umtali as accountant. Chapman had an acute and intimate knowledge of the growth of the railways and of their intricate financial structure with the several private companies so closely allied with the powerful British South Africa Company. He took charge when the territories served were generally in a very prosperous state and traffic was at a peak, a happy situation very soon to be changed by the world-wide depression, the effects of which hit the Rhodesias severely in 1930–1.

Many settlers in Southern Rhodesia had ventured into the growing of tobacco, often with insufficient experience, and overproduction in the 1929 crop had resulted in a slump and the failure of many farmers. In other directions trade had been booming but the world depression by late 1930 began to be felt with increasing severity in the two Rhodesias and the effects were accentuated by the severe outbreak of foot-and-mouth disease which struck ranches early in 1931 and stopped the export of cattle. The only bright spot was the development of the northern copper mines which were just coming into production and having extremely low working costs were able to compete successfully with producers in other countries. With agriculture badly hit and the base metal industry drastically curtailed, spending power gradually dropped and the depression led to a severe reduction in the traffic offering. The total earnings at £4.1 million were down by over £1 million (22 per cent) in 1930–1 and it became essential to reduce staff and put the workshops and running sheds on short-time working, while restricted train services came into operation. The erection of 130 open and 50 livestock trucks just delivered from Britain was deferred and the material stored at Umtali, while engines of older classes were stabled.

The world depression continued with serious effects and a further drop of £1.5 million revenue was suffered in 1931–2, which compelled further stringent economies. Salaries and wages were reduced, allowances and expenses cut and further considerable reduction in staff became essential. Premature pensions were offered to many long-service men, while the native employees, some of whom were paid off, had their pay fixed on a lower scale. The remaining staff carried on with their jobs in an uneasy state, wondering about their future and whether settling in Rhodesia had really been worth while. It was a distressing time for the general manager who had many meetings with the railwaymen's unions in endeavours to alleviate the effect of the severe economy measures.

Coupled with economies was an increase of rates and fares by 5 or 10 per cent, with a few special exceptions for low-rated exports. The severe drop in earnings through the depression was so serious that it was not possible to meet the interest due to the holders of certain BR, RR and MR debentures and the drastic step of declaring a moratorium in respect of this interest was resorted to in an agreement with the bondholders applicable from the end of 1932 to May 1934. This moratorium was terminated in May 1935, by which time the financial position had been restored.

In the meantime various new works started before the depression had to be completed. With the opening of the Nkana branch line in 1930 work had soon begun on the extension to Nchanga (Chingola) to serve the copper mine being developed there, and though completion was delayed by very heavy rains the new branch line, 42 miles long, was opened to traffic on 20 June 1931. Originally the Mufulira mine was given rail access via the BCK line from Mokambo, but as soon as the Nkana—Nchanga line was open, work began on a branch from Chambishi, 20 miles from Nkana, to link Mufulira direct with the RR system. Though this line, 21 miles long, was completed in Jannary 1932, no public train service was introduced until 1 April as mining was suspended at Mufulira in consequence of the world slump. The BCK line then fell into disuse.

An innovation in Rhodesia was the completion of bulk petrol and oil storage depots at Bulawayo close to the Raylton golf-course and in 1930 the first ten bogie tank wagons were placed into service to carry supplies from Durban. Apart from water tank wagons, these were the first vehicles provided by the RR for the bulk carriage of liquids and at that time it was hardly visualised to what extent petrol and oils were to be conveyed in tankcars. Salisbury soon followed with bulk storage depots and sixteen more tank wagons came into use in 1936 to cope with the growing trade. By 1937 the oil companies had erected storage at Beira and in April petrol and oil supplies began to travel over RR lines entirely, instead of from Natal, and gradually as road transport developed storage depots were established in other large towns.

Another new traffic in 1930 was the export of chilled and frozen meat from the cold storage works at Bulawayo to South African ports en route to Britain. For this, nine bogie refrigerator wagons were supplied by Metro-Cammell Carriage & Wagon Co. With wooden bodies lined with lead sheeting, they had two sections over 15ft long with ice chambers at ends and centre, the ice blocks being loaded through side doors just below roof level. With a tare of 65,000lb, the trucks had a capacity of 1,524cu ft. One of these new vehicles was fitted with a Lightfoot-Stones mechanical refrigerator plant, this being operated by a belt drive from an axle, while it had brine tanks for storage to maintain low temperatures during standing time in transit. It was ill luck that the foot-and-mouth disease outbreak stopped all exports almost at once, but by late 1932 the restrictions were lifted and meat railings resumed to Cape Town and Durban for shipment overseas.

Care was taken in selecting high-class cattle for slaughter, and conveyance from loading point to abattoirs was arranged in bogie cattle trucks having special padding to prevent bruising, which it is important to avoid in the chilled beef trade. While frozen beef was stacked on the floors of refrigerator trucks, roof rails with hooks were installed to permit chilled beef carcases to be hung so that the cold air could circulate. Trials were carried out with the Lightfoot-Stones truck and the more conventional top ice bunker wagons in use on the SAR, the wagons being attached to the Bulawayo—Cape Town passenger train for the first part of the journey to give the quickest possible transit over the 1,354 mile run. Initially the Lightfoot-Stones truck gave good results and plant was ordered for the other eight RR bogie wagons, but trouble was later experienced with the mechanism of the axle drive, which proved unreliable. Nevertheless, the keen co-operation of the railways played a major part in the establishment of this export trade, which was of much benefit to the cattle ranchers in Matabeleland.

With the growing development on the Copperbelt and the coming transfer to the Northern Rhodesian capital to Lusaka, it was decided to move the district superintendent and his staff from Livingstone to Broken Hill so that the control of the northern district was more centrally sited. Offices and some housing were obtained from a mining company and other quarters built, so that early in 1932 the move was effected and staff, families, furniture, office equipment and files were all packed off on a special train bound for Broken Hill. At that time James Hopwood was the district superintendent, while S. P. J. Fry was engineer for no 4 district and these two officers had charge of all railway activities throughout the northern territory.

The move was not very popular as, despite Livingstone's intense heat, the fishing and boating on the Zambesi provided recreation for many enthusiasts, while its proximity to Victoria Falls brought many visiting sporting teams to compete with the railwaymen at cricket, soccer and other games. Broken Hill was also hot and its comparative isolation at that time, when roads were merely rough dust tracks, meant that distance cramped the visits from elsewhere, so that the little township divided itself into three—mine, civil service and railway—around which social activities resolved.

173

The railway housing area grew with increasing staff and a clubhouse was erected, later to develop into a rival to the mine club, and to have sports fields and bowling greens.

For some years the Union of South Africa had hoped for a direct rail link with Rhodesia from the Northern Transvaal as an alternative to the line through Bechuanaland from Mafeking. The Beit Trust in 1928 provided funds to construct a road-and-rail bridge across the Limpopo river, near Messina, to provide uninterrupted communication between the two countries and by government agreement the SAR extended its line from Messina by ten miles to the new bridge and for another mile into Southern Rhodesia. A township named Beitbridge was established on the Rhodesian side of the river and the cost of the railway from the bridge was borne by government. The SAR has operated and staffed this line ever since it was opened in August 1929, but it was not long before RR introduced road motor services linking West Nicholson and Fort Victoria with Beitbridge. Passenger traffic, mainly Africans, soon developed and some types of South African exports began to use these routes into Rhodesia.

Later on road competition was to develop with private enterprise carrying goods from Beitbridge to Rhodesian towns, as the main roads were improved, while the route became very popular for tourists travelling by car. The one mile of line in Rhodesia was transferred to RR ownership in 1961 but is still worked by the SAR.

Depression and economy had been the watchwords with RR during 1931 and 1932, the total earnings having dropped from the high of £5,297,768 in 1929–30 to £2,634,266 in 1931–2, but there was a gleam of sunshine in 1932–3 when there was an increase of over £250,000 in revenue. General goods traffic was improving and mining activity was brisk with reviving copper development in Northern Rhodesia and asbestos and gold in the south, while a heavy maize crop allowed a return to the export of this grain. As many as fifty-three locomotives had been put into store during the slump in traffic and it was not until late in 1934 that the first ten were returned to work.

Despite the depressing times efforts were made to retain and increase business with new attractions, especially for passengers.

The acceleration of passenger trains had been continued in line with the SAR, while a new facility was the 'tourist motor car concession', by which holders of two return tickets could rail their car to their holiday destination at very low rates for the return trip. This inducement was attractive in the days of motoring long distances over indifferent gravel roads and retained many people to rail travel, particularly those who availed themselves of the 'Rhodesia residents' concession', which gave a return journey for single fare over RR lines once a year.

With the increased passenger business it was essential to obtain more dining-cars and eight had been supplied by Cravens of Sheffield in 1929–31. These seated twenty-four passengers at tables for four and two separated by a gangway in a 24ft 8in long saloon, while service was given from a kitchen 12ft 5in long, and a pantry of 10ft 0in; there was a small bar, with refrigeration, at the opposite end to the kitchen. These cars had clerestory type roofs with fans and good lighting and access was gained from the adjoining coaches over open gangways, as at that time all carriages had open balcony ends. It was no mean feat for the catering staff to serve three or even four sittings on crowded trains in the time available.

Cravens had also supplied in 1929 two private saloons—designated 'Reserved' on the sides. These had a lounge with large observation windows at the trailing end, three single bedrooms and a bathroom, and a kitchen and larder at the leading end with accommodation for the catering staff. The length over headstocks was 60ft 6in and the tare 89,000lb. These saloons looked impressive and were very comfortable, having easy chairs, a settee and a folding table, with good lighting and fans in the lounge and bedrooms. One was normally allocated to the governor of Southern Rhodesia, who made many journeys by rail, while the other was used by the resident director of RR and other distinguished visitors. At this period the general manager had his own saloon (old no 89050), which had been built in the Bulawayo workshops in 1921, but an older and more interesting private saloon was no 89040, which had been used for many years by George Pauling and his associates until it was purchased by the RR in 1923. This vehicle had four bedrooms as well as a large lounge, a bathroom, and staff accommodation and kitchen, and apart from being used by senior officers for line inspection tours it was sometimes hired as a 'family' saloon for shooting parties and holiday trips. The internal decoration with beautiful grained panels, ornate carving and old-fashioned lamp brackets gave a somewhat Victorian appearance and one could picture Pauling and his friends enjoying the ample meals, with no lack of liquor, for which he was renowned on his railway travels. Later on the interior was modernised.

Two other saloons were nos 89000 and 89009 built by the Electric Railway & Tramway Carriage Works in 1905 for visiting directors and senior officers. Both had new bodies of modern design fitted after some twenty-five years service, one supplied by Cravens in 1931 and the other constructed in the Bulawayo workshops. Normally all these private or 'Reserved' saloons had the varnished teak livery but for certain royal visits one or two were painted white with gilt lettering and lining, and looked most striking.

In order to maintain contact with the staff at wayside stations, to undertake investigations into new works, to meet the public at small centres, or to supervise varied jobs along the line it often was necessary for senior and district officers to spend several days at a time away from their homes. For this reason a railway stretching over such long distances as RR had to own a number of service coaches of varying types in which officials could undertake tours; as such vehicles were self-contained it was simple to put one off a train at a convenient station. Stabled in a siding senior officers were able to give hospitality to local businessmen and so ensure good relations with some of the users of the railway system. It was a pleasant custom to throw a small party in the 'gin palace', as the larger saloons were irreverently called, and when the practice of taking one's wife on line tours was encouraged by a new general manager the 'men only' gatherings were enlivened by mixed company. Negotiating the steps down from the saloon to ground level at the end of the evening was apt to unsettle the dignity of the most sedate visitor.

Other service coaches were used by the paymaster and store-men who travelled on the 'Pay and Stores' trains, which travelled over the system early each month, sometimes accompanied by a doctor in a medical coach, fitted up with a surgery as well as living quarters. At platelayers' cottages when one of the family was ill a circular sign bearing a red cross was displayed towards the track as an indication to the enginemen to stop so that the doctor could make a call.

The scales inspector, who tested and maintained all the weighing machines and scales at stations for goods and parcels—very important to fulfil government assize regulations—had a specially equipped caboose, while boiler inspectors, pumpfitters and truck-fitters also had service vehicles designed to carry the tools and equipment of their trades. While most of these vehicles were eight-wheelers, some of the older cabooses were short four-wheelers with a minimum of comfort and convenience. An unusual service coach was that used by the railway medical officers on the Plumtree—Mafeking section; it was a six-wheeled vehicle with a bogie at one end and two wheels at the other. Painted white for coolness it had a red cross on the doors and 'RMO Francistown' on the sides, and was numbered RR 89004.

Over the years, the standard of comfort in these travelling homes was raised by better design, automatic couplers instead of bell buffers, and improved internal fittings. Showers or baths were installed, and better electric lighting and fans, while for food storage, gas refrigerators were provided; such refinements, how-ever, came into vogue only in the 1950s and 'older hands' put up with relatively rough conditions in their travels on duty. The Victorian tin hip bath was part of the equipment in some of the service coaches and many of the older staff recall their 'caboose boy' filling the bath from paraffin tins boiled on the wood-burning kitchen stove and the difficulty, if one was large or tall, of getting some sort of a bath at the end of a long day. Others had to be content with a shower and a sudden cessation of the water supply if the roof tanks were not kept filled.

Other coaching stock of a specialist nature were the two specie vans belonging to the Southern Section, which worked a shuttle service between Bulawayo and Johannesburg conveying boxes of gold bars from the Rhodesian banks for export to London by the weekly Union Castle mail ships. These vans had a large built-in safe and provided accommodation for the two specie guards who were locked into their heavily barred van and travelled with the gold on all journeys. For the Umtali—Beira passenger trains, two postal vans were supplied for the Portuguese mail sorters who handled the bags of mail from overseas and elsewhere on the journey down to Beira. One of these, no 158, was built in 1899 as a first-class saloon for the Mashonaland Railway and after conversion to a baggage van in 1919 was altered for postal use in 1927, while the other, no 8, had been built in 1900 as the Train de Luxe baggage van and was converted to a postal van in 1931.

An unusual vehicle was the native infectious diseases coach, usually known as the 'leper coach'. This was a four-wheeled guards' van, the interior of which was fitted up as two compartments, one for the patients and one for the attendants, and had a stove, lavatory and water supply. This van had been converted in 1931, as a leper institution had been established in the Fort Victoria district, where lepers from all parts of the Rhodesias were treated. After each trip the 'coach' had to be disinfected and it was noticeable that there was always a reluctance by the wagon staff to undertake the job.

In 1934 one of the most senior officers, with over thirty years' experience of the trials and difficulties of life on the BMR, retired, namely T. Beach Smith. Beach Smith had joined the Traffic Department in 1901 at Umtali and played a notable part in the development of the railway, having filled various posts up to that of traffic manager and in 1927 had become the first chief superintendent of transportation. He was a good violinist and in the early days at Umtali was a member of a small orchestra mainly composed of railwaymen, who brought good music to the town, as well as helping at local dances. It is probably by his introduction of no 14 Up Through Port Goods train that Beach Smith was best remembered by his staff, as this train, giving a through transit from Beira to Northern Rhodesian stations in particular, was a notable addition to the train service. It was always believed that

178

when extra offices were built on the upper floor of the station where his staff were housed, Beach Smith moved to an office on the platform side of the building, despite the lack of sun, in order to have a view of 14 Up coming in. Woe betide if the train was late.

Beach Smith was succeeded as chief superintendent by W. Barron Dawson, an officer of wide experience on the SAR whose energy and ideas were an asset to RR at a time when traffic was reviving at a rapid rate and the maximum usage of power and wagon stock was vital to move the growing business. He also fostered a sense of taking responsibility and prompt action among his staff, and believed in delegating work to his subordinates.

The rapid rise in business and the upward trend in new developments were a tribute to the virile nature of Rhodesians. The low ebb in railway earnings was £2,634,000 in 1931–2 with a net operating revenue of only £73,000, but by 1934–5 the total earnings had shot up to £4,559,000 with a net revenue of £1,934,000, and this happier position enabled the companies to bring payment of all interest on debentures up to date and so cancel the moratorium. The staff also benefited as pay deductions were restored and full-time working in the shops was resumed. From this time until World War II traffic showed an almost continuous upward trend and the tonnages carried of various commodities achieved new records year by year.

Interesting developments in 1934–5 included the introduction of the motor trolley gang system for the maintenance of the track. Hitherto gangers had cottages, often in isolated spots with their labour housed close by, at about eight-mile intervals along the line. They made their track inspection and journeys to place of work by hand-operated pump trolley but the new mechanically propelled 'flying gang' trolley, capable of hauling one or more trailers, speeded up transit to the site of the job. This enabled the number of gangs to be reduced and as a start the system was tried out on the Fort Victoria branch, followed by the Selukwe branch a few months later. It soon proved a success and the 'FGT' method was introduced on the Copperbelt branch lines and elsewhere.

179

The visit of Prince George to Rhodesia in March 1934 was an event of importance and satisfaction to the railway staff, as all the travel was by rail and involved not only journeys over the whole main line between Bulawayo and Umtali and later north to Sakania, but also over the Fort Victoria, Luanshya and Nkana branch lines. For his tour throughout South Africa the prince travelled in the SAR White Train originally provided in 1925 for the visit of his brother, the Prince of Wales, but on arrival at Bulawayo the RR provided much of the coaching stock and, of course, the locomotives. Two of the White Train special carriages were lent for the prince's use on his tour of the Rhodesias and went on through the Belgian Congo and Angola to Lobito Bay, as did the SAR twin dining-car *Protea*.

The general manager, Henry Chapman, travelled in private saloon no 89040 attached to the royal train and with his intimate knowledge of the system was able to inform the prince of much local detail. The royal train manager was Frank Barnett, chief trains clerk, who with various inspectors ensured the smooth running of the whole operation. At the conclusion of the Rhodesian tour the prince bade farewell to the RR officials and paid tribute to the manner in which his comfort had been studied.

Diesel-engined railcars for passenger traffic had been advocated by Beach Smith before his retirement and he had even envisaged fast railcars over the Bulawayo—Salisbury run. A petrol-engined 'rail motor coach' had been supplied by the Drewry Car Co in 1916 and had been tried on various services but its small size— only twenty seats—limited its suitability and it fell out of use after a few years. It was decided in 1934 that with the successful development of the diesel engine and the use of railcars in many countries an experiment would be made on the Shamva branch line from Salisbury and an order was placed with Ganz of Budapest.

Carried on two four-wheeled bogies, the car seated sixteen first-class and forty native-class passengers, with a compartment to hold $2\frac{1}{2}$ tons of parcels traffic. Delivery was effected in mid-1936 and in September railcar no M1, in a green and cream livery with aluminium coloured roof, went into service with trips from Shamva every morning except Sundays. It returned from Salisbury in the late afternoon, daily except Saturdays, so giving time for shopping and business to the residents along the line. The weekend break at Salisbury enabled mechanics to service and repair the vehicle as needed. The run of eighty-six miles was timed for $3\frac{1}{2}$ hours, including 30 minutes for stops en route, and this new service soon became very well patronised; indeed the natives overflowed their seats and usually quite a number were standing, while cream cans and parcels congested the luggage compartment. T. H. (Tommy) Grey, a main-line driver, trained as railcar driver and was in charge of M1 for several years. Little did he think then that some twenty-five years later he would be chairman of the railway board of a nationalised railway system.

Before going to Salisbury to inaugurate the new service, the Ganz railcar was called upon to display itself to a group of Bulawayo 'VIPs' who were invited by the general manager to come on a trial trip. An officer had been sent specially to Budapest to see the railcar built and tested and he was deputed to demonstrate the diesel's efficiency on a run from Bulawayo. The party assembled and with a cheerful send-off M1 set out at a good speed down the bank along the north main line, but after only a couple of miles a detonator, placed by a ganger working on the track, exploded with a loud report beneath the railcar. This explosion so unnerved the driver, already tensed up with his important load, that he clashed the gears in a hasty movement and to his horror the gear locked and the brand new railcar came to an undignified stop. Despite all his efforts the luckless officer was unable to restart the car and an urgent message was sent back by runner for a shunting engine to come out and tow the railcar back to the station. This 'SOS' was greeted with much hilarity by the protagonists for steam and there were many red faces among the railway officers in the 'VIP' party. Doubtless Henry Chapman managed to control himself until his guests dispersed and he was able to blow off steam.

An experiment by Dawson at Easter 1935 was a 'Round Rhodesia' tour by special train from Bulawayo to Fort Victoria,

Sinoia, Umtali and Salisbury with motor car trips to Zimbabwe ruins, Sinoia caves, Vumba mountains and Mazoe citrus estates. This 1,354 mile rail trip cost £11 10s for first-class travel, with all meals, car tours and the use of an observation-lounge car—borrowed from the SAR—as an added comfort. While the tour was quite successful it was not repeated owing to poor support when mooted the following year.

The inclusive fare excursions to Victoria Falls with accommodation at the Falls Hotel, advertised for both first- and second-class travel, were however always popular and these special fares originally confined to Bulawayo and Salisbury were extended to benefit people from centres in the north as well as other points in Southern Rhodesia. Such special fare trips were not available at Easter, July and Christmas holiday seasons; the hotel was always fully booked then and had a long waiting list for cancellations.

The expansion of the railway road services had shown that motor transport could play a big part in the movement of goods in Rhodesia and several private operators acquired lorries to run over the main roads between the larger towns, such as Umtali—Salisbury and Bulawayo—Salisbury. These services were in direct competition with the RR and, as in other countries, the hauliers went for the cream of the rail traffic, that is the easily handled high-rated commodities. Some success was achieved, especially from Umtali where clothing, textiles and other goods imported from Beira by rail were handled through a depot near the railway station and taken to Salisbury by lorry. As the rail rates Beira—Umtali and Umtali—Salisbury were calculated separately instead of on the through mileage, the road competitors were able to cut in with a slightly cheaper rate, which attracted a number of traders.

The growth of this competition was of much concern to the railway, as it spread to local industries distributing their products, an advantage being that there was door-to-door conveyance without local cartage fees, and sometimes quicker deliveries. Efforts were made to give better transit to high-rated rail traffic and Dawson introduced a 'Red Label' service for light, easily

handled packages of an urgent nature. These were specially con-
signed at no extra charge and were carried in vans on mixed
trains, receiving urgent collection and delivery arrangements by
the cartage contractors. This measure was partly successful in
stemming the loss of traffic to road and the staff became imbued
with enthusiasm in dealing with Red Label packages until merchants began using these labels on all their goods. There were the
odd failures and in one instance an angry smallworker, whose
urgent mine pump part had been delayed between Bulawayo and
Que Que, wrote to Dawson complaining bitterly and suggesting
that he put red pepper on the fundaments of the railwaymen concerned! Dawson used this letter to drive home to his staff the
importance of his Red Label service.

With the retirement of M. N. Varvill as chief engineer, E. M.
Rice was promoted to the position in 1935. His main concern at
first was the condition of the old 60lb round-top rails, some of
which had been in use up north since the construction days and
which, on the Bulawayo—Salisbury section particularly, were
giving trouble with alarming breakages. It was clear that heavier
metal was needed to stand the strain of the rising traffic and at
last sanction was given for relaying with 80lb BS rail in 40ft
lengths, together with increased stone ballast. As a start the Salisbury—Hunters Road section of the main line was chosen.

This was the first time 40ft rail had been used on RR and one
snag was that no trucks of sufficient length were available. The
difficulty was overcome by borrowing from the SAR 100 of their
new drop-sided wagons in exchange for a similar number of new
RR high-sided trucks. After some time it was found that a batch
of new drop-sided wagons could be lengthened by the insertion of
an extra 5ft panel in the main underframe and an extra door on
each side, which gave a length of 42ft, and this enabled the trucks
on loan from the SAR to be returned. All future orders for drop-
sided wagons specified the longer bodies.

Work on this relaying programme was skilfully organised and
started in February 1936 from a depot established at Salisbury.
With two departmental relay gangs and two contractors, the job
was carried out at good speed and in two years the 290 miles to

Bulawayo had been completed. This heavier track was a decided step forward in view of the increase in axleloads of locomotives and wagons since the line was first laid and orders for 80lb rail for a further two years' work were placed to enable the relay organisation to go straight on with the line north of Bulawayo to Northern Rhodesia. Here the job was stopped at Batoka in 1940 as the war interfered with supplies of rail. To relay some 750 miles in almost exactly four years reflected great credit on the engineers responsible.

When the rail was ordered for the third year's work, which included the severely curved Dett—Wankie section, is was specified that enough sorbitically treated rail should be supplied for all curves sharper than 12 chains. Such treated rail had been tried with success on a few sharp curves earlier and it was found to last at least twice as long as ordinary rail. Sorbitising is carried out when the rails are cooling off after rolling, by subjecting the rail crown to a finely sprayed stream of brine. While rail wear was undoubtedly reduced, an unexpected repercussion was the serious effect sorbitic rail had on locomotive wheel tyres, which brought a protest from the CME. To ameliorate this, a number of rail and flange lubricators were installed on the sharply curved sections of line and this relieved the trouble.

Coincident with the 80lb re-railing an extensive series of deviations and regradings was carried out between 1938 and 1940 on the 61-mile section between Bulawayo and Sawmills in order to permit the haulage of increased loads in both directions. The original ruling grade had been 1 in 80 uncompensated, with 10-chain curves, but the new route which involved eight separate deviations was designed to give grades of 1 in 130 in the down and 1 in 110 in the up direction, both compensated, with 20-chain curves. This had been surveyed by the location engineer, A. M. Close, and eliminated the steep grades and sharp curves of the original line.

The last deviation to be completed, just outside Bulawayo, was nearly twelve miles in length and introduced two features new to RR practice. For the first time in Rhodesia two bridges were constructed to carry road traffic over the railway, a first step in level-crossing elimination, while another 'first' was the fly-over track leading to the explosives magazines, which crossed the main line by the first rail-over-rail bridge on RR. The main-line approach into Bulawayo station at the west end was considerably re-modelled in conjunction with the deviation, in order to separate the Victoria Falls and Cape lines from the shunting in the main traffic yard. For this, signalling and interlocking were installed and gave a greater measure of safety in working a very busy area.

In the years immediately before the outbreak of World War II in September 1939, the territories served had been enjoying con-tinued expansion and prosperous trade conditions, and with rail-way revenue buoyant the time was considered opportune by the London boards to carry out a conversion of the debenture stocks. Thus in 1937 the Beira Railway Co 6½ per cent stock was replaced by new debentures at 5 per cent, while Rhodesia Railways Ltd raised £21,750,000 of new 4½ per cent stock to redeem its own various debentures as well as those of the Mashonaland Railway Co, providing for a sinking fund to redeem the new issue over forty-four years. This RR conversion scheme involved the acquisi-tion of the Mashonaland Railway so that only one company now owned the whole railway system between Umtali and the Congo border including branches, except for the separately owned Shabani Railway.

This financial transaction resulted in a total annual saving of over £244,000 to the Beira and Rhodesia Railways, a very useful reduction in expenses. The disappearance of the Mashonaland Railway Co brought to an end its association of forty years with the fortunes of the two Rhodesias. It had done splendid work as a pioneer company in opening up the country and its name will always be linked with the romantic early days of railway develop-ment. With this step the marking of certain locomotives and roll-ing stock with the initials 'MR' was to cease and gradually as shopping occurred 'RRM' was substituted. The various initials placed on engines and vehicles over the years, to designate owner-ship were as follows:

MR   Mashonaland Railway
MRKB Mashonaland Railway (Kalomo—Broken Hill)

RR   Rhodesia Railways (Vryburg—Bulawayo)

RRM   Rhodesia Railways (North of Bulawayo)

RKR   Rhodesia Katanga Junction Railway (Broken Hill—Congo border)

BT   Beit Trustees (This was affixed to stock bought on loans advanced by the Beit Trust to the RR or MR).

Although the initials RRM were placed on a few engine tenders, it soon became the practice to use RR only, though for coaching and wagon stock the RRM designation was general. The Beira Railway Co never owned any rolling stock after the line was widened to the standard gauge. A considerable number of old wagons no longer fit for main-line use were allocated for 'Beira Port Use' and confined to the conveyance of imports and exports between ships, sheds and dumps in the port area, and these were appropriately marked.

One interesting feature of the conversion of the RR and MR debentures in 1937 was that before the scheme could be effected an assurance had to be obtained from the governments of the United Kingdom, on behalf of the Bechuanaland Protectorate, and of the Union of South Africa that they would not exercise their powers to expropriate the section of line between Vryburg and Palapye. These stemmed from the construction days when the British and Cape Colony administrations authorised the building of the railway. It was now agreed by the two governments that Rhodesia Railways would be free from any possible expropriation of this section of line for a term of thirty-three years.

CHAPTER EIGHT

From Private Ownership to Nationalisation

WITH record tonnages being handled as a result of development of trade and industry the future outlook of RR was bright. The copper mines in the north were expanding rapidly and in early 1937 the line between Chambishi and Chingola was re-opened to serve the Nchanga mine. Locomotive power was pressed to the utmost to cope with rising traffic, the pooling of engines among crews had become general, and it was only by skilful planning and much overtime on the part of repair staff that the available power met the demands. The average monthly mileage run by train engines was 2,129 in 1936, rose to 2,815 in 1937, and was up to 3,144 in 1938, a very fine achievement by the staff.

The rising European population and the higher spending power of the indigenous people called for more frequent passenger services. On local mixed trains first-class accommodation was provided by the conversion of old first-class coaches into 1st/2nd class composites, while on some branch lines additional mixed trains were run. The Northern Express was again accelerated to give a 40min earlier arrival at Ndola, while over the Mafeking—Bulawayo run an extra train in the summer season in each direction catered for the holiday business, making five trains weekly on the service to South Africa. The Bulawayo—Johannesburg service was also speeded up and so gave a better connection by the fast train on from the Rand to Durban, while in the reverse the Johannesburg train was faster by 6½ hours to Bulawayo. The SAR also replaced a slow train from Cape Town with one in express times reaching Bulawayo on Saturday mornings, a cut of 14hr 25min in the overall journey, very welcome to long-distance travellers, particularly those with a family of children.

While the standard of comfort for passengers was quite high, some people found that sleep at night was not easy on the relatively hard beds in a rocking train. To help poor sleepers special de luxe mattresses were introduced as an experiment at a fee of 3s a journey. Made of foam rubber, suitably covered, these soon became popular with passengers and over the years the stock was considerably increased on trains. So travel conditions changed in forty years from the pioneer passenger with his own blankets and 'skoff box' to the modern traveller with a de luxe bed with fresh linen and all the amenities of a dining-saloon.

The number of routes of the Road Motor Services (RMS)—the road feeder services of RR—had been increased over the years but some of their finest work was the special transport of material for the bridges built by the Beit Trustees to give better road connections between distant centres. One of these was the Birchenough bridge over the Sabi river on the main road from Umtali to Fort Victoria, which hitherto had only been passable through a drift when the river was low. The RMS built special trailers to carry 2,600 tons of steelwork, some of it in sections 40 to 53ft long, this having to be hauled over eighty miles of rough gravel roads with many long and steep grades winding among the hills. Another similar job was the carriage of 3,000 tons of steel, cement and other material from Lions Den, near the terminus of the Zawi branch line, to Chirundu, 146 miles away. Here a site had been chosen for the Otto Beit bridge which provided a crossing of the Zambesi river and linked Salisbury and Kafue directly by road, so aiding inter-territorial communication.

These special jobs taxed the ingenuity of the RMS staff in coaxing heavily loaded large lorries and trailers through sandy bush tracks in wild country, much of it sparsely populated save for game. For the trip to Chirundu much of the run was through tsetse fly areas and all vehicles had to be thoroughly sprayed in fly chambers at the border of the infested area.

In 1937 the design of diesel oil engines had so improved that a start was made on the conversion of the RMS Thornycroft lorries from petrol to oil fuel by the fitting of Gardner diesel engines, and gradually the whole fleet was changed over. The first passenger coach, a Thornycroft vehicle with Gardner engine, was placed in service on the busy passenger route between West Nicholson and Beitbridge, where connection was made with SAR trains to the Rand.

Sir Henry Chapman, who had been general manager since 1930, retired and was succeeded on 1 April 1938 by Mr W. J. K. Skillicorn, who had been assistant general manager of the South African Railways. Chapman had been with the railways for thirty-four years and had devoted himself whole-heartedly during the long years of booms and slumps. Of a somewhat austere disposition, he did not suffer fools gladly and was apt to lose his temper irrationally with his staff; nevertheless he had a kindly heart for those in trouble. On retirement, his keen financial knowledge was retained as he was appointed to the board of directors in London and soon after became resident director in place of Sir Drummond Chaplin, who had died. This position was to entail regular visits to Rhodesia and it was during one of these in 1939 that war broke out, with the result that Chapman was retained at railway headquarters in Rhodesia as liaison with the London board. Capt Harry Allen, another long-service railwayman, was appointed principal assistant to Skillicorn, and with his close knowledge of the system and his popularity with the staff in the sporting fields was a valuable help to the new general manager.

It was ill luck for the new manager that on 4 April 1938 there occurred the worst railway accident ever to happen on the lines of the RR. This was at 1,282 miles, near Vakaranga, in the only curved cutting between Plumtree and Tsessebe, when the Bulawayo—Cape Town passenger train collided head on at speed with a northbound goods train. Twenty-six people, including eighteen passengers, were killed and twenty-seven injured in the wreck, which destroyed or damaged the two RR trainsmen's cabooses and several SAR carriages and wagons, and resulted in the two RR 10th class locomotives involved, nos 153 and 241, being scrapped as beyond repair. An enquiry found that the SAR stationmaster at Tsessebe had issued a wrong train order and this official was later charged in a Bechuanaland court. The cost of the damage, claims and so forth, amounting to some £80,000, was by agreement shared equally between the SAR and RR administrations. A feature of the accident was the fine work done by railway members of the St John Ambulance Brigade, who were sent by road to the scene from Bulawayo, and assistance was also rendered by masters and scholars from the Plumtree School, who helped the dining-car staff and other surviving trainmen in freeing trapped passengers from the wreck.

There had been serious difficulties with water at this period, as not only was the rainfall very poor in the 1937–8 season, resulting in failures at several watering points, but impurities in raw water supplies were causing a bad condition in many loco boilers. The treatment of boiler feed waters was carefully studied as engine failures, due largely to leaking tubes as a result of heavy scaling of boilers, were having an effect on engine availability. In several areas the high mineral content of raw water had its effect on boilers and this was particularly so in the Broken Hill district. It was ironic that the valuable minerals providing much traffic, in turn caused the railway difficulties by their presence in locomotive water supplies.

Matabeleland in particular had very poor rains and by August 1938 the Khami dam near Bulawayo had practically dried up, seriously affecting the water supply for locomotive and workshop needs. Various wells were re-opened for pumping, while water tank trains were run from reliable watering points and the tanks decanted into troughs alongside the south main line close to Bulawayo and the water run into temporary reservoirs. Thirty-two open short wagons were converted into tank wagons for use as extra tenders on the worst sections, or for supplying domestic water to stations and cottages whose supply had failed. This drought situation remained precarious until, by good fortune, heavy rains fell early in November and December.

The much-needed rains continued into 1939 until by March there had been too much. As usual, it was the Beira line that suffered most and washaways occurred, with embankments slipping and water up to the track between 33 and 48 miles; all night services were suspended for a fortnight, though the line was not closed entirely. In Mashonaland the Hunyani river rose in heavy flood on 16 March reaching a maximum of 4ft over the rails on the bridge, while the approach embankment was washed out for 300ft to depths of 3–10ft. The main line was closed here for four days, while about the same time the Fort Victoria branch was cut by a washout at the 121½ miles bridge, the approaches to which were damaged causing the bridge itself to shift. The line was re-opened after ten days' hard work but a second flood came down and tilted the temporary bridge spans, so that it was closed again for another week. This was the last spasm of the 'Rain God' as the weather dried up and eased the worries of the RR engineers. Contending with nature's assaults on the steel way made life interesting but such troubles were rather too frequent.

It was times like these, when accidents and washaways occurred at isolated spots, that highlighted the very inadequate communication facilities. Station-to-station speech was over an iron wire phonopore line, which limited the range of conversation and suffered much interference during thunderstorms when the crackles on the wire almost deafened the listener trying to pick up what the speaker at the other end was saying. In 1933 Bulawayo and Salisbury were linked with intermediate stations when a selector telephone system was installed by the Southern Rhodesian postal authorities over their wires, and this had vastly improved the co-ordination of traffic arrangements between the district offices in the two towns. By 1935 this form of telephone had been extended to cover the Bulawayo—Livingstone section and as it made possible direct speech with Wankie, it greatly facilitated control at the colliery centre.

The experience gained was so marked that sanction was obtained for the extension of the selectorphones to the main line north of Livingstone as well as over the Salisbury—Umtali section. Reliable communications were essential for effective traffic control and the 'selector' enabled senior operating officials to discuss problems with ease and speed, in contrast to the old days when a conversation could only be held through a telegraphist laboriously tapping out question and answer on a morse key. Present-day railwaymen dialling reliable trunk telephones for speech and using teleprinters for written messages have little conception of the frustration and difficulties with which their predecessors had to contend and of the misunderstandings that arose through imperfectly heard phone messages. Such was especially the case when using the phonopore line in getting information from the agitated guard of a train at the scene of an accident.

The heavy pressure on locomotive power resulting from the rapidly rising traffic had led the chief mechanical engineer to review the methods of shopping engines and early in 1939 Sells introduced the 'progressive system of loco repairs' at the Bulawayo workshops. This system aimed at (i) reducing the time locomotives were in shops and so increasing their revenue earning capacity, (ii) avoiding delays in waiting for new or repaired material by planning the various operations to a time schedule, (iii) lowering the cost of repairs per engine, and (iv) increasing the capacity of the workshops without extension of buildings.

Tender engines were given general repairs in thirty-eight working days—reduced to thirty-four for 12th class—instead of an average seventy-three days before the progressive system was started. Under this arrangement locomotives were 'proposed' for shopping by the district officers and with consultation at headquarters a programme for several months ahead was drawn up for which the workshop staff could prepare. The success of the system at Bulawayo led to its introduction at Umtali where the Garratt type was repaired, their general repairs being averaged at thirty-nine working days. There is no doubt that the speedier passage of engines through workshops contributed appreciably to the availability of power during the war, which was a time of great pressure.

Similar measures were introduced for the repair of wagon stock, both at Umtali and Bulawayo, resulting in the time for a general being cut from fifty-three to twenty-three working days per wagon. This improved repair rate of trucks had become possible by the opening of a new wagon shop at Umtali and the extension of the Bulawayo shop, coupled with the better planning of work.

With the threat of war looming up in Europe, the demand for base metals such as copper, chrome, lead, zinc and asbestos on the world markets stepped up pressure on RR and fortunately with heavier locomotives, improved track and the sterling efforts of the staff new records were achieved in the operating results, and revenue mounted. A general reduction of rates and fares was possible in January 1939 and this removed all the surcharges imposed since 1932, so restoring more harmonious relations with the railway users.

When World War II broke out in September 1939 the Rhodesias were fortunate that the railways were geared to cope with heavy traffic and that there was a backbone of well experienced staff. With compulsory military service on a part-time basis in Southern Rhodesia, a large number of younger employees was soon lost when their units were mobilised. A company drawn from the 2nd Rhodesia Regiment at Bulawayo, including many railwaymen, was at once rushed to Victoria Falls to protect the famous bridge, the safety of which was so vital for communications to the north. Manpower control regulations were soon enforced in both Rhodesias to ensure the retention of staff in essential services and this had a braking effect on many who wished to join the forces but had to be reserved for railway work. Within a year 373 men were released for war service, a total which finally reached 560, of whom fifty-eight were killed in action or died.

The war years meant long hours of overtime and the postponement of leave for the remaining staff, while to replace men on service, pensioners and others over normal age were employed. Many women were recruited for clerical work and some acted as stewardesses on dining-cars. In the railway workshops military requirements were manufactured and with the CME as a member of the Government War Supplies Committee an ordnance factory, known as 'Rofac', was built close to the Bulawayo workshops and run by seconded RR artisans with some eighty women operatives. This factory produced bomb pistols, striker heads, practice bombs and similar equipment for military and air training purposes.

The offer by Southern Rhodesia to provide facilities for an RAF training group as part of an empire scheme was gladly accepted by the British government and this had a heavy impact on rail services. Nine flying schools were established around Bulawayo, Gwelo and Salisbury and all meant extensive work on the construction of runways, hangars and housing, calling for the movement of many thousands of tons of material and equipment, which were followed by crated aircraft to be assembled at air stations. At several aerodromes private sidings were constructed by RR to facilitate the delivery of aviation spirit, and as the flying increased so the volume of petrol from Beira and Durban rose rapidly. This called for stringent control over the transit and shunting of the tankcars, which included some on hire from SAR.

The thousands of air force personnel, both flying and ground staff, brought very heavy pressure on passenger trains as, apart from men on duty, many sporting teams and men on leave travelled between the larger centres. For these reasons, and also because of petrol rationing, passenger traffic rose rapidly and though trains were strengthened with extra carriages, the civilian population often had much difficulty in obtaining train bookings, as well as losing excursion fare benefits which were cancelled. With overseas holidays no longer possible South Africa became the magnet for holidays for Rhodesians and people from the Belgian Congo and Nyasaland, so further swelling passenger travel. Dining-car services were taxed to the limit and in order to cope with the demand four dining-cars were rebuilt as twin units to seat 40 or 42 instead of the small cars seating 24.

Close co-ordination over military passenger travel was effected by RTOs at the larger stations to liaise with RR, and red-capped military police became a familiar sight on platforms. For some few years the coloured luggage porters employed at Bulawayo and Salisbury stations had been issued with red covers for their peaked khaki caps as an easy distinction for passengers, but the arrival of military 'Red Caps' caused some confusion. Eventually RR bowed gracefully to the armed forces and station porters lost their red cap covers.

At very short notice, late in 1940, due to military operations in East Africa against the Italians, who had just entered the war, RR was called upon, in co-ordination with SAR, to move to the north many trainloads of South African troops and equipment. These trains were worked to special schedules allowing the north-bound troops a short break at Bulawayo, while the empty stock trains were speedily returned south from Broken Hill where an army depot had been set up.

The entry of Italy into the war led to the internment of a number of Italian permanent way staff with many years of service, so adding to the shortage of trained men. Some gangers' cottages were closed and adjoining gangs covered longer lengths.

In June 1940 the Mafeking—Bulawayo main line was cut by a disastrous explosion on Foley bridge when the weekly train carrying explosives for Rhodesian mines was almost completely destroyed. The 100ft span bridge was demolished and fourteen explosive trucks, a caboose and a wagon disappeared, but while other vehicles were damaged the locomotive escaped almost un-scathed. Three Bechuanaland police bridge guards, three other natives and a caboose attendant were killed and two European trainmen seriously injured. Despite exhaustive enquiries the cause of the explosion could not be definitely established.

With the shortage of staff, and to some extent material, new facilities had to be curtailed apart from the relaying of track and the completion of various deviations for which rail was available. The 80lb relaying of the main line was continued as far as Batoka in the north, while the growth of traffic over the Nkana branch, originally laid with secondhand 60lb rail, called for new 80lb track with extra sleepers. On the Vryburg—Bulawayo line much of the original permanent way was deteriorating to a serious degree under the heavy traffic and some 350 miles of track needed renewal. The difficulty in obtaining new material was extreme and it was only after suppliers in Britain and India had cancelled orders that one hundred miles of rails and fastenings were obtained from North America as well as 61lb rail from Iscor in South Africa. The provision of stone ballast and hardwood sleepers was begun with this relaying, which eventually got under way in 1943.

The war brought extreme pressure on all resources of RR, which were constantly overtaxed by the demand for important minerals for the allied war effort. Copper, chrome and asbestos to the ports rose to new records, while coal and coke railings leapt up to 1,203,000 tons in 1943, including 78,000 tons to Beira for bunkers and export. For five long years the operating staff—enginemen, guards and shunters especially—willingly worked long hours with very little leave so that the maximum movement of traffic was achieved. Concentration was primarily on these long-haul mineral exports and at times the staff were instructed to 'give empties preference' in making up trainloads in the direction of coal and chrome loading points. The slogan 'Trucks—Trucks—Trucks' to speed the release and prompt movement of empty wagons became a fetish with the operating staff.

It was a testimony to the efficient manner in which the system was worked that record operating results and tonnages were achieved each year and a comparison between the years of 1939 and 1944 illustrate the remarkable volume of traffic:

	1939	1944	Increase
Tons carried	3,118,782	4,658,222	49.4%
Passengers carried	1,021,758	2,486,315	143.3%
Train miles	6,612,705	9,110,307	37.8%
Net ton miles (000s)	1,498,880	2,192,313	46.3%
Total earnings £	5,496,621	7,505,631	38.4%

The engine stud and all coaching and goods stock were flogged to the utmost and only the good work of the maintenance staff kept them running. It was therefore welcome relief when nine heavy Garratt locomotives and one hundred open bogie wagons were delivered during 1943–4 through the auspices of the British government, to assist in moving strategic minerals.

Due to the difficulty in obtaining goods from overseas the development of local manufactures was stimulated and many secondary industries were started. This led to internal short-haul traffics demanding an increased share in the truckage but much still came up from South Africa. The growth of northbound tonnage over the Mafeking—Bulawayo line exceeded the capacity of RR locomotives available and power was hired from SAR to help move the rising trade. This flow of imports from the south was to have an adverse influence on the truck exchange position between the two railways as the excess of SAR wagons on RR lines not only raised the hire charges but posed a problem in returning empty trucks to the south.

The delivery of four new 15th class Garratts in 1940 introduced grease lubrication in place of oil, and Sells soon found the change gave excellent results. Experiments with the 10th, 11th and 12th classes showed that grease was more reliable than oil under conditions of indiscriminate pooling of engines, which was so necessary to secure maximum usage, and resulted in complete freedom from overheated axleboxes, side-rod bushes and crank pins. As a result, Sells decided to convert lubrication to grease generally since equipment could be obtained and this had its good effect on engine availability. Nevertheless, as the war dragged on with engines running excessive mileages and longer periods between general repairs, failures in service became more numerous, and by 1945 the locomotives were beginning to show the strain.

With the heavy demand on coaching stock it was decided to speed up maintenance by painting the exteriors instead of varnishing, and spray guns were introduced for this work. The internal state of carriages deteriorated under the heavy wear, coupled with some vandalism and pilfering of fittings, until by the war end passenger stock became very shabby. No new coaches had, of course, been obtained.

For some time the municipality of Gwelo had been anxious to expand the town by extending building sites to the south but this was impeded by the first $2\frac{1}{2}$ miles of the Selukwe branch line which left the station at the Bulawayo end and ran through an area suited for housing. Agreement was eventually reached in 1941 for the Selukwe line to be linked with the Fort Victoria branch by about one mile of new track to a junction named Selvic, $1\frac{3}{4}$ miles from Gwelo on its western side. This freed the old railway

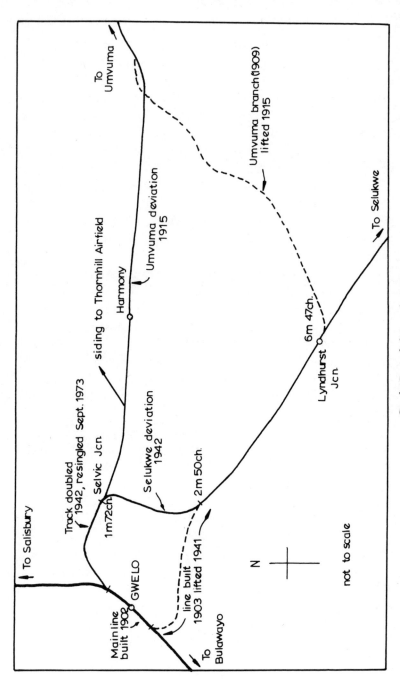

Gwelo Branch lines: deviation

To Salisbury

Main line built 1902

GWELO

Track doubled 1942, resingled Sept. 1973

Selvic Jcn

1m 72ch.

siding to Thornhill Airfield

To Umvuma

Harmony

Umvuma deviation 1915

Umvuma branch (1909) lifted 1915

To Bulawayo

line built 1903 lifted 1941

Selukwe deviation 1942

2m 50ch.

Lyndhurst Jcn.

6m 47ch.

To Selukwe

N

not to scale

strip for improved town planning, and it is interesting that Bulawayo and Salisbury were in later years to enjoy deviations of a
like nature. The name Selvic Junction did not remain long as it
was soon found that the handicap of an unattended junction on
train services could not be sustained and the line from Selvic into
Gwelo was doubled in 1942.

High pressure on movement continued to the end of the war in
1945 by which time excessive overtime and lack of leave were
causing sickness and fatigue particularly among the running staff.
There was a shortage of men in various grades as recruiting had
been impracticable, while the lack of artisans and shortage of
building material delayed new housing for possible recruits. The
acute position with gangers had led to extended lengths and as
there seemed little likelihood of many Europeans taking up life
in the bush a start was made with the training of coloured men
as gangers, while pay rates were improved.

By mid-1945 the air training was discontinued and the repatria-
tion of RAF personnel, in many cases with wives and families,
temporarily imposed a heavy burden on passenger services. The
return of Rhodesian servicemen from Europe added to this, but
soon with the lifting of petrol and tyre restrictions on private
motorcars a drop in upper class passengers was noticed although
the native class continued to rise.

The end of the war left RR in the position of being unable to
move all the traffic offering, as engines and rolling stock, track
and other facilities needed extensive maintenance before there
could be a return to previous high standards. Many railwaymen
returning from active service were disenchanted with their old
jobs and were unsettled, while many resigned as the boom in
industry and commerce led to more attractive employment offers.
As shift working and posting to lonely wayside stations were
inevitable to railwaymen, RR lost its appeal to many young men
and new staff had to be sought overseas among the many
ex-servicemen who desired a new life in a sunny developing
country.

There is no doubt that RR served the Rhodesias and adjoining
territories extremely well during the war and made a material

contribution towards the allied cause. Local developments now made it obvious that the railway system was faced with high capital expenditure on new equipment, rolling stock and facilities over the coming years to counter the sudden postwar expansion. For this to be financed from London by the company was recognised to be no easy task and discussions began with the governments of the territories served. After considerable negotiation it was agreed that Rhodesia Railways Ltd would be acquired by the Southern Rhodesia government, which purchased the RR share capital for £3,150,000 with effect from 1 April 1947. A loan of £30 million was raised by Southern Rhodesia to cover this purchase as well as to redeem the balance of £21,750,000 $4\frac{1}{2}$ per cent debenture stock outstanding and to provide additional capital for railway development amounting to some £6.3 million.

Though Southern Rhodesia assumed responsibility for the financial arrangements necessary and carried out the transaction, Northern Rhodesia and the Bechuanaland Protectorate were involved by guaranteeing 20 per cent and 5 per cent respectively of any deficit in future in the loan service. Thus private enterprise relinquished control of 2,445 miles of railways in the two Rhodesias and Bechuanaland, including the 112 miles of line within the Union of South Africa, and the whole system with the exception of the Beira Railway (203 miles) and the Shabani Railway ($62\frac{3}{4}$ miles) came under state ownership. The curious position thus arose of one government owning the railways running through other governments' territories.

For some fifty years the various railway companies so closely linked with the Chartered Company had played their important role in the progress of the Rhodesias. As the era closed it is fitting to pay tribute to the wide vision and acute financial skill with which the directors in London had managed the expansion of a very fine railway system. Cecil Rhodes himself had been the first chairman, while the names of Rochfort Maguire, Henry Birchenough, Dougal Malcolm and Drummond Chaplin, among others, stand out in the history of RR.

In the period between the end of the war and the settling down to state ownership many difficulties and problems arose. As soon

Page 201 (*above*) Bechuanaland Railway 4–6–0 no 1 became CGR 6th class no 582 when erected at Salt River, 1897; (*below*) Sunday evening at Salisbury, 1939, with classes 6A 4–8–4T, 12th 4–8–2, 13th and 14th Garratts at ease

Page 202 'The Weekender' from Livingstone on Victoria Falls bridge. MR 4–4–0 no 3 with compo carriage, 1913

as practicable the company had placed orders early in 1946 for the supply of thirty Garratt locomotives from England, twelve 4–8–2 engines from Canada, 450 open and covered wagons, 21 refrigerators, 25 petrol tankcars, 97 passenger coaches and 15 baggage vans as a start towards building up the urgently needed fleet of rolling stock. Unfortunately, deliveries were not to prove as speedy as hoped.

Staff had become a major problem as commerce, industry and mining attracted any skilled labour, already at a premium in Rhodesia, although steady immigration was taking place. Apart from this serious shortage, there was discontent over pay and working conditions, which led first to a strike of the native employees leading to a government commission of enquiry, and later a dispute with the RRWU ending with an arbitration tribunal for the white and coloured staff. Increased pay and allowances were granted to all staff, while in the case of the natives a new department was formed under a chief officer (Dr E. M. B. West) to handle African affairs, such as working conditions, welfare, housing and rations. This innovation was to achieve much success in happier relations in future years.

The boom in industry and on the copper mines produced heavy tonnages of machinery, plant, cement and general goods, largely imports from overseas through Beira and from South Africa. This led to congestion of traffic at depots and reacted on the turnround of trucks, which in turn caused a decline in base metal and coal railings. The reduced colliery loadings seriously affected stocks of coal at power stations and mines, and chrome despatches had to be cut to divert wagons to Wankie. This surge of general traffic completely overtook the facilities at the larger goods depots and embargoes had to be enforced on the acceptance of goods from SAR. A strike on the copper mines lasting several weeks led to a cessation of copper loadings and of the mines' ability to offload coal, which fortunately could be diverted to build up power station and railway stocks.

Over several years this picture of constant juggling with insufficient engine power and wagons, with cramped traffic yards and goods sheds, and with a shortage of trained staff was a daily routine for the supervisory officials. With much reluctance, restrictions on traffic had to be imposed and the business world suffered many frustrations, often with a lack of appreciation of the real battle railwaymen were having in trying to cope with the ever-growing demands. At Bulawayo, Salisbury, Gwelo, Umtali and Ndola extra goods sheds were rapidly provided, while more tracks were put in to enlarge traffic yards where space permitted, sometimes merely to give standing room for trucks awaiting discharge, as merchants in their turn were often overwhelmed or dilatory with customs clearances and other paper work.

Not only was more staff needed to run trains but additional engineers had to be recruited to organise the planning and construction of the urgent expansion of tracks, houses, and so forth. It had become obvious that large marshalling yards, modern signalling and train control, track relaying and the strengthening of bridges were all needed to transform the run-down and now quite inadequate railway into a modern well-equipped system to cope with present-day business.

In the interim between Southern Rhodesia acquiring the assets of the company and the legislation establishing Rhodesia Railways as a statutory body on 1 November 1949, the Portuguese government exercised its right to expropriate the Beira Railway Company between Beira and the border near Umtali. The purchase of the Beira line was completed on 6 April 1949, while under the Van Laun agreement the Portuguese had also acquired Beira Works Ltd, the company responsible for port operations. To assist in the change, RR continued to control the line and port working until 1 October 1949, when the long alliance between the Beira and Rhodesia Railways ceased, though the same co-operation in close working was to continue happily in future years with the new Portuguese regime, several officials being ex-RR staff.

The London board of RR had been augmented early in 1947 by Sir Arthur Griffin, who had recently retired as chief commissioner of Indian Railways. He arrived in Rhodesia in March as resident director, replacing Sir Henry Chapman, and then succeeded Skillicorn as general manager on 1 May 1947. Griffin had had wide experience in India and with his strong personality, energy and knowledge was well suited for the change to state ownership, and he tackled with vigour the many problems. His experience of government control in India was invaluable in the formative period of state ownership in Rhodesia. It would be true to say that he, together with two other ex-Indian railway officers—S. E. L. West and F. E. Hough—who arrived soon after as CST and CME respectively, found conditions on RR in many ways dissimilar to those to which they were accustomed in the East, and initially acclimatisation was needed.

Early in 1948 the RR directors in London retired and a new board was constituted in Southern Rhodesia, while the London office became the agency for the railway's business in Britain. The head office of the various railway companies had been housed since the early days with the British South Africa Company at 2 London Wall, where directors' meetings were held, while a London manager and staff handled financial business, purchase of rolling stock, stores and equipment from overseas suppliers, and recruiting. With the outbreak of war in 1939 this office had moved to Bexhill-on-Sea, but later went inland to Ascot. This was as well, as in the blitz on London a bomb burst and set fire to a gas main in London Wall, and 'no 2' was entirely burnt out. A few old records in a basement safe were not burned, though severely damaged by water, but most of the old history was lost. In 1946 the office went back to the City and at Salisbury House, London Wall, the staff remained until the London agency closed in June 1961, Oliver Naylor being the last agent. So ended the direct link between RR and London.

The Railway Commission referred to in Chapter 6 was to disappear under the Southern Rhodesian legislation with the formation of a new railway board in October 1949. The first chairman was Lt-Gen Sir Clarence Bird, KCIE, CB, DSO, with J. S. H. Grant (ex-chairman of the Railway Commission) for a time as vice-chairman, while other members were appointed to watch the particular interests of Northern Rhodesia. This board was to continue with periodic changes of members until Zambia achieved independence and a split of control occurred.

Just before Skillicorn completed his term as general manager, RR was faced with a most pleasurable task, that of arranging the rail journeys of the Royal Family in Rhodesia. Their Majesties King George VI and Queen Elizabeth, accompanied by Princesses Elizabeth and Margaret, honoured Southern Rhodesia by including it in their South African tour early in 1947. For their extensive visit the SAR provided a luxurious newly built White Train, which was readily made available for the Rhodesian section of the tour. While many of the SAR staff remained on the train, RR was in charge with James Hopwood (the CST) as train manager and senior officials and inspectors travelling on the local journeys. RR enginemen and guards naturally handled the trains.

For the royal tour, involving journeys from Salisbury to Victoria Falls and back to Bulawayo prior to returning south by train through Bechuanaland, very extensive plans had to be made in conjunction with the government to suit the programme of visits to intermediate towns, for the quiet and secure staging of the royal and pilot trains, the re-stocking and watering of saloons, postal, radio and telegraph facilities, laundry and other matters. The Royal Family flew from South Africa to Salisbury on 7 April, the two trains having arrived the previous day and stabled in a special siding at Government House. At Victoria Falls the main party was accommodated in the Falls Hotel which was reserved entirely and this involved major re-furnishing and equipping for the occasion.

For the haulage of the royal train, which weighed 810 tons, the four 15th class Beyer-Garratts, nos 271–274, were specially prepared and painted in a most attractive royal blue livery. For each journey two locomotives were used, separated by a bogie water tank, also painted blue, while the pilot train, weighing 634 tons, was double-headed by two 12th class 4–8–2 locomotives in RR black livery. The appearance of the two trains was outstanding and a great credit to the railway staff concerned in this memorable event. (Picture, p 220.)

The tour went off smoothly and according to programme, the only unrehearsed incident of note being at Matetsi where, when the train stopped for water en route to Victoria Falls, their

Majesties seeing a small gathering at the station decided spontaneously and without warning to alight. The stationmaster (Charlie Wise) at once stepped forward respectfully to greet the King and Queen and escorted them to the thrilled group of onlookers. Everywhere crowds had loyally and enthusiastically welcomed the royal visitors but this informal reception made a great impression.

At the conclusion of the tour King George invested Mr Skillicorn with the CVO in honour of the part played by RR in the success of the royal visit.

CHAPTER NINE

Modernisation Schemes

THE postwar boom in business and industry, with its constantly rising demand for rail transport, had been straining the worn-down facilities of RR but with capital funds now becoming available through governmental and international sources it was at last possible to implement some of the ideas in the minds of the railway's officers. The main centres, Salisbury, Bulawayo and the Wankie area, where traffic movement was at its heaviest, called .for early attention, along with certain deviations to improve main-line grading or other special needs, such as the Hunyani Poort water catchment for the capital city. These and many other lesser extensions were to take up much time over several years in what became a ten-year development scheme for modernising the system.

Salisbury, as the junction for the branch lines to the tobacco and maize growing Mazoe and Lomagundi districts, was having to cope with much greater farming traffic, as well as that arising from the rapid industrial expansion around the city itself. The successful development of Rhodesian tobacco to supply a large share of world consumption led to the establishment of many buying, marketing, packing and manufacturing concerns around Salisbury, while industries producing fertilisers, farming equipment and packing materials were a natural outcome. All these required private sidings and added to the seasonal very heavy traffic burden, with its problems of meeting tobacco sales and export shipments. At this time Salisbury became the largest single tobacco marketing centre in the world and its sales floors, probably the finest and best run anywhere, were reliant in the developing years on the efficient services of RR.

In the immediate postwar period the only traffic sidings were close to the station itself, and while a smaller yard alongside the goods sheds had been laid down this did not lend itself to any major development owing to land restrictions, and the reception and sorting of trains had become increasingly difficult. By good fortune Lochinvar farm, some four miles on the Bulawayo side of Salisbury, became open for purchase by RR and this provided for ample future growth. On one side of the main line a village was set out with much-needed housing for European staff, both married and single, with canteen, schooling and sporting facilities. On the other side a start was made in 1950 with a reception and sorting yard, initially for traffic from the Gwelo direction, while service lines from Salisbury station yard were extended and eventually linked with Lochinvar, so making possible the shunting of trucks directly to the innumerable private sidings that serve the industries, tobacco sale floors, oil installations and so forth.

With Lochinvar yard in operation it was at once practicable to consider the relocation of the branch line to Mount Hampden, which ran from the Umtali end of Salisbury station across frequent road-rail level crossings round the east and north of the city boundaries through Avondale and other suburbs. After land negotiations, a cut-off was planned from near Mount Hampden through the Tynwald area well to the west of Salisbury to join the main line at Lochinvar. Almost twelve miles of line running through the outskirts of the city could then be lifted and the land handed over to the municipality, with considerable benefit to future town planning, as well as the removal of dangerous level crossings. The length of new construction was nine miles and the new line was more easily graded. This deviation was opened in September 1953 and branch-line goods traffic was much reduced from Salisbury yard.

Over subsequent years the volume of traffic in the Salisbury area made it necessary to double the main line between Salisbury and Lochinvar and to expand the marshalling yard with a second set

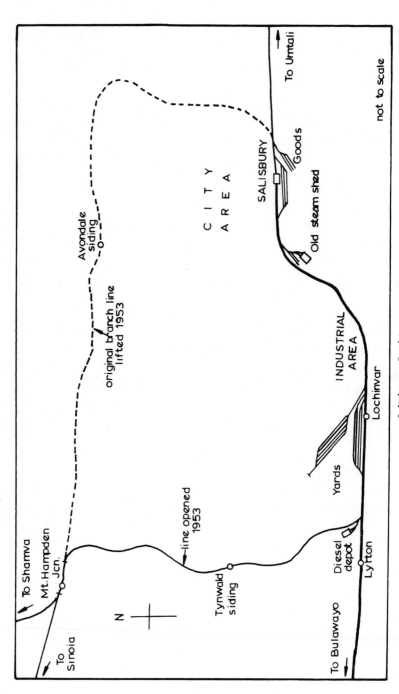

Salisbury—Lochinvar section

of reception and sorting tracks, while facilities for the handling of livestock and vehicles were installed, as well as weighing and dumping sites for minerals. The Lochinvar area also provided for an extensive township, housing African staff and their families, and so permitted the old 'location' near the goods sheds in Salisbury to be cleared for further expansion.

Before the early stages of Lochinvar yard had been completed, an extensive deviation of the main line between Norton and Salisbury was necessitated by the large dam constructed to impound water from the Hunyani river to provide for Salisbury's rapidly growing needs and for an industrial area at Norton. This deviation was a major scheme, as a bridge over the Hunyani and some miles of track were to disappear under the area flooded, and a new location of the main line had to be found north of the range of hills skirting the dam. Fourteen miles of new track were constructed on the northern side of these hills, while a bridge 360ft in length was provided over the Hunyani just below the dam and spillway. This deviation called for heavy cuttings and banks, three crossing loops, and a loading loop for farmers, and was opened to traffic on 29 October 1951, before much of the new track had been ballasted. The old bridge and permanent way were dismantled and recovered only just before the old track was covered by water filling the dam.

The Hunyani deviation coincided with a very heavy rainy season and in places the track did not settle very well, while in the cuttings heavy rain loosened boulders which broke away and fell on the line. For some weeks this trouble caused delay to trains and an almost routine operation was devised to rescue passengers by bus from the incoming morning Bulawayo—Salisbury mail train, which was often stranded by rockfalls or washouts during the night. By early February 1952 the rains brought the Hunyani river down in flood to such an extent that the new dam was filling very much faster than ever expected. The spillway was still in the contractors' hands and suddenly its early completion became a matter of extreme anxiety as the rising water neared the top. For some days it was a close thing and RR engineers maintained a day-and-night watch, since an overflow with the concrete

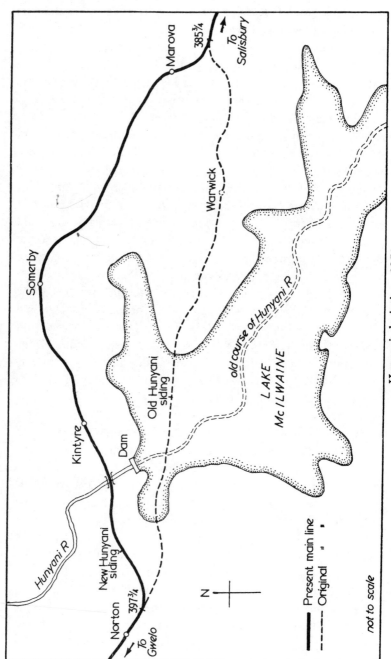

Hunyani deviation, 1951

spillway incomplete might have led to a disaster involving the main-line bridge downstream from the dam. Fortunately, with the help of railway material the contractor just finished the job in time.

Other important works in the Salisbury area were the construction of lengthy service sidings into the extensive industrial sites on each side of the main line to Lochinvar and Lytton, the provision of rail access to factories in the Msasa-Rodia area off the Umtali line, and the remodelling and expansion of the yard at the east end of the station. The station itself was much improved with a two-storey parcels office of modern design, extra lower class waiting rooms and booking office, and an attractive building housing a restaurant and bar.

While Salisbury had had its difficulties in meeting rising traffic, at Bulawayo the boom was bringing much worse problems for the overtaxed facilities and the staff grappling with the torrent of imports from the south. Beira was unable to cope with the heavy shipments, many of a bulk nature requiring immediate clearance up line to Rhodesia, and with delays to imports becoming more frequent merchants in the Rhodesias were diverting their overseas purchases to South African ports, so throwing a heavier burden on the main line from Mafeking. Added to this was the rapid growth of trade with South Africa, whose manufactures were filling many local needs. Engine power was hired from SAR for the Mafeking—Bulawayo section and although this increased movement, it also accentuated yard and handling difficulties in Bulawayo, which was already dealing with larger local traffic as well as the increasing copper and coal passing through from the north.

Bulawayo traffic yard was hemmed in by the passenger station, the goods sheds and railway African housing, much of which required replacement elsewhere before yard expansion could be effected, while the engine shed facilities were not only now quite inadequate but to some extent also hampered development. An immediate expedient was the construction of a nest of sorting sidings at Kumalo, to which point a shuttle service moved traffic for Gwelo and beyond, so easing congestion in Bulawayo yard.

Extra goods sheds and sidings at the eastern end of Raylton enabled the removal of the old shed and banks abutting the traffic yard to permit more tracks to be laid for sorting and marshalling.

It is opportune here to pay tribute to the yard inspectors and shunting staff who coped during years of acute congestion in Bulawayo and its many private sidings. The names of 'Bull' Liddle, Chalmers and Eric Davies, among others, come to mind as leaders of the overworked shunting crews who frequently faced twelve-hour or longer shifts cheerfully to clear rakes of wagons needing sorting. During very bad periods in winter the power station was often short of coal and on occasions within hours of closing down. Then an 'SOS' from the city electrical engineer would lead to a search party of senior railway and municipal officials scouring the sidings for the odd wagons known to be somewhere but 'lost' in the congestion. One railwayman quipped that while Queen Mary reputedly died with 'Calais' on her heart he would have 'Coal' on his.

While the Bulawayo station and yard staff were battling with the flood of traffic in the boom period, which at times almost brought the yard to a standstill despite the palliatives adopted to provide more track space, planning was urgently going ahead for the Greater Bulawayo Development Scheme. In 1943 the city engineer had put to RR a proposal to deviate the main line to Salisbury round the north and west of the city and so eliminate busy level crossings at several points, while the station itself would be converted from a through to a terminal type. This municipal proposal fell in with railway planning but had to be held over during the war years.

Now, however, planning was pushed on and soon a start was made on the largest single undertaking since railway activities were centralised in Bulawayo nearly fifty years earlier. This Greater Bulawayo scheme costing over £1,100,000 included:

(1) the deviation of the Cape main line between Bellvue and Bulawayo
(2) the deviation of the north main line from Bulawayo via Westgate to Mpopoma

(3) the provision of a goods marshalling yard at Mpopoma, four miles from Bulawayo, at the junction of the deviated Salisbury and north main lines

(4) the construction of a new main line from Mpopoma through the northern outskirts to Cement station and the lifting of the original Salisbury main line through Suburbs halt and Kumalo.

The re-aligning of the Cape main line was to give a better approach and release space for a new running shed, and later a reception yard at Westgate for Mafeking trains. This deviation was completed in 1951 and was followed by the north main line through Mpopoma, where a start was made on the new marshalling yard. The new Bulawayo—Westgate—Mpopoma line was double-tracked with colour light signalling.

Mpopoma, as RR's first major yard, was the subject of very detailed planning as it involved fifty-six tracks and sidings covering over 170 acres. Extensive earthworks were needed in flattening the land for the laying down of twenty miles of track, the erection of two road-over-rail bridges, two modern signal cabins for the colour light signalling, floodlighting, wagon repair, coal and water facilities, and so on. Work was hampered in the early days by heavy rains and those concerned have lively memories of the quagmire which bogged down earthmoving machines. Gradually work went on until, to the relief of the strained traffic staff, Mpopoma came into operation with its reception, sorting, exchange and departure sidings for all north and east traffic. Now Bulawayo local traffic and wagons from and to the south were shuttled from and to Mpopoma, so eliminating pressure on Bulawayo yard and speeding up handling generally.

Concurrently with the opening of Mpopoma by Sir Roy Welensky in May 1955 the new main line was brought into use to Cement with $9\frac{1}{2}$ miles of double track replacing the shorter single line from the east end of Bulawayo station through Kumalo. The effect of this deviation was to convert Bulawayo into a terminus, all trains entering and departing at the west end, and also to practically eliminate goods trains from the station yard. This

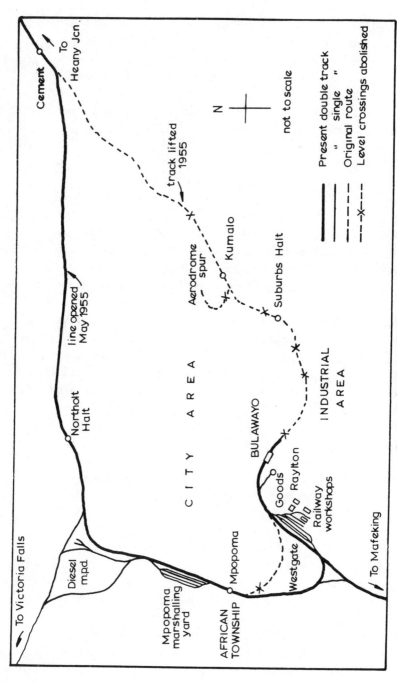

Greater Bulawayo Development Scheme, 1955

To Victoria Falls

Diesel m.p.d.

Mpopoma marshalling yard

AFRICAN TOWNSHIP

Mpopoma

Westgate

Railway workshops

Raylton

Goods

BULAWAYO

INDUSTRIAL AREA

To Mafeking

C I T Y   A R E A

Northolt Halt

line opened May 1955

Suburbs Halt

Kumalo

Aerodrome spur

track lifted 1955

Cement

To Heany Jcn.

N

not to scale

Present double track
"   single   "
Original route
Level crossings abolished

new section of main line involved the erection of seven road-over-rail and four rail-over-river bridges, the longest being a 100ft span over the Umgusa river near Cement.

With these extensive improvements it was essential to install modern three-aspect colour light signals and track circuiting. These were controlled by a three-storey cabin at Bulawayo West, and two-storey cabins at Westgate and at each end of Mpopoma, while the double line thence to Cement was worked with block bells, there being three automatic block sections. Cement station was remodelled and signalled with a small cabin and later the double track was extended to Heany, junction for the West Nicholson branch, and improved signalling installed.

In the meantime a new locomotive running shed had been provided at Bulawayo at a cost of £300,000, to replace the old engine shed dating back to 1906, which was completely outgrown by the modern fleet of locomotives mainly of the Garratt type. This installation included a 100ft turntable—the first in Rhodesia and the largest yet in Africa—repair and ash pits, offices, stores, mess and wash rooms, and an electrically-operated coaling plant. This impressive shed layout was opened by the Governor of Southern Rhodesia, Sir John Kennedy, on 18 April 1953.

The concentration of train movements at the west end of Bulawayo station enabled a start to be made on its conversion to a terminus. The existing platform layout was altered to provide five platforms of the peninsular type with a circulating area, customs shed and other facilities at the east end, while an overhead bridge led from no 1 to the other platforms near the west end. Various passenger amenities were modernised over the years including more spacious offices, better lighting and public address systems, and an expanded parcels office and cloak room. All these benefited the growing traffic. With the opening of Mpopoma and the increasing expansion of African housing townships and amenities in close proximity, it was decided to build a station to serve the large African population there. This station with full passenger facilities was opened in 1960 and proved a great convenience to the public, at the same time easing congestion at Bulawayo station.

It was in the Wankie colliery area that the third major development was made. This was first to construct deviations over the main line for forty-five miles from Dett to provide a ruling grade of 1 in 120 compensated as against 1 in 80 uncompensated, so increasing the single Garratt goods load from 785 tons to 1,300 tons to cope with the rapidly rising down-line traffic. This project cost about £1,500,000 and was linked with an avoiding line from Mbarira (New Wankie) to Thomson Junction, eight miles long, which skirted the mining area. This line included the only tunnel on RR, 278 yards long, driven through a hillside of shale. The line was two miles longer than the original but it eliminated banking up the heavy grade and relieved the south end bottleneck at the old station, while it also ensured that the main line was moved clear of underground workings.

In December 1953 no 3 colliery of the Wankie complex had been brought into production and this, together with no 2 colliery earlier, linked in with Thomson traffic yard. This in turn called for extensive remodelling and the provision of a running shed and wagon repair yard to replace the cramped and obsolete facilities at Wankie. In the mid-1950s power station, copper mine and railway coal orders were leaping up, as well as those from many new consumers, and the supply of truckage was one of the RR's chief headaches. In 1951 2.1 million tons of fuel were carried, rising to 2.5 million in 1954, 3.0 million next year, then 3.3, followed by the record of 3.7 in 1958. While a record of 460 wagons were loaded out by the collieries on 1 August 1955, an even flow always improves movement, and it was in October 1957 that the record month of 351,983 tons of coal and coke in 8,969 trucks was achieved. This gave an average of 332 trucks per working day with a highest of 389. By then the benefit of improved facilities and adequate engine power had been felt and the colliery company was seeking new customers.

It would be impracticable to detail all the schemes that were carried out throughout the system to bring it from almost derelict conditions immediately after World War II to the up-to-date and efficient organisation functioning by the mid-1950s. Extensive remodelling of traffic yards, new goods depots, new and additional

Page 219 (*above*) First three 15th class 4–6–4: 4–6–4 Beyer-Garratts at Salisbury shed, 1940; (*below*) one of the last 12th class Mountains, RR no 257

Page 220   The royal train heading for Victoria Falls behind 15th class Garratts in black l...

running sheds, mechanical coal handling for locomotives, work-shop expansion for the extra rolling stock, relaying of track, new stations, hundreds of new houses for staff and countless minor improvements were made over the ten years or so.

To appreciate the pressing need for this rapid expansion of rail facilities one must remember the influx of new settlers in both the Rhodesias, attracted by good prospects, a delightful climate and an atmosphere of pleasant living conditions free from the con-fines of crowded life in Europe. Opportunities were there for an outdoor life if desired, while developing the produce of the country provided attractive business investments, giving employ-ment in commerce and industry to all races. Many of the families of early settlers had expanded their farming, while services for the growing population had called for professions, artisans and the like, and for training labour in all walks of life.

In Southern Rhodesia the population has risen at a tremendous rate as is shown by these figures:

	1946	1955	1971
Europeans	82,380	165,000	255,000
Asian and Coloureds	7,470	12,500	26,600
Africans	1,770,000	3,090,000	5,310,000
Total (approx)	1,859,850	3,267,500	5,591,600

While in the north—now Zambia—where the land area is 290,323 square miles compared with the south's 150,333, the population has also increased rapidly, viz:

	1945	1956	1969
Europeans	21,000	64,810	43,390
Asian and Coloureds	1,700	6,950	14,961
Africans	1,630,000	2,000,000	3,998,600
Total (approx)	1,652,700	2,071,760	4,056,951

Here the copper mines were the mainstay of development but

industries of various kinds were also being fostered to meet the local demands, while cattle, grain and tobacco farming were expanding under European direction.

All this brought much greater employment and spending power for the indigenous population, who little more than half a century ago, were nearly all still living in a relatively primitive state under tribal conditions, feeding almost entirely on the grain from crops dependent on seasonal rains. Only eighty years ago wheeled transport was practically unknown. Peaceful conditions had improved living, and good health services had effects which contributed to the population explosion; rail transport had to grow rapidly to meet the demands.

THE LINK WITH LOURENCO MARQUES

The provision of an additional rail outlet to the East Coast became essential soon after World War II. It was soon clear to Sir Arthur Griffin that the amazing development in the two Rhodesias, with the demands of the rapidly rising population, was beyond the capacity of the port of Beira and its rail route to the hinterland. Discussions of the problem eventually led to the choice of the Mozambique port of Lourenco Marques as a second sea terminal and an initial reconnaissance was carried out in 1949 by a Rhodesian survey team. This survey envisaged a railway between 220 and 240 miles in length to link with the Portuguese line at Pafuri at the junction of the Rhodesian, Mozambique and South African borders.

After further negotiations a second survey was begun in 1951 along a route north of the Nuanetsi river instead of to the south of it, and eventually an excellent route was found to a point twenty-two miles north of Pafuri. A Portuguese survey had now reached the Rhodesian boundary, nine miles south of the RR team's line, and a compromise was soon agreed upon by fixing a point between the two.

By mid-1952 work started on the Rhodesian section of line at Bannockburn, then a siding on the Somabula—Shabani branch line, and a nest of sidings with storage areas was laid out with nearby housing for the construction staff. The terrain is very hilly to the Ngezi river and cuttings of 20 to 30ft deep, mainly through serpentine or granite rock, alternated with embankments of almost a similar height through this broken country. The Ngezi is crossed by a bridge with four 90ft spans and the line then passes through lightly cultivated land until it reaches the Fort Victoria—Beitbridge road at Rutenga. From there to the border, where the CFM established its terminal at a new settlement called Malvernia, in honour of the famed Rhodesian and Federal Prime Minister, Lord Malvern, the line ran across flat, arid and desolate country, almost uninhabited except for wild game ranging from elephant to the smallest buck. There were no roads at all and a great scarcity of water.

The ruling grades in both directions are 1 in 80 from Bannockburn to Sarahuru, and thence to the border 1 in 125. This permitted a through goods load of 1,100 tons from Bulawayo to Malvernia behind a 15th class Garratt, with 1,000 tons in the reverse direction. Since the introduction of diesel power the goods loads are 1,200 tons down line and 850 tons up. Over the flat Sarahuru—Malvernia section loads can be appreciably increased.

The line involved 199 miles of new construction by RR and the relaying with 80lb rail of the forty-nine miles from Somabula to Bannockburn, to bring the section up to main-line standards. In Mozambique the CFM line from Lourenco Marques to Guija was extended by 200 miles to the border at Malvernia. This involved a crossing of the Limpopo river and as the line neared Rhodesia it passed through a dusty flat stretch of uninteresting country for many miles.

An imposing station building was erected by the CFM at Malvernia and here the exchange of traffic is effected. RR locomotives refuelled there at the CFM depot and an extensive village grew up accommodating the Portuguese railway, police and customs staff. A Rhodesian customs post was established at the RR border siding, which was named Vila Salazar as a compliment to the Portuguese prime minister.

A feature of the construction by RR was the use of a special platelaying train devised by A. M. Hawkins, a senior engineer.

This train consisted of a rake of eleven flat wagons and a canti-lever crane on a twelfth wagon. Each wagon was fitted with a pair of carrier rails and the gaps between wagons were spanned by 'bridge rails' so forming a continuous carrier track. The pre-assembled 40ft panels of rails with steel sleepers were loaded on to the train, six panels per wagon, the bottom panel being sup-ported by four single-rail roller carriers on the carrier rails. The loaded rake was then propelled to the railhead where the crane wagon was standing and the six panels on the leading truck were winched on to the crane truck. The top panel was run out and lowered on to the formation, fishplates fixed, and the train was then propelled forward and the operation repeated. The crane hoist and winch were electrically operated from power supplied by a petrol driven alternator on the crane truck. Each rake of wagons carried half a mile of track so that the work progressed quickly, stone ballast being run out behind the platelaying train.

The South-East Connection, as this line was known, cost approximately £6 million and was opened to goods traffic on 1 August 1955. Until stone ballast had been laid both on the RR and CFM sections, it was not considered desirable, due to speed restrictions and the dust nuisance, to inaugurate a passenger service. Even when this was eventually done, on 20 July 1956, the weekly passenger train had a dusty trip, but this soon im-proved and the service was then increased to twice weekly.

The opening of the link with Lourenco Marques was an im-mediate relief to the Beira line which had been grappling with exceptional traffic difficulties. Shiploads of drought-relief maize, wheat, sugar, timber, cement, rock phosphates and other fertilisers had been making heavy truck demands which led to bunching and delay at inland factories and elsewhere, while the increasing seasonal tobacco traffic had to be handled in addition to the export flow of copper, chrome, asbestos and the like. These mineral exports were at once divided between the two ports and incoming bulk shipments were phased to spread the burden over the two rail routes.

As well as being an alternative route for exports and imports the new line served mineral developments, as asbestos, chrome and iron ore deposits were waiting for rail transport. Later on, in 1964, the highly developed and well irrigated low veld agricultural area was served by a 56-mile branch from Mbizi to Triangle and Chiredzi, whence sugar, citrus, wheat and other produce created significant traffic. This branch was extended another eight miles in 1965 to serve Nandi estates.

Somabula now became an important junction, having additional tracks, fully signalled and controlled from a cabin. Shabani branch trains were run from Gwelo while those to Malvernia normally originated from Bulawayo with caboose working. To avoid shunting complications with through trains to and from Bulawayo, which had to reverse direction to gain the new line, a 'balloon' was constructed at Somabula round which these trains ran and this simple solution was known to many as 'Pegrum's balloon', after the chief superintendent of transportation.

At the time when the South-East Connection was being surveyed, strong efforts were made by South Africa to sway Rhodesia to consider an alternative route to the sea by a link of some ninety miles from the West Nicholson branch terminus to Beitbridge, the end of the SAR line from Pretoria and Pietersberg. Such a link would have been of great benefit to South Africa as the SAR would have secured more revenue on Rhodesian traffic by providing a direct SAR route from the Transvaal and Natal. This route would have been strongly competitive with the RR main line between Mafeking and Bulawayo, which, given adequate engine power, was by no means near saturation level and was extremely remunerative to RR finances.

However, by the late 1960s the traffic density over the Botswana route was rising to such an extent that a second link with South Africa would become essential within a few years. With the Somabula—Malvernia line now crossing the originally bare south-eastern area and bisecting the Beitbridge—Fort Victoria main road at the wayside station of Rutenga, eighty-five miles from Beitbridge, a rail connection to this point became a very live issue as an alternative to the previous idea of the West Nicholson link. Much argument ensued between the protagonists of the two routes, with Bulawayo pressing for West Nicholson and those with interests in the Midlands and Salisbury urging the merits of Rutenga. The Rhodesian government arranged full enquiries, followed by detailed surveys of both routes with costs, and early in 1971 the announcement was made that Rutenga was favoured and would be constructed within five years.

ADMINISTRATIVE CHANGES

In 1953 the Federation of Rhodesia and Nyasaland was created, resulting in a change of control for RR. For many years the thought of an amalgamation of the two Rhodesias had been present in the minds of numerous Rhodesians. The two territories had much in common, sharing the same railway system and the port of Beira, while several technical services such as airways, currency and statistics had been shared over recent years. A series of conferences over three years at government level between the United Kingdom, the Rhodesias and Nyasaland had been held, culminating in the recommendation of a Federation. A referendum was held with the voters of the self-governing Southern Rhodesia in April 1953 and the majority was in favour. A federal ministry ensued under Sir Godfrey Huggins, for twenty years prime minister of Southern Rhodesia, who included in his cabinet Sir Roy Welensky with the portfolio of transport and communications. RR then became a federal responsibility, although it is interesting that the Nyasaland Railways, which also had a link with Beira, and the Trans-Zambesia Railway in Mozambique, remained as private companies.

These distinguished political leaders of the federation both had connections with RR. Sir Godfrey Huggins, when he first came to Salisbury in 1911 as a doctor, was for a time a railway medical officer in partnership with Dr F. E. Appleyard. The other, Sir Roy Welensky, who was born in Salisbury in 1907, joined the BMR as a fireman in 1924. In those days he achieved fame as a heavyweight boxer and was champion in 1926–8, before he was transferred to Northern Rhodesia where he served for many years as a fireman and driver. Becoming keenly interested in politics, Welensky entered the Northern Rhodesia Legislative Council in 1938, was appointed a member of the executive council in 1940, and was director of manpower from 1941 to 1946. For these duties he was released from active railway service, to which he never really returned, as in 1956 he succeeded Lord Malvern as prime minister of the federation until its dissolution in 1963. Throughout his political career he always maintained a very keen interest in the well-being of the railways and of the Railway Workers Union.

Sir Arthur Griffin became chairman of the railway board in January 1953 and was followed as general manager by Lt-Col H. B. Everard, DSO, TD, who had had many years with British Railways (London Midland Region), while the chief engineer, B. H. Johnson, was appointed assistant general manager. The following year saw an organisational change with the introduction of the Commercial Department under J. H. Allen, which relieved the Transportation Department, in which over half of the total European staff were employed, of responsibility for rates, fares, claims, publicity and advertising, and control of commercial staff at stations and goods depots.

For some time there had been agitation in the Northern Rhodesia Legislative Council for a senior railway officer to be placed within the territory, to liaise directly with local bodies as the representative of railway headquarters in Bulawayo. Views had been expressed that the needs of the north were neglected and as an example the difficulties of the copper mines in obtaining their coal supplies were cited. The rapid growth of demands on the Wankie collieries from all consumers had raced ahead of the supply of new motive power and rolling stock to RR, and to maintain production the copper mines had had to import coal through Lobito over the Benguela and Katanga railways to Ndola, while extensive wood cutting in the local forest areas, with road haulage to the mines, was an expensive and unsatisfactory supplement to coal.

Thus the appointment of a railway representative at Lusaka early in 1953 was welcomed as providing closer contact with government, commercial, mining and other bodies. At the same time extensive railway developments already planned were seen by the public to be progressing. These included the extension of traffic yards at Broken Hill, Kafue, Livingstone, Ndola and Nkana, and large new goods depots at Lusaka, Nkana and Ndola, the latter on new sites more convenient to users. Soon the arrival of a batch of 16A class locomotives, followed in 1955 by the first of the larger 20th class, was to accelerate the flow of traffic and move greater tonnages in the north without the delays of the past.

The change to federal control and the political trend towards more opportunities for the advancement of the Africans were to have effects on RR. Already the designation of the lowest class of travel had been changed from native to fourth class and the sign-posting of all station facilities was altered from a racial term to that of the class of travel. Dining-cars became available for meal service to all races when properly attired, as the number of Coloured, Asian and African passengers travelling first and second class rose. On mixed trains specially designed buffet cars were introduced to serve the third and fourth classes and soon became popular.

A major policy change was the decision to open to Coloureds, Asians and Africans recruiting for grades such as firemen, shunters, lorry drivers and dining-car waiters; progression to the grade of driver and guard was also provided for. The ability to speak and understand English and the attainment of certain educational standards were essential for the knowledge and under-standing of train working and other regulations, and many appli-cants had to be turned away for lack of these vital needs.

The Railway Training Centre was opened at Bulawayo in 1953 to give intensive theoretical and practical courses of instruction for the grades of guard, shunter, fireman, station foreman, clerk, checker and platelayer, before the men were sent out to stations and depots to complete their training. The loss of staff to other employment continued to be a problem and apart from Britain and South Africa men were recruited in Holland, Italy and Greece. For these the training centre had to run classes in the English language. Satisfactory results were achieved with these courses and the railwaymen-instructors, some of them pensioners, deserved much credit for their efforts.

OWNERSHIP OF THE SOUTH LINE

The line from Vryburg to Mafeking and Bulawayo had been operated by the Cape Government Railways and subsequently by the SAR under a working agreement which had continued over several decades. This curious anomaly of one administration running a lengthy section of main line for another railway company, which owned the line passing through three separate countries, must be unique in railway history. In the 1894 agreement for the construction of the Bechuanaland Railway a right to purchase the line from Vryburg to Palapye, with terms and conditions regarding the price, was granted to the governments concerned, and in 1937 a further agreement gave this purchase right to the Union of South Africa, subject to the consent of the British government on behalf of the Bechuanaland Protectorate. At the end of 1959 the SAR took up the option on the section between Vryburg and Ramatlhabama, on the border between South Africa and Bechuanaland, and after negotiations the 112 miles of line with land, buildings and movable assets (excluding engines and rolling stock) were purchased from RR by the SAR for £1,350,000, so eliminating this 'foreign' railway from South African territory.

From 1 December 1959 RR took over the SAR-operated line between Bulawayo and Mahalapye, a distance of 269 miles, and the latter point became the handover station for traffic. Extra sidings were installed as an exchange yard and locomotives and crews from Bulawayo and from Mafeking turned round at Mahalapye, which became an RR-staffed station.

J. W. S. Pegrum, deputy general manager since 1956, had become general manager in 1958 in succession to Lt-Col Everard whose term of contract had expired. Pegrum had joined RR as a guard and was the first Rhodesian-trained railwayman to achieve the highest post, after a wealth of experience in many transportation positions throughout the system. He was responsible, in conjunction with the Minister of Transport, for the final negotiations with the South African administration which led to the purchase of the Vryburg—Ramatlhabama line and the takeover by RR of the operation of the Bulawayo—Mahalapye section.

That the arrangements went off so smoothly was characteristic of the happy inter-railway relations between SAR and RR over long years of association. It was followed in 1965 by the opening of discussions for RR to take over the rest of the line within Bechuanaland as a more convenient operational arrangement, and on 26 September 1966 the handover by SAR was effected. This coincided with the granting of independence to the protectorate under the name Botswana. Thus seventy years after the line was built RR actually controls the working of its railway south from Bulawayo. RR trains now run into Mafeking, as running rights have been granted by SAR over the 16-mile section from the border into Cape Province. Locomotives and crews based at Bulawayo work round trips over the whole line, the caboose working now being a reversal of the longstanding round-tripping from Mafeking with SAR staff, while RR staff have replaced SAR employees at all points within Botswana. All the African employees were absorbed by RR.

The passenger trains from Cape Town to Bulawayo are made up with SAR coaches and carry SAR bedding services but SAR dining-cars are detached at Mafeking and RR diners picked up at Artesia for the journey into Rhodesia. A similar arrangement works in the opposite direction with dining-car services. The Bulawayo—Johannesburg passenger trains are, however, made up with RR coaching stock so that the cream and teak livery of Rhodesian carriages penetrates the SAR and the grey and brick red South African livery is familiar in Bulawayo.

CENTRALISED TRAIN CONTROL

The difficulties experienced by station staff in the control of trains with the outmoded telegraph order system increased very rapidly in the postwar years as the train service became more intensive. Over the long sections between manned stations train crossing arrangements were apt to go wrong and upset time-keeping for various reasons, such as a hot box, an engine steaming badly or shunting time being exceeded, while some drivers were better 'runners' than others. Unless the station foreman was a Celt with a gift of second sight the poor man had almost to arrange his crossings by guess or by God. Trains became 'out of course' and affected the running in adjoining sections, so that punctuality suffered as more and more trains were run.

The most critical section of line was that between Gwelo and Bulawayo, 110 miles long, where the daily service had risen from seven trains each way to thirteen or more. Webb & Thompson electric train staff machines had been introduced at Bulawayo, Kumalo and Cement, but morse telegraph messages were still exchanged between stations thence to Gwelo. This heavier service brought delays, with consequent high overtime for train crews, and the cost of splitting sections by opening extra stations, each with three foremen needing housing, was high. Thus there were cogent arguments for trials with a more modern form of train control.

With the upsurge of traffic thought was given by the signal and telegraph engineer, E. W. Dennison, to the advantages of Centralised Train Control, a method developed and used extensively in North America, whereby long stretches of single line railway could be controlled from a central point. At this time there were only one or two CTC installations in the British Empire and none in Africa and, while some operating officials strongly supported the idea, there was hesitancy in higher circles about becoming committed to a little-known, new and expensive system, with track circuiting and electric colour light signals over long stretches of line.

Dennison was instructed to make a model of his CTC proposal and his demonstrations soon convinced the authorities to recommend its installation between Bulawayo and Gwelo. As a result an order was placed in 1948 for equipment from the Siemens-General Electric Railway Signal Co in England. Soon after, as the Greater Bulawayo project and the doubling of the line to Cement were planned, it was decided to install CTC from Heany Junction to Gwelo and in September 1951 the first section as far as Shangani came into operation.

For the first two months of working trainmen were still issued with paper orders over the CTC section as they had been strictly brought up to the necessity of holding a written authority showing

231

the train crossings en route. During this introductory period the crews became used to the practice of looking for colour light signals and, equally important, the panel operators gained practical experience.

The illuminated panel of a CTC installation contains a diagram of the whole of the line controlled, showing by lights the individual signals and the progress of each train over the track-circuited sections. The setting of signals is effected by switches operated on the panel of the control machine and the signals then operate automatically. After each signal has been set, its aspect is repeated back to the control machine and so the panel shows the local conditions set up. Thus the operator can watch the progress of each train and is able to plan crossing arrangements well in advance, so as to ensure minimum delay to the running of trains.

Some initial difficulties were experienced with the installation, especially with electro-mechanical axle counters on lengths of track with steel sleepers, but the work was pressed on to Gwelo and the whole section came under CTC on 13 May 1953. Much of the equipment had to be fabricated locally in the small signal workshop, to keep costs low, and with inexperienced staff the job proved lengthy. The original control machine was placed in the trains office at Bulawayo, where it was convenient for study by all concerned in the project, which was soon to revolutionise operating methods on RR.

CTC was proved a great success, though the economy of having hand-operated main-line points at crossing places was soon found to be false, and power-operated facing points worked from the panel were recognised to be a valuable time-saver. Power points were soon to become a standard feature in future installations and the existing ones were converted. So trainmen on night trains passing through the Wankie Game Park were relieved of much anxiety when the need arose to walk forward to reverse points at a siding. Lions and elephants were quite prevalent in this area and their presence at the points was not welcomed. It was just after power points had been installed that a driver going round his locomotive on foot mistook the whirr of the points machine for the low growl of a lion and beat the speed record for regaining his footplate.

It became clear that full CTC not only increased line capacity but had other important features in that it allowed: (i) much safer train control (ii) better, standardised supervision by central control (iii) higher average train speeds (iv) economies in station personnel (v) avoidance of an electric token system which could later become redundant (vi) postponement of track doubling. The safety factor was of primary importance as with a heavier train service failures by the human element had resulted in more frequent telegraph order irregularities and collisions.

The policy of extending CTC was soon accepted and by 1958 it had come into operation on the 116-mile Wankie—Gwaai section, with control at Dett, and on the 89-mile Gwaai—Mpopoma section, controlled from Sawmills. An installation was also on order for the line from Wankie to Zimba, 142 miles, with control at Livingstone.

In the meantime the boom in traffic throughout the system was taxing RR to the utmost, and with the safety aspect and other factors in mind it was decided to complete CTC over the whole of the remainder of the main line from Gwelo to Umtali on the eastern border, and from Zimba to Ndola throughout Northern Rhodesia. This involved a further 726 miles of line with 128 intermediate crossing places, all controlled from six control rooms. With the need for early completion contracts were spread between three British companies, Westinghouse, Siemens-General Electric and AEI/GRS. These contracts incorporated various improvements resulting from the extensive experience gained with CTC in both the operational and technical spheres.

Work on these extensions proceeded until in 1964 the whole of the 1,215 miles of main line, with the exception of the short double-line sections, was under CTC. This was a most notable achievement by any standards and completed the transition of RR from an unsignalled pioneer concern to a most modern organisation, handling the growing business of rapidly developing countries. At the time of its completion no other railway outside North America had such an extensive system of CTC.

233

CHAPTER TEN

Recent Events—The Split with Zambia

IT is no longer true, as once seemed to be the case, that a railway's history never ends, since in some countries railways have gone out of fashion, many miles of track have been pulled up and some lines have disappeared completely. In Africa, however, there is still much railway construction and, certainly for the foreseeable future, no other known form of transport can possibly replace RR in serving such productive and highly mineralised territories.

In a constant effort to provide the public with a satisfactory service RR is continually improving its equipment and methods. Briefly, the more outstanding of many developments in recent years are the following:

The Stores Department has been completely reorganised, with vast improvements in methods and purchasing, and the discontinuation of buying in London.

In 1959 the relaying of the main line with 91lb rail, first on hardwood and then on concrete sleepers, was begun, to permit heavier axleloads and higher train speeds.

New locomotive depots brought into use at Broken Hill and Livingstone in 1960 and 1962 have been valuable assets to Zambia Railways.

To control shunting, radio-telephony has been introduced between yards and locomotives in the Bulawayo—Mpopoma area and elsewhere.

Two twin dining-lounge cars, *Zambesi* and *Kafue,* designed and built in Bulawayo workshops, afford a new standard of travel comfort, while smaller buffet cars have also been constructed.

In 1960 bulk tank wagons for cement were introduced, the first in Southern Africa. Tallow, molasses, crude tar, glycerine, ammonia, acid and bitumen are also carried in tank wagons as well as petrol and oils.

In 1964 the Chiredzi branch line was opened; it has the longest rail bridge in Rhodesia, 1,389ft, over the Lundi river.

In 1959 the new six-storey headquarters building was opened in Bulawayo to accommodate the managerial, operations, commercial and personnel branches.

The medical and health services for employees of all races and their families were completely revised and much improved during the 1950s.

Data processing by computer has been developed in many fields of accounting and statistics.

Road Motor Services has been expanded to cover 8,338 route miles on 62 routes by 1970, using 189 lorries and 216 trailers.

The phenomenal expansion over the twenty years since World War II can best be illustrated by a few statistics.

| | Years ended | | |
	30.9.1945	30.6.1965	Increase
Route miles	2,446	2,711	265
Train miles	7,835,089	14,703,347	6,868,258
Passengers (All classes)	2,490,755	4,213,950	1,723,195
Tons hauled—			
Coal and Coke	1,687,176	2,422,988	735,812
Chrome Ore	240,280	593,415	353,135
Copper	283,413	1,125,468	842,055
All traffics	4,352,624	12,950,479	8,597,855
Locomotives			
Steam	215	324	109
Diesel	—	69	69
Coaching Stock	379	638	259
Wagon stock	4,190	12,428	8,238
Staff:			
Europeans	4,378	10,285	5,907
Others	12,201	19,139	6,938
Working A/c			
Rly Revenue	£6,084,413	37,088,919	31,004,506
Rly Expenditure	£3,965,069	30,615,349	26,650,280

These figures appear in published reports, those for 1965 being for the last year prior to Rhodesia's declaration of independence. They give comparisons before the effects of political pressure and sanctions reacted on RR, and before the subsequent split of the system at the Rhodesian—Zambian border.

One of the most striking features is the enormous growth of copper traffic, and the tonnages quoted do not include short-haul copper ore in the mining area. While the Zambian copper has been by far the largest source, the Congo (now Zaire) and the expanding Rhodesian mines provide significant contributions. World market prices have in the past drastically affected both production and railway earnings for short periods, but in general the traffic has been constantly rising.

The prosperity of Northern and Southern Rhodesia always depended to a large extent on world demands and in consequence definite peaks and troughs have formed a feature of RR traffic returns throughout its history. Economic growth during the years of the federation was on a continued upward trend, until in 1958 a shadow of doubt was cast by the political uncertainty engendered by the rising clamour for independence throughout Africa, and business suffered a setback.

Trade revived in 1960 and many new records were achieved, being aided to some extent by the diversion to RR of Congo traffic normally conveyed over other routes which were disrupted by the internal disturbances following the granting of independence by Belgium to its colony. It was soon seen to be inevitable that the call for the abolition of colonialism would end the Federation of Rhodesia and Nyasaland, and RR, as a federal asset, faced an uneasy future. This uncertainty led to some drift away from the Rhodesias, and railwaymen were affected, especially in the north. Wastage of staff and recruitment difficulties had a harmful effect.

Upon the dissolution of the federation the ownership of, and the financial responsibility for, RR passed to the governments of Southern Rhodesia and Northern Rhodesia in equal shares from 1 January 1964. It was decided that RR would continue as a unitary system under the control of a board of management responsible for the railways' continued function, and a Higher Authority was constituted with four members, two from each government. From the practical point of view the Railway Board, then under the chairmanship of A. R. Kemp, had wisely argued at high-level discussions that economically and operationally it would be to the greatest benefit of all parties for RR to continue as a single unit.

The granting of independence to the northern partner, which became the Republic of Zambia in October 1964, was followed by a feeling of antagonism and political tension towards Rhodesia, which had dropped 'Southern' from her name, during the latter's endeavours to negotiate with the United Kingdom for independent status. A period of uneasy stress ensued for RR and finally, in November 1965, Mr Ian Smith's government unilaterally declared Rhodesia's independence. This step at once led to greater reaction from Zambia and it was soon to become most difficult for RR officers in that territory to cope with the direct interference into operational matters. One such step was the diversion of as much as possible of Zambian export copper to other routes, all longer and more costly, as well as being unreliable, while another was the reduction to a minimum of the import of Wankie coal, until politicians realised their dependence on Rhodesian services.

By early 1966 the Zambian ministers on the Higher Authority had advised the Railway Board of their inability to continue to function as members and it was becoming clear that a break-up of the system was inevitable. The Board of Management assessed the problem of division and as a result of its report it was accepted that Rhodesia and Zambia would establish autonomous railways in their own countries from midnight on 30 June 1967.

The creation of Zambia Railways, with 669 track miles from the centre of Victoria Falls bridge to the Congo (Zaire) border, plus the Copperbelt branches, has reduced RR lines to the following:

	Miles
Main lines:	
Mozambique border—Victoria Falls bridge	765
Somabula—Malvernia	248
Bulawayo—Ramatlhabama	468*
Branch lines in Rhodesia	532
Total Route Miles	2013
Main line: Double track	
Salisbury—Lochinvar	5
Bulawayo—Heany Junction	21
	2039
Beit Bridge Railway (operated by SAR)	1
Total mileage of track	2040

*Of this total 390 miles fall within the Republic of Botswana.

So, over seventy years, the picture of the railways in Central Africa has changed from the spreading system born from the dreams of Cecil Rhodes into more compact units organised on a national basis. Rhodesia Railways now consists of a central network of important trunk lines forming vital links between many surrounding territories, along which traffic can pass when demand arises and politics permit, from, for example, Lobito in Angola to Beira and Lourenco Marques, from South Africa to Malawi via Mozambique, and from Zaire to Beira. Airways have eliminated any passenger travel by such circuitous routes, though the really adventurous could still undertake such journeys purely as an interesting experience. Over the years goods traffic has passed in varying quantities along these long lines of communication and brought revenue to the railways concerned, but local prejudices have brought restrictions on trading in troubled Africa.

In Zambia a new development will be the opening of the lengthy Tan-Zam railway connecting the territory directly with the Tanzanian east coast port of Dar-es-Salaam. This railway is being constructed with capital and engineering aid from the People's Republic of China and coming down from the north-east will join the Zambian main line at Kapiri M'poshi, between Ndola and Broken Hill (now Kabwe). It will provide a new route for the export of Zambia's copper and for some of her imports from other than the immediate south.

What effect the loss of Zambian traffic will have on RR is difficult to forecast at a time when Rhodesia's rapidly increasing production is taxing the capacity of her rail system. The copper revenue will be missed but it has been dropping since Zambia's independence and other business will replace it. Suffice it to say that with funds for expansion being made available one feels confident Rhodesia Railways will be ready to meet any problems of rising traffic with the ingenuity and vigour of those who have followed the pioneer railwaymen of Rhodes's railways.

ZAMBIA RAILWAYS

Events in Zambia since the establishment of ZR are difficult to trace precisely owing to the sparseness of authoritative news released by the Zambian government. However, as the RR management withdrew it was partly replaced by expatriate British colonial service railway officials and engineers from various countries. By 1967 only 157 European employees from RR had chosen to sign on with ZR, all the others (over 1,000) having opted to remain with RR. In the meantime extensive recruiting of contract expatriate staff had been carried out by RR and later by the Zambian government in the United Kingdom, East Africa, Sudan and India to secure experienced railwaymen, and while some were obtained their general calibre does not appear to have been high. A staff training centre with an apprentice school had already been provided by RR at Kabwe for local recruits and this was expanded.

Shortage of experienced men led to difficulties in undertaking essential maintenance of locomotives, rolling stock and track and to some degree in manning trains. Services have been reduced with consequent severe delays in movement of traffic and turnround of wagons. A Zambian minister has admitted that the standard of staff discipline was appalling and that there were 369 derailments, 13 main line collisions and 53 severe siding accidents in the first year of local control. Many accidents were due to gross negligence, speed, slack maintenance and drunkenness. In 1970 it was known that at least nine diesel and steam locomotives had been written off in accidents, while a further three diesel and several steam engines had been very badly damaged. One locomotive suffered a burst boiler through failure to maintain the water level.

After stating in 1969 that its own staff would take over from Bulawayo future general repairs to its steam locomotives, ZR urgently requested a few months later that RR should resume such major repairs. Several locomotives were then despatched from Livingstone but their mechanical condition was so indescribably bad that they were returned from Victoria Falls as unrailworthy. Others on arrival at Bulawayo were in a shocking state of disrepair and neglect. New railway workshops have since been built at Kabwe (Broken Hill) but these apparently concentrate on diesel locomotives and rolling stock with what staff ZR have been able to obtain.

At the time of the split there were approximately forty-one 20th/20A class, twelve 16A class and eight 15th class Garratts and twenty 12th and four 9B class steam locomotives in Zambia, a total of eighty-five engines. These have now practically all been replaced by diesel-electric units from North America and West Germany, while three ex-RR Wickham railcars and others from Japan have taken over much of the local passenger services. The first of twenty-six DE6-type General Electric diesels entered ZR service in May 1967.

A 'one-for-one' exchange of locomotives and rolling stock at Victoria Falls was imposed by the Rhodesian government to ensure a proper balance of stock, but despite this, serious congestion of traffic has occurred on ZR, resulting in periodic embargoes on goods from the south. In 1969 the through passenger service was discontinued and RR trains terminated at Victoria Falls, though goods traffic was worked through to Livingstone. The few rail passengers from Rhodesia to Zambia travelled by bus.

Early in 1971 the Zambian government signed an agreement with Canada for a team of Canadian National senior personnel to administer the management and operations of ZR for five years.

CHAPTER ELEVEN

The Troubled Years

FROM 1970 onwards the position on RR began to deteriorate, causing great anxiety among the members of the management team. However, despite the worsening political situation, and the imposition of sanctions, progress and expansion continued.

In 1972 the Makabusi river in Salisbury was canalised over a 2¾-mile stretch enabling a very large new covered goods area to be developed. This covered ninety-one acres between the station and the river. Track improvements continued and by this time, except for a short section of line between Bulawayo and Gwaai the whole main line from Salisbury to Thomson Junction was laid in continuously welded rail on concrete sleepers. Steady further progress was made thereafter until in 1981, sixty-three per cent of all running lines were equipped in this way. Even some of the balance was in continuously welded rail but on steel sleepers.

In November 1972 to mark the 75th Anniversary of the arrival of the first train in Bulawayo, a railway museum was opened near to the station since when considerable progress has been made, and, by the end of 1981, thirteen locomotives, eleven coaches, and a variety of goods rolling stock were installed in suitable surroundings. The committee responsible for this museum have also indulged in running highly successful vintage trains almost annually, to various destinations, hauled by a variety of locomotives. The first ran at Easter 1973 hauled by two 12th Class locomotives, and went from Bulawayo to Balla Balla through the Ncema Gorge.

By this time, it was becoming obvious that dire trouble was

coming and in February 1973 the border between Rhodesia and Zambia on the Victoria Falls Bridge was closed, though, in fact, wagons never ceased to cross the bridge, being propelled on to it by a locomotive from one country, and being picked up later by a locomotive from the other. Moreover, from then on, due to sanctions, all types of goods vehicles were produced locally, to be followed in 1974 by 3rd/4th class coaches as well. Local manufacture has continued ever since, so that the railways are no longer dependent upon imported rolling stock.

Staff shortages were beginning to make their presence felt from the middle of 1973, and one result was that through diesel-hauled goods trains were reduced to two-man operation, that is with a driver and a guard. This method of working proved to be very successful and has continued ever since. The Road Motor Services, which operated mainly in the eastern part of the country bordering Mozambique, were beginning to experience great difficulty in keeping services going because of sabotage and ambushes, and there was to be no let up for eight years.

It was becoming increasingly obvious, too, that a new route to the south was an urgent necessity, and after a great deal of discussion on possible routes and initial go-ahead in 1971 it was finally decided to build the eighty-three mile stretch of line from Rutenga to Beitbridge. This line set a construction record and was completed in October 1974 after only six months' work and this included two major bridges over the Bubi and Nuanetsi Rivers. The line became fully operational in April 1975, when a new station and marshalling yard were opened at Beitbridge.

To cater for this increase in mileage the DE 5 diesel electric class was ordered; thirty-five were erected locally in 1975/6. One of these locomotives was subsequently marooned in Mozambique only being returned to its home railway in 1981 after four years in exile. To accommodate these additional locomotives and the existing fleet a new and very modern diesel motive power depot was built at Mpopoma outside Bulawayo. This allowed the removal of the very cramped diesel depot which had been in the steam running shed area.

With the completion of the new Beitbridge connection it was decided that the time had arrived to build a long-planned hump marshalling yard at Dabuka outside Gwelo, and work commenced in November 1974. This was a very large construction job in virgin country, and it was five years before the whole scheme came into full operation, by which time it had already been extended to accommodate a container transfer depot.

Unfortunately the imposition of sanctions and the closure of the northern border were having a serious effect on RR revenue, and towards the end of 1975 it was decided that there would have to be a ten per cent increase in rates, which were still relatively low in the national interest. Unfortunately this was not too successful as costs continued to rise and the traffic to fall with the result that deficits continued. In September 1975 an historic conference was held in the middle of the Victoria Falls Bridge using the South African Railways' Presidential 'White Train'. The conference was intended to resolve the political situation, but unfortunately it failed and the 'placing' of trucks on the bridge had to continue for a further period.

About this time the local demand for steel rose considerably because it could not be imported, and therefore it was decided to carry raw materials to the steelworks near Que Que, by block liner trains. These trains of special air-braked wagons run non-stop from Mukwakwe carrying iron ore, and from Wankie carrying coal. They are usually double-headed by DE 8As and sometimes triple-headed by lighter locomotives. They run at passenger train speeds. The terminals for both loading and unloading are laid out as loops and trains run on the merry-go-round principle, being loaded and un-loaded as they pass slowly without stopping through a hopper complex. Since that time further liner trains have been added to carry chrome from Selukwe.

Early in 1976 the political situation worsened even further, and this resulted in the closing of the Mozambique borders at Machipanda (seven miles east of Umtali) and Malvernia in March. This was done so rapidly that five locomotives, 1,897 wagons and nineteen staff were trapped in that country. Although the staff were subsequently returned through South Africa, the rolling stock remained exiled until July 1980 when the locomotives and all but 230 wagons were returned, the remainder having succumbed to lack of maintenance.

At this stage the internal war was beginning to affect the railways badly, firstly by reducing the staff by two and a half per cent, a figure which subsequently grew considerably because of military service, and secondly by the commencement of incidents designed to disrupt the train service. The latter started on 18 April 1976 when three diesel locomotives were mined on the Beitbridge section and derailed with most of their train. As a result of these incidents the night passenger trains between Salisbury and Umtali were withdrawn on 4 June and armoured trolleys were deployed to patrol those sections most likely to be trouble prone. Despite this a passenger train was mined south of Victoria Falls in December 1976 and that caused the cessation of the service until after the war. Fortunately, the track had been improved and strengthened gradually, and continuously welded rail on concrete sleepers had been installed on the Sawmills to Gwaai, Somabula to Chiredzi and Rutenga to Beitbridge sections. At the same time track maintenance had been totally mechanised, all of which helped to keep the lines open.

In April 1977 Mr T. A. Wright retired as general manager and he was succeeded by Mr W. F. Sievwright, who had made his previous career in the civil engineering department. So ended the longest period of tenure of an RR general manager, and certainly Mr Wright had guarded its fortunes through a very eventful period. As if to mark the departure of Mr Wright there had been major washaways at the Bubi Bridge in March and these caused a considerable suspension of train services, as if there were not enough other troubles all over the system during this period. The repair teams, though, had become so well organised that very rarely was there a delay of more than twenty four hours through these difficult times.

Another landmark in the history of the railways also took place around this time when the railway missioner retired, and thus the railway mission service to staff, which started at the turn of the century, came to an end and the special mission coach was placed in the railway museum. However, despite the fact that the war was becoming ever more difficult the historical committee still arranged odd trips and a special train was run from Salisbury to Marandellas and back on 14 May 1978 using a 15th class locomotive. This was the first time a steam locomotive had been seen in Salisbury since

1973. By strange coincidence this even coincided with the announcement that steam traction would be retained for a further fifteen to
twenty years until electrification could be well established and that
all existing 14A, 15, 15A, 16A and 20th class steam locomotives
stored at that time would be rehabilitated. This programme, which
was almost complete at the end of 1981, necessitated the almost
complete rebuilding of eighty-seven Garratt locomotives. This
involved the provision of new tanks, bunkers, boilers, fireboxes and
roller bearings; the locomotives were totally stripped and rebuilt
from scratch which is a great credit to all those involved. The first
locomotive to be commissioned was 16A class no 643, and it emerged
from the works in July 1979. It was followed shortly afterwards by
15th class no 420 which was named *Indlovu*, and subsequently all
15, 15A and 20th class locomotives are being named after animals,
Matabele regiments and rivers. Then on 17 August 1978 another
notable event took place with the renaming of the railways as
'Zimbabwe Rhodesia Railways', a title which was to be in existence
for only a short time, and never appeared on locomotives or rolling
stock.

Despite the continuing war which had caused the cessation of all
night passenger trains, progress of new works continued and in
September a new line around the town of Que Que was opened,
complete with a new station and goods yard. At the same time CTC was
completed from Somabula to Beitbridge, all controlled from one
central cabin at Dabuka, which constituted a big step forward in
signalling technology on the railways, and was also a forerunner to
bringing the line from Dabuka to Salisbury under the control of the
Dabuka cabin.

Towards the end of 1979 the first sign of improvement in the
general situation showed in the re-opening of the Victoria Falls
Bridge in November. At last the shuttling of trains on and off the
bridge could stop and everyone on the staff hoped for further easing
of the situation. On 17 December DE 2 class no 1200 and its train
were derailed by a landmine and this proved to be the last of 482
'scrambles' which had caused a tremendous amount of damage and
killed six enginemen, six running staff, eight track staff and eleven
others, to say nothing of forty-seven staff injured. It is true to say

that with the difficulty of obtaining supplies of vital materials and spare parts, in addition to the constant interruptions to the train service, this period was one of the most difficult and challenging in the history of Rhodesia Railways and was overcome only by the loyalty, bravery and ingenuity of the staff, several of whom were decorated for these qualities.

With the political settlement during the winter of 1979/80 and the emergence of the legally constituted state of Zimbabwe from the original Southern Rhodesia, things at last began to return to normal, though, as with the two previous world wars, the railway was fairly run down. The locomotive stock in particular, was in a very poor state with the result that a number of locomotives were hired from South African Railways. This hiring started with steam in the form of six 15Es from 1970 to 1973, followed by six 15Fs from 1978 to 1979, continuing with fifteen GMAs from late 1979 to August 1981 and finally eighteen 14Rs. During the same period class 33 diesels were hired from the middle of 1980 to the middle of 1981 followed by DNPCF locomotives similar to class DE 6. In February 1980 the Mozambique border at Machipanda was re-opened and trains started to run again, though at rather infrequent intervals and with loads limited to 800 tonnes by the lack of reliable locomotives on the DNPCF Beira line.

The general manager, Mr Sievwright, retired in April 1980 and was succeeded by Mr N. Lea-Cox. At the same time the name of the railways was changed again to 'The National Railways of Zimbabwe', (NRZ); this time it was more permanent, appearing on all vehicles by the end of the year. By the middle of 1980 all the night passenger trains had been reinstated, though the Cape Town and Johannesburg trains had been reduced to one a week and the branch line services were not reinstated, mainly because of a shortage of motive power.

Plans for electrification were also well advanced and a test section was installed between Gado and Samwari in the middle of the country. For this section a 25kV electric locomotive was borrowed from South African Railways and ran for about a month with the result that practical experience was gained for the proposed electrification of the 206 miles from Dabuka to Salisbury. Towards the end of the year rerailing with 54 kg/m (approx 108 lb/yd) rail was commenced at Dabuka, and as this work progressed, various remodellings at the main centres were carried out in order that everything should be ready for electric trains to commence running. Work finally started on electrification from Dabuka to Salisbury in the middle of 1981 and it is planned to be opened for traffic at the end of 1983.

In October 1980 all the through routes to the sea were operating again with the opening of the line through Malvernia, now renamed Chicualacuala. This re-opening involved the complete relaying of about 40 miles of track before any trains could pass, and this, like the Beitbridge section, was completed in record time. A further major work in this area was the opening of a 21-mile extension from Nandi to Mkwasine in the south east of the country for transporting large quantities of sugar for export.

At the end of 1980 two events, showing the signs of the times, took place. The first was the opening of Dabuka container yard in order to cope with the vast increase in container traffic to and from the ports, and the second was the closing of the Gwelo civil engineering district because of the considerable shortage of staff. This situation has continued in all departments just as a great expansion is required, and the shortage of staff is most critical. However, as in the past, NRZ staff have accepted the challenge and will, no doubt, restore the system to its previous high standard.

CHAPTER TWELVE

Locomotives—Early Days

It is with the first engines supplied to the Beira Railway itself that the conscientious locomotive historian runs into difficulty. The Brush Electrical Engineering Co was completely re-organised in 1938; all the old records of the Falcon engines and rolling stock were destroyed and only a few old catalogues survived. From the catalogue details, and from photographs, one has to build up a picture of the various types of locomotives that gave service over the eight years of BR narrow gauge.

In the early days of the line the contractors must have managed entirely with their five tank engines, as it is not until July 1894 that reference is made to the BR owning two 'large' locomotives which, due to the track, could then only run as far as the 40 mile peg. BR Locomotive no 1 must have been one of these two engines. This little engine, with its spark arrester chimney and cowcatcher, had a single-roofed cab with open sides and large oval-shaped driver's windows; the safety valves were on the dome and the whistle was on top of the firebox. From a photograph of this engine outside Beira shed (picture, p 65) it is apparent that the wheel arrangement was 0—4—2, while the tender was the small four-wheeled type. No 1 was one of three engines 1-3 built as 0—6—0s and was rebuilt as an 0—4—2 for Beira Docks. The London magazine *Engineering* reported that in 1893 Falcon Works supplied a locomotive which bears the number 3 on the side of the boiler barrel and on the tender. No photograph of this six-coupled engine is extant showing it in service; its outstanding feature was the dome type sand container mounted on the boiler between the chimney and the steam dome. Apart from the six coupled wheels and the 'sand dome' this engine closely resembles the BR Falcon-built 4—4—0s, of which there are many photographs. (Picture, p 66.)

Another explanation is that BR no 1 was originally of the 0—6—0 wheel arrangement, as was no 3, and that when the line was extended up the escarpment with its sharp curvature, the rigid wheel base with six coupled wheels gave difficulty and a local conversion was made by removing the rods between the second and third pair of wheels, the engine so becoming an 0—4—2. Such an alteration is known to have been carried out with other 0—6—0 engines on light railways in Rhodesia many years later.

The mainstay of the BR were the Falcon 4—4—0 tender engines which served the line so well and were later to achieve fame on other narrow-gauge lines in both Rhodesia and South Africa. Described by Brush as being admirably suited for light narrow-gauge lines, they were known as Falcon 'Class F, types 2 and 4' and were available in three types with slightly differing dimensions. So far as the Beira Railway was concerned the first order was for the smaller boilered version; this had cylinders 8in by 15in, coupled wheels of 2ft 8in diameter, a total heating surface of 225sq ft and a tractive effort of 3,000lb. A four-wheeled tender carrying 500 gallons of water and 45cu ft of wood fuel was hauled, and the whole unit in full working order weighed only 18 tons. The makers stated that the locomotive could haul 158½ tons on the level and 24 tons up a 1 in 40 grade. This batch had spark arrester chimneys and differed from the engraving of BR no 3 in that the sandbox had been removed from the boiler top and replaced with small boxes on the running plate, the engine number being affixed thereon in brass numerals. BR no 9 at the head of a mixed train is illustrated on p 65 and it can be seen that the boiler, cab side panels and the tender sides were all lined, probably with yellow paint on green livery. No cowcatcher is provided and the large oil headlamp is a prominent feature.

Unfortunately, owing to the absence of records, it is not possible to state exactly how many of this type were supplied, but photographs have been seen of 4—4—0s nos 4, 6 and 9, while from no 11 onwards all engines were of the larger type of 4—4—0. The main differences here were that the cylinder diameter was 9in instead of 8in and the boiler was larger, having a heating surface of 275sq ft with a larger grate area; this resulted in the engine weighing 15cwt more. The tractive effort was 3,987lb. A six-wheeled tender was provided with capacity for 650 gallons of water and 50cu ft of wood fuel, giving a total inservice weight of 20 tons 17 cwt. In appearance, apart from the longer boiler and smokebox, the engine had a normal chimney with a lipped top, the safety valves were mounted on a turret close to the cab, and the dome had a rounded top; the whistle was fixed to the front of the cab, while the running plate was at a higher level than the cab floor. Both designs of 4—4—0 had louvres for use at the side windows and double-roofed cabs to give the best possible conditions for the enginemen. BR no 21, after many years on a logging line in Matabeleland, was recovered and is now preserved in the railway museum at Bulawayo.

The catalogue price of the larger type is given as £1,000 but at railway directors' meetings in 1897 it was stated that the price was £1,250 and orders were approved for twenty such engines. As the lowest running number on record is no 11 and the highest is 44, it would seem clear that thirty-four Falcon locomotives of the larger 4—4—0 design were acquired by the BR between 1896 and 1898. The last eight were built by Glasgow Engineering Co.

Despite references to a black livery with yellow lining, it is clear from the excellent photograph of BR no 24 resplendent in new paint, that a lighter colour, probably green, had been used with yellow and a dark lining, the chimney and smokebox being black. Whether this was for some special occasion is not known but the effect must have been pleasing to the eye.

These were the first engines provided for the group of railways comprising the BMR and were replaced in 1900 by standard 3ft 6in gauge locomotives when the Beira—Umtali line was widened. Meanwhile Cecil Rhodes's Cape to Cairo route had been pressing northwards and in October 1897 had reached Bulawayo. The line from Vryburg to Bulawayo had been opened with the aid of the CGR, which had undertaken by agreement with the Bechuanaland Railway to operate the section and initially to provide locomotives and rolling stock.

However, late in 1896 the CGR must have asked the Bechuanaland Railway to assist with engine power as the famous Glasgow builders, Neilson & Co, received orders for three 4–6–0 and four 4–8–0 locomotives for urgent delivery by early 1897. Reliance was placed on two well tried CGR types and these orders were, in effect, extensions of CGR orders for batches of the same design. Bechuanaland Railway nos 1 to 3 were identical to the Cape 6th class and eventually became the SAR 6B class. (Picture, p 201.) Already these 4–6–0s had become famous throughout the CGR and some were busy on the Vryburg—Mafeking line.

The other order was for four of the CGR 7th class which arrived as Bechuanaland Railway nos 4 to 7. Designed by H. E. Stephens, then chief loco superintendent of the CGR, they had an axle loading of 9.6 tons, while the engine weighed 48.35 tons and the eight-wheel tender 34.65 tons, so that they were admirably suited to the sand-ballasted 45lb and 60lb track.

Neilsons and other Glasgow builders supplied a considerable number of these locomotives to the Cape railways between 1892 and 1902, while a batch of similiar design was shipped to the Sudan Railways in 1897. It is clear that others than Cecil Rhodes were imbued with the idea of the Cape to Cairo railway and *Engineering*, referring to the Sudan order, commented on the similar gauge and design and suggested that 'this was a forecast of the connection which will no doubt be ultimately made by railway between these widely separated countries'. Alas, this was not to come.

It is curious that, though delivered by Neilsons as Bechuanaland Railway locomotives, upon erection by the CGR at Salt River they appear to have 'lost' their number plates and came into CGR service as nos 582–4 and 347–50. As we shall see no 348 was eventually to reach BMR ownership.

In the meantime construction of the Mashonaland Railway had been begun with the line from Umtali to Salisbury and for this Paulings bought two locomotives from the CGR. These were shipped to Beira and were carried over the 2ft-gauge line to Umtali where they were erected and placed into use by the contractors. They had been built by Neilsons in 1882 as CGR 4th class 4–6–0 tender locomotives, becoming nos W59 and W71. Now, after main-line use between Cape Town and Beaufort West, they were to run out rails and sleepers and other requirements for the construction of the new line across Mashonaland.

These two 4–6–0s had been erected at Umtali by June 1898 and received new number plates N1 and N2. Their distinctive feature was a long platform, complete with railing, between the front of the smokebox and the buffer beam. It was possible to place a chair on this platform and ride along with a clear view of the track ahead, a privilege afforded to few, however. The Salter valves on the dome were another unusual feature.

After a year in the ownership of Paulings, they were taken over by the MR in 1899 and it was these locomotives that hauled the two trains from Umtali on 22 May 1899 for the official opening of the line to the capital town of Salisbury. For this occasion MR no 1 had been named *Cecil J. Rhodes,* which was painted on the splasher over the centre coupled wheels. (Picture, p 83.) These two engines ran for several years but when new lines were opened they were relegated to branch lines, no 2 being allocated in 1906 to work the Gwelo—Selukwe round trips, with a load of 220 tons on 28 axles. Soon after, they were withdrawn from service.

Not long after the advent of the two CGR locomotives, the MR purchased two 4–4–0 tender engines from Nasmyth Wilson & Co of Patricroft and these became nos 3 and 4. They were shipped to Beira and were also erected at Umtali after transit over the narrow-gauge line. It is curious that the makers had started work on these two in 1891 but they were not completed for delivery until 1897 when bought by the MR. They must have been ordered for another railway of similar gauge but not sold for some reason until the MR was known to be looking for engine power for its new line. They were quite attractive, having a chimney with a copper band at the top, and a dome of burnished brass. The very roomy cab had two side windows with elegant curved tops, while the tender could carry 3½–4 tons of wood but only 1,670 gallons of water.

They soon followed nos 1 and 2 into service on construction and were named *Salisbury* and *Umtali*, names which they retained for several years. No 4 *Umtali* suffered serious damage in an accident near Tsungwesi in 1898, when due to excessive speed on a curve the locomotive and several trucks became derailed and the driver and fireman, a timekeeper and four Africans were killed, while four Europeans and eighteen Africans were injured. This mishap occurred during the period of construction by Paulings.

These two 4–4–0s were not capable of anything but light loads and in later years were mainly used on local passenger services, such as between Salisbury and Avondale, the Gatooma—Eiffel Flats branch and the Matopos train from Bulawayo. Another duty was the Livingstone—Victoria Falls weekend trips in pre-World War I days. Eventually they were put into store and in 1929 scrapped.

Two tank engines with an interesting history had been purchased by the MR late in 1899 and were nos 5 and 6, later receiving the names of *Inyanga* and *Paulington*. These two locomotives were bought secondhand, having been built in 1896 by J. Fowler & Co of Leeds for the Metropolitan & Suburban Railway which ran from Cape Town to the suburb of Sea Point. The story goes that these six-coupled tanks were unsuited for the curves on the Sea Point line and frequent derailments led to their withdrawal. The Metropolitan & Suburban Railway was closed in 1897 after a chequered career and the two tank engines, then named *Sea Point* and *Green Point,* were taken over by the CGR against outstanding debts. In 1899 they were sold to the MR for £2,167 each, shopped to Beira, carrried over the narrow gauge and put into service at Umtali in January 1900.

With their brass-capped chimneys and polished domes these tanks must have looked smart at the head of trains on the Umtali—Salisbury section. Records show that *Inyanga* ran 26,160 miles in 1901, while *Paulington* notched up 19,812 miles in 1900 —quite good performances then. This did not last and soon they were mainly engaged in shunting at Salisbury and Umtali, one being nicknamed *Pretty Polly*. Eventually growth of traffic and heavier rolling stock overtaxed them and they were sold in 1921 and 1924 to a contractor at Elisabethville.

In the meantime Paulings had brought to Umtali a light saddle tank named *Jack Tar*, which was used on the gauge widening of the Beira Railway. This little 0–6–0, which made history with the BMR, was built in 1889 by Manning, Wardle & Co of Leeds and weighed just over 19 tons. Originally the engine was of 3ft gauge and was purchased by an English contractor named J. P. Edwards, who was building part of the Midland Railway's Dore to Chinley branch line. After use by another contractor, *Jack Tar* was altered to 3ft 6in gauge and with some modifications was shipped out to Paulings at Beira. Later, the MR bought the little engine which then became MR no 7 in 1900. (Picture, p 151.)

For many years this busy engine shunted at Beira—in the early days there was no other shunting engine needed—and in any case this 19-ton machine was the only one light enough to cross the Chiveve creek bridge to place trucks at the customs wharf on the opposite side of the inlet from the station and yards. It was an auspicious day when the Portuguese governor of Beira rode on the footplate with the railway superintendent and loco foreman, while *Jack Tar* propelled an open bogie wagon which, newly painted and carpeted with a tarpaulin, carried gaily dressed ladies and other guests reclining in easy chairs for the colourful ceremony of opening the Mozambique Company's wharf.

For a spell in 1904–5 *Jack Tar* was sent to Victoria Falls for use during the construction of the famous bridge. During its career there it distinguished itself by being the first locomotive to cross the bridge. One night while hauling two loaded trucks to the north bank, its side-rod killed a leopard that had strayed on to the uncompleted bridge and was crouching beside the track.

When the bridge was finished *Jack Tar* returned to Beira where at times the shunting duties only called for two hours work a day. The years passed and it was not until 1927 that the job needed heavier engine power. The next duty was works shunter at Bulawayo, where a life of activity continued. By 1935 re-boiling was necessary and other changes in appearance were made. These included the provision of a brass dome and cap to the chimney, while a new fully enclosed cab was fitted in place of the original open shelter. The black livery was replaced by dark green, lined with yellow, and looked very smart. One loss was the little anchor fitted in front of the chimney which was eventually replaced by a polished V during World War II, but this ornament did not have the significance of *Jack Tar's* anchor.

By 1942 the work at Bulawayo was too heavy and the little locomotive was moved to Umtali for workshop shunting until withdrawn for preservation. Exhibited at the Rhodes Centenary Exhibition at Bulawayo for three months in 1953, *Jack Tar* was then stored, until later loaned to the Umtali Museum. Now it is in the railway museum at Bulawayo.

With the extension from Bulawayo to Salisbury begun and the Beira gauge widening in hand, the railway companies placed orders with Neilson, Reid & Co of Glasgow for more locomotives. Guided by the CGR experience with its 7th class 4–8–0s, of which the Bechuanaland Co had already purchased four, the BMR ordered twelve in 1899, two specifically for the Beira line, and followed this up with another twelve in 1900. The sturdy 7th class design was very suited for the light pioneer track of the BMR and the locomotive superintendent, N. Gibbons, was doubtless glad to receive the first batch at Beira to augment the mixed stable already in his charge.

The second batch, RR 11 to 22, was landed at Cape Town and went into service on the CGR-operated Vryburg—Bulawayo section; there they remained for several years until some were moved to BMR control north of Bulawayo. Under a revised working agreement with the CGR, the RR now had to provide the engine power for the line from Vryburg.

All the Neilson Reids had the conventional round-top boilers but in 1901 Kitsons supplied eight 7th class fitted with Belpaire fireboxes, as were the two subsequent orders, each for ten locomotives, placed with the North British Loco Co in 1903. The earlier engines were re-boilered with the Belpaire type in 1925–30.

Until 1905 the 7th class provided the power for practically all trains over the main lines, Beira—Bulawayo and Vryburg—Victoria Falls. At that time only three 7th class were needed to work the entire train service between Salisbury and Gwelo, the Salisbury crew booking off for rest at Globe & Phoenix (now Que Que) while the engine took the train on to Gwelo with a relief crew. The fitter at Salisbury had a hard task to get an incoming locomotive ready for the road again in the time available, as late arrivals were normal in those days.

At that time the main traffic flow was inland, being made up of imported goods and railway construction material. From Beira the load was fourteen bogie wagons over the flat section to Bamboo Creek, and thence to Umtali on the 1 in 38 adverse grade with 5 chain curves the 7th class managed to pull seven or eight loaded wagons, 210–40 tons gross. Such load was maintained on to Salisbury over the undulating country, while on to Bulawayo over the 1 in 80 grades 400 tons was the load.

Much of the traffic consisted of rails and sleepers for Paulings, as work was pushed on with extensions in the north. Several of these engines were allocated to Paulings for the Victoria Falls—Broken Hill extension in 1905–6 and RR no 14, which in 1904 had headed one of the first trains into the terminus at the falls, had the honour of being ferried over the Kafue river by pontoon to work construction trains north before the long bridge was completed.

Altogether fifty-two 7th class locomotives were built for the BMR and in order to avoid confusion with the early MR engines, much re-numbering was undertaken, first in 1901 and later in 1906. In addition to the fifty-two ordered direct two others were obtained in 1909 by Paulings from the CGR, nos 348 and 398, for the building of the RKJR from Broken Hill to the Congo border. These were taken over by the RKJR in 1910 for £1,800 each and were later acquired by the MR in 1928; they retained their CGR numbers until scrapped in 1938. Engine no 19 appears to have been scrapped early on, as it was replaced by a second no 19, which had been owned by the Imperial Military Railways, their no 110, during the Boer War.

By 1914 the need for suitable shunting engines had arisen and W. J. Hosgood started the conversion of some 7th class into tank engines. Two types were evolved by extending the frames, one having a 4–8–2 and the other a 4–8–4 wheel arrangement. Provided with side tanks holding 480 gallons, and a bunker tank for 500–650 gallons and $3\frac{1}{2}$–$4\frac{1}{2}$ tons of coal, these engines weighed $63\frac{1}{2}$ and 68 tons respectively. With a stumpy chimney and no cowcatcher, they were hardly recognisable as having been of the 7th class. The nine 6th class 4–8–2 tanks and the four 6A class 4–8–4 tanks emerged from conversion between 1914 and 1923 and ran from fifteen to forty years, the last being set aside for workshop shunting in 1956.

While in due time many of the old 7th class were scrapped, others were sold to various new owners, and curiously in 1915, when World War I had temporarily reduced traffic in Rhodesia, the SAR bought five for use in South-West Africa, which had just been taken over from the Germans. One of these was the ex-IMR no 110 (RR no 68) which thus returned to South African lines. The Zambesi Saw Mills Railway, operating into the forests from Livingstone, became the home of eight 7th class, three remained with the CFM at Beira in 1949 and three others were sold to a Congo contractor. Yet another has ended life on the steelworks private line near Que Que.

On the level Beira—Vila Machado section the 7th class continued to work practically all trains until replaced by the 9th class in 1931. The Salisbury branch lines also saw this class well into the 1930s and others were placed on the shunt at smaller depots.

No 72 ran the Matopos trains until the last trip in June 1948, while No 43 was workshop shunter at Bulawayo for several years and rejoiced in a blue livery. Subsequently no 43 worked the Selukwe branch jubilee train in 1963 and has now been set aside for the railway museum.

In 1903 when the little 7th class engines were battling up the mountain section to Umtali, the loco superintendent was looking round for a more powerful engine to take their place. The opportunity came when Kitson & Co of Leeds produced its early example of an articulated locomotive of the Jean-Jacques Meyer design, and so offered a solution to the problem of increasing train loads without double heading. It is clear that the two Kitson-Meyer 0–6–6–0 engines bought by RR in 1903 were the first articulated machines to have been used in Africa, though the Cape and Transvaal railways each had a very similar locomotive in 1903–4. Some twenty more years were to pass before RR received its first Beyer-Garratt articulated locomotive, the type which finally solved the problem of hauling heavy loads over hilly sections.

The two unusual Kitson-Meyers arrived at Umtali in 1903 and became RR 51 and 52. They were of the simple four-cylinder type with the drive on to the leading coupled wheels of the two six-wheel units. The boiler and bunker were supported by a pair of braced girders, which in turn rested upon the two power bogies which carried the load on pivots as near as possible to the centre of the wheelbase. As well as the normal chimney a second chimney mounted on the bunker served the exhaust of the rear unit, steam having passed through a long pipe from the smokebox to the rear cylinders. Fitted with Walschaerts valve motion, the cylinders were placed at the trailing end of each unit and this, in the case of the front unit, led to the unusual placing of the cylinders very close to the firebox, in contrast to the normal practice which separates these features as far as possible for cleanliness. The steam and exhaust pipes had ball and socket joints fitted, the centre of the ball coinciding with that of the spherical pivot casting. The reversing and hand-brake gear was provided with universal joints.

The drive on the leading wheels of each unit was found to cause heavy wear on the flanges when working the sharply curved line and this, coupled with the dusty unballasted track, led to heavy repairs after short service on the long pull from Bamboo Creek. The Kitson-Meyers had a tractive effort of 75 per cent boiler pressure of 34,900lb, compared with the 18,660lb of the 7th class, and this enabled them to haul up to fourteen loaded trucks on up trains and twenty empties in the direction of the port. (Picture, p 152.)

With a design so ungainly in appearance and having a chimney at each end, it is not surprising that when erection was nearing completion in Umtali workshops one of the fitters asked his foreman which way the engine was meant to go. From the illustration it will be seen that the cab, while roomy, was almost entirely enclosed, and this led to much complaint from the well warmed enginemen. The small bunker section was quite inadequate for the usual coal consumption of about 110lb per mile and so an ordinary tender holding 3,250 gallons of water and seventy tons of coal was hauled. This in turn led to delays while the unfortunate fireman threw coal forward from the separate tender to the engine's coal bunker.

After some while on the mountain section it was decided to try the Kitson-Meyers on the Umtali—Salisbury run where the climbs and curves were not so arduous. Speed however had to be limited to 8mph over much of the light track so that the goods train trip was a lengthy journey. A Kitson used to leave Umtali with a train in the morning and on reaching Rusapi in the afternoon, after 62 miles' run, the crew banked their fire and took their blankets into the van to sleep overnight. Early next morning steam was raised and the Kitson-Meyer pushed on to Salisbury, another 108 miles over somewhat easier track. The story goes that a driver once invited an African who was walking past at a siding, to ride on the engine to Salisbury—really to get some help with the firing—but the native replied, 'Mina funa hamba checha' (I want to go quickly!).

In 1907 the Kitson-Meyers were moved to Bulawayo to work on coal trains from Wankie, being mainly used from Dett to which point cross-trips were worked by other trains from the colliery to make up a good load for the articulated locomotive to haul to Bulawayo. Here on the 1 in 80 grade they hauled a load of 700 tons inclusive of a 45-ton water tank and a 14-ton caboose but again their slow speed and heavy coal, oil and water consumption proved a serious disability. By 1912 the two engines had been withdrawn from use, as the 9th class 4–8–0s were arriving and later they were dismantled. They had covered a mileage of 163,317 and 158,892 respectively in a working life of some eight years. One boiler was used for the Umtali workshop power station while the other went to Victoria Falls to operate the hotel laundry. So ended the lives of a curious and unusual class of locomotive in Rhodesia.

Although ready to experiment with the Kitson-Meyers, the management decided to order a slightly larger 4–8–0 than the 7th class and in 1904 the North British Co delivered a batch of ten 8th class engines, nos 53 to 62. These were to the well-proved design of H. M. Beatty, chief locomotive superintendent of the CGR. Eight were initially placed on the Mafeking line while the other two worked between Bulawayo and Gwelo.

They worked with saturated steam and had Stephenson link valve gear, and with a tractive effort of 24,370lb they were an advance on the 7th class, especially on the long Mafeking—Bulawayo round trip working. In 1910 a second batch was supplied and numbered 73 to 79. These had a deeper firebox and the boiler was placed a little higher, with a shorter chimney and lower dome; they also had a larger tender holding 8½ tons of coal, compared with 6 tons in the first batch.

While some of this class spent most of their lives on the Vryburg—Bulawayo section, others gave useful service on main and branch lines in Rhodesia. Three were later sold to Zambesi Saw Mills and two others went to the Union Lime Co in the Cape. By 1941 no 60 was the last of its class in service and this engine remained on shunting for many years until sold to Zambesi Saw Mills in 1956, where it is still running in the forests.

In 1904 Gibbons, the first loco superintendent, resigned and in May 1905 W. J. Hosgood was appointed to succeed him. Hosgood was a Welshman and had served with the Barry and the Taff Vale Railways before becoming engineer-in-chief of the Port Talbot Railway. Owing to his beard and likeness to the famous Japanese admiral of the time, it was not long before Hosgood was nicknamed 'Togo', a name which stuck to him throughout his twenty years of good service with the BMR.

At this time Umtali was the home of the only railway workshops, apart from also being railway headquarters, and practically all locomotives and other rolling stock were erected there. The pin-and-link coupling was universal and engines went on their way bearing a dim oil-burning headlamp of imposing proportions. It was for 'Togo' Hosgood to change all this and much more over his years of office.

In the next few years much-needed improvements were made to the permanent way while bridges were strengthened, all to give freer and better running of the train service. By 1912 Hosgood was able to persuade the board to accept his specifications for the first locomotive designed for Rhodesian requirements as opposed to adopting a CGR design. An order was placed with the North British Co for eighteen of his 9th class 4–8–0s which were numbered 80 to 97 and went into service at Umtali, Bulawayo, Livingstone and Mafeking.

The 9th class were the first superheated engines on the system. A feature was the larger boiler with a grate area of 31.2sq ft compared with the 8th class 21.35sq ft, and a total evaporation surface (with the superheater) of 1,580.7sq ft as against 1,314sq ft. They proved an economical design and popular with the enginemen. The class was augmented during the war years by two orders for six each; first from Beyer Peacock in 1915 were nos 105–10 and then from North British in 1917 came nos 111–116.

It was soon clear that the 9th class was a success in shifting more traffic over the main line, their goods load being 380 tons between Umtali and Salisbury rising to 650 tons thence to Wankie, with a low coal consumption of 60–5lb per mile. No 91 hit the headlines in 1922 by hauling the first passenger train to do the run of 299 miles from Salisbury to Bulawayo in less than twelve hours. This was in an emergency; driver F. G. Williams who drove the engine from Salisbury found on arrival at Que Que that the relief Bulawayo crew had not arrived so he took the train on to Gwelo. The newspaper report of this exploit caused much comment and a public demand for a regular service at this speed was not received with enthusiasm at headquarters.

World War I progressively called for greater efforts by the BMR to move more mineral exports and, with Britain fully engaged, an order was placed with the American Loco Co's Schenectady Works for the supply of six 4–8–0s of a design similar to the 9th class. These engines were designated the 9A class, coming into service as nos 117 to 122 in 1917. Their slightly different appearance was accentuated by the American practice of placing number discs on the smokebox door, while the cab had one large window instead of two small ones. At 111 tons 5cwt they were nearly three tons heavier than the 9th, mainly due to the larger tender capacity. While initially used from Umtali to Vila Machado, after some twelve years they were relegated to shunting duties, losing their cowcatchers in the process, but they continued to perform, noisily but well, in the bigger yards for many years. Two were scrapped in 1946 while the others were withdrawn in 1964.

After the arrival of Major M. P. Sells as CME, the earlier 9th class were due for reboilering and under his direction a redesigned and larger boiler with a wider firebox was specified with a working pressure of 180lb. Four of the 9th class were fitted with these modifications in 1939, which had the advantage of adding fifty tons to their load capacity. These reboilered engines became the first of the 9B class and as the improvement was so successful a further twenty-two were converted from 1944 onwards; thus most of the 9th class were rejuvenated to give many extra years of service.

Late in their service the 9th/9B class were mainly used on branch lines, though from Beira they had replaced the 7th on the main line to Vila Machado. Four were never converted to 9B and after ballast and shunt service at Mafeking they ended up with Zambesi Saw Mills in 1963–4.

Traffic at Beira port called for more shunting power for the new deep water wharf and in 1929 two 0–6–0 side tanks were ordered from Hudswell Clarke & Co, Leeds. These became RR nos 1 and 2 and were 36-tonners. It was found fairly soon that the tight curves on the wharves led to frequent derailments for which their rigid wheelbase was blamed and before long they were withdrawn to Umtali. After some years they were brought into use for workshop shunting, one at Umtali and the other at Mafeking. Later no 1 was brought back to Umtali, where she was eventually named *Genevieve*. Meanwhile no 2 had been busy at Umtali and in 1941 was named *Churchill* as a tribute by the staff to the great leader. The engine was given a special livery of green, with red and yellow lining, and had the name, with RRM above, painted in a crescent on the side tanks.

Some time after, *Churchill* was sent to Bulawayo in its green livery. Here one of the shop foremen, H. Hawkins, discovered a supply of royal blue paint left over from the Royal Train Garratts in 1947 and he had *Churchill* repainted in a blue livery. A little later cast brass nameplates *Winston Churchill* were provided and at the same time a polished brass dome cover was fitted and a copper top to the chimney. The engine was then again repainted in GWR dark green with gilt lettering and in this new livery the little shunting engine was for years the pride of the workshops.

The last of the small locomotives was also a workshop shunter. This was RR no 5, purchased in 1929 from the SAR for use at the mechanical shops at Mafeking, which undertook heavy repairs to the RR locomotives working the Southern Section. Built in 1901 by Chapman & Furneaux, Gateshead-on-Tyne, for the Port Elizabeth Harbour Board, this 0–4–0 saddle tank was the smallest locomotive ever owned by RR. This little 'pug', after many years running round the harbour at Port Elizabeth, had come well inland, to dry and dusty Mafeking, to end its days on RR duties though in the hands of SAR staff. No 5 was eventually scrapped in 1940.

CHAPTER THIRTEEN

Locomotives—Mountains and Garratts

WITH the growing development of the territories served, and increasing travel by the rising population, it was realised that some improvement was needed to the main services between Bulawayo and Salisbury and over the 484-mile run from Mafeking to Bulawayo. Hosgood's thoughts turned to the new Mountain type 4–8–2 wheel arrangement which had been introduced to the world in 1906 by D. A. Hendrie, then loco superintendent of the Natal Government Railways, and which had since proved successful in several variations of the design. Hosgood's specifications led to an order for seven 4–8–2 tender locomotives being placed with the North British Loco Co of Glasgow in 1913. They were built for work on 60lb track which was still sand ballasted and, as they were mainly needed for heavier passenger trains over the easier graded sections of main line, driving wheels of 4ft 6in diameter were chosen.

The 10th class, as these 4–8–2s were designated, became nos 98 to 104. They were landed at Cape Town and erected by the SAR at Salt River for working up to Rhodesia. The first three were allocated to Mafeking for the long round-trip to Bulawayo and back of 968 miles, while the other four went to Bulawayo for the Salisbury run. These superheated engines weighed 120.3 tons in working order and had an eight-wheel tender with capacity for 8½ tons of coal and 3,500 gallons of water. An attractive locomotive, designed for speeds of 40 to 45mph with passenger trains, they soon made a name for themselves and were popular with engine-men as a free-running and hard-working machine easy on coal and water. All the original batch were fitted with oil headlamps but soon a gradual conversion to electric headlights was begun, as had already been started with a few 7th and 8th class locomotives. These 10th class cost some £5,700 each.

For a time some were used in Northern Rhodesia, together with some of the second batch, nos 153–8, which, again, were supplied by North British. The whole class however gradually found its way to Mafeking and so it was chiefly in Bechuanaland that this handsome and useful class earned its keep. Working with regular crews—two drivers and two firemen, who shared their cabooses with two guards on the 2–2½ days round trip—these locomotives were carefully nursed and so were light on maintenance. That their charges were popular with the Mafeking men was obvious as all brasswork was kept brightly polished and one often saw a name in brass such as *Daisy* affixed below the headlight. A feature of the class were the three-paned side windows of the cabs, pro-viding good ventilation through the heat of the line skirting the Kalahari.

The second batch was erected at Umtali, but when an order was placed for an extra engine, no 159, in 1924, it was landed at Cape Town and erected at Salt River. The main improvement in these later orders was an increase in tender capacity of one ton of coal and a thousand gallons of water, so necessary for the long run between watering points. The last batch of six, nos 241–6, was supplied in 1930, once again by North British, and went direct to Mafeking. These cost £8,600 each compared with the high cost of £18,000 of the 153–8 order built in 1922 during the postwar boom.

As well as the 1899 running shed at Mafeking, RR later built a small workshop for the overhaul of engines allotted to the Southern Section. Here the staff of the SAR, who worked the line under agreement, carried out all repairs except for urgent jobs which had to be done at Bulawayo during a round trip. In 1932 a modern machine and erecting shop was added. Eventually in

1949 a start was made on transferring periodic heavy repairs to the Bulawayo workshops as an economy. This was a gradual process, until in 1954 the importance of Mafeking had declined to such an extent that the workshops were finally closed.

The free running 10th class locomotives showed a fine turn of speed on the easy grades through Bechuanaland and then coped with the heavy climb from Francistown into Rhodesia with its rise in altitude of some 1,600ft. They helped considerably in the reduction of passenger train timings in the 1931–3 period when the Rhodesia Express and other faster trains were introduced. Over the years they gave good service but two—nos 153 and 241—had to be scrapped after suffering severe damage in the disastrous head-on collision at Vakaranga in 1938. Four were sold to Zambesi Saw Mills in 1959–60, while others were scrapped from 1961 onwards. For a period in 1961–2 three of the class went to Nyasaland on hire but their heyday was over and the few left are now in store.

Towards the end of World War I the BMR was hard-pressed to meet traffic demands and tenders were invited for a more powerful Mountain type locomotive. Eighteen 4–8–2s of the 11th class were ordered from the Montreal Loco Works in Canada and these were delivered during 1918–19 for erection at Umtali. In the interval before delivery it was possible to hire six 2–8–2 tender locomotives from the CFK and these were mainly used on the Vila Machado-Umtali section during 1918.

The 11th class, nos 123–40, were superheated and their larger boiler and firebox, as compared with the 10th class, made them eminently suited for working heavy trains over 60lb track with the 35mph maximum speed which applied on the main line until the 1930s. They were used extensively for heavy coal traffic from Wankie both north and south, being shedded at Bulawayo and Livingstone. Later, as the copper mines were developed these locomotives did most of their work in Northern Rhodesia. With a tractive effort of 37,026lb at 85 per cent boiler pressure they proved a very useful acquisition and a second batch of twelve, nos 141–52, was ordered from the same builder in 1921. While the first batch had cost £15,400 each in 1918, the second lot came out at £19,000 only three years later.

The first of the class, no 123, had been run in steam at Montreal before shipment and was found to be an easier runner than the rest. For this reason no 123 was christened by the enginemen 'The Prairie Belle', though she never received a nameplate. In later years over the easy grades between Monze and Kafue a load of 1,400 tons was hauled by this class, being reduced to 750 tons for the 1 in 64 climb from Kafue to near Lusaka, though by double-heading a through load of 1,400 tons could be taken.

For many years the sharp distinctive exhausts of the 11th class echoed throughout the line in the north, as the whole class was shared by Livingstone and Broken Hill sheds. Having their numbers on a round plate on the smokebox door and a large Pyle National electric headlight, which also showed the engine number on its side glasses, they had a rather American appearance. Unlike all other modern RR classes, the footboard was stepped up from the cab floor level, so spoiling the fine line of the machine.

No 129 was scrapped in 1937 after an accident, while six of the latest batch were sold to the CFM in 1964 for service from Lourenco Marques and so maintained a distant connection with Rhodesia.

In 1924 'Togo' Hosgood, who had headed the locomotive department since 1905, retired and was succeeded by E. H. Gray. Gray had had much experience with the SAR and his first task was to provide the additional power needed for another boom in traffic. He had two main problems, the heavily graded section from Vila Machado to Umtali and the provision of a general purpose locomotive for main-line duties, particularly between Salisbury and Wankie. For the former the answer was the first batch of Beyer Peacock Garratts, while the latter was met by Gray's Mountain type, the 12th class. (Picture, p 219.)

In appearance the 12th class might be likened to an enlarged 9th class. It had the 4–8–2 wheel arrangement, the boiler was longer and larger with 190lb pressure and the firebox was deepened to the level of the pony wheels. Engine and tender weighed 131.37 tons, the tender carrying 10 tons of coal and 4,250 gallons of water. Using Gray's specifications with the axleload limited to 13 tons for 60lb rails, North British was asked to submit a suitable design, after which twenty 12th class were ordered.

The first lot arrived in 1926 and became 172–91 and of these 182–91 were supplied with Lentz poppet valves as an experiment. Three more came next year and with the success of the design manifested by the very good performance another twenty were ordered in 1928.

Initially the class was allocated to Salisbury for working to Gwelo, but as more came into service they spread to Bulawayo and then Livingstone. These sturdy locomotives became very popular with the staff, both enginemen and artisans, and they handled all types of trains without difficulty, being light on coal and water. The Lentz valves did not prove suitable, as it was found impossible to keep the gear correctly adjusted for very long, and they were replaced by Walschaerts gear, with which all the others were equipped. Oil lubrication of bearings and side rods was originally provided but from 1940 they were converted to grease lubrication.

A further twelve, nos 247–58, were supplied in 1930, which enabled the class to be rostered for main-line duties over the whole system. With improved track, as stone ballasting was extended, and as the 12th class had proved its reliability, the long-desired speed-up in passenger trains became possible.

Until the mid-1930s engines were normally allotted to individual drivers and their regular crews took great pride in maintaining a high standard of external cleanliness, apart from the mechanical efficiency of their locomotives. Many were decorated with leaping buck, swooping birds or fierce lions in brass on the smokebox door, and being brightly polished these added to the smart appearance of the engines.

It was an exhilarating sight to see a shining 12th class heading the daylight express of varnished teak saloons speeding on its way from Bulawayo to Salisbury, a run which soon included the 110 miles to Gwelo with only one stop for water. That handling a 420-ton load of twelve saloons was well within the capacity of the class is instanced by two runs with heavy trains at holiday

Page 269 (*above*) Canadian-built Mountain at Bulawayo in 1949
—11A class 4–8–2 no 315; (*below*) experimental condenser
locomotive, RR 19c class no 336, built by Henschel, 1954, with
elephant ear smoke deflectors

Page 270   The largest RR Garratt, 20A class no 740 in green livery at Livingstone in 1962. Other unusual features are the nameplate and the capuchon on the chimney

weekends, recorded by the author. In July 1931 no 183 with train no 11 Down had an eighteen-coach load on leaving Bulawayo and reached Gwelo in 4hr 30min with 49min at stops, so cutting the schedule by exactly 60min. This was an average of 24.4mph and compared with the booked time of 4hr 20min with 23min stopping time of the then Rhodesia Express with its load of twelve carriages.

A year later no 204 in charge of driver Lawler hauled a heavily laden seventeen-coach train of 660 tons to Gwelo and cut the time to within 15min of the schedule for the daylight express. This trip was run at an average of over 26mph. Speeds of up to 45mph were noted on many journeys by passenger trains, this being quite usual on the newly laid Victoria Falls—Deka deviation with its 80lb track. With goods trains, loads of 1,000 tons were hauled without undue difficulty, and the operating department found these locomotives of very real value because of their versatility. Speeds were low compared with Europe but these were heavy trains running over light track in undeveloped country.

Throughout World War II these 4–8–2s did yeoman work with the heavy passenger trains and growing volume of export minerals, but with the advent of pooling the old individual care of the engines lapsed. High mileages were run and signs of bar frame failures appeared, which was attributable to inherent design weakness. This, however, was overcome by modification and the need for frames to be replaced was avoided.

In 1944 three of the 12th class—nos 198, 212 and 213—were fitted with the wider shorter 11th class boiler, the conversion being undertaken in Bulawayo workshops. At the same time their tenders were enlarged to 12½ tons of coal instead of 10 tons. These three were designated the 12A class. No 198 was scrapped after serious accident damage, but the other two gave good service until sold to the CFM in 1964.

The original 12th class engines continued to run over the main line and later the Copperbelt branches, but some had been allocated to the Southern Section at the end of World War II to assist the 10th class on the long run from Mafeking. Here, too, they performed well and in 1959 a batch of thirty-two 12th class was transferred to Bulawayo to work all trains south, while the SAR had others at Mafeking along with the RR 19th class. However by 1963 they were all taken off the main lines and put to work on shunting, branch lines and ballast trains. As a class they will always be remembered by the staff with affection, as having been one of the most successful and hard-working locomotives on the railways.

Gray's other great success on the BMR was the introduction of the Beyer-Garratt. There was an urgent need for more powerful locomotives to work over the most difficult section of the Beira line. From an altitude of 125ft at Vila Machado, the line climbed over two escarpments, on gradients of 1 in 40 uncompensated and with frequent unchecked five chain curves, to 3,552ft at Umtali, 143 miles later. Before coming to the BMR Gray had had experience of Beyer-Garratts on the SAR and these British-built articulated engines had given very good results. The operating economies appealed to the BMR management, as the answer to this difficult line, and specifications were sent in 1924 to Beyer, Peacock & Co, Manchester.

The Beyer-Garratt type of locomotive was evolved from the ideas of an English-born engineer, H. W. Garratt, in collaboration with Beyer Peacock in 1907 and his design revolutionised the operation of railways in many parts of the world. In brief, the Garratt consists of a boiler slung in a cradle between two engine units, these being pivot-mounted to the boiler unit. This boiler arrangement, of a separate cradle frame held between the two engine units, permits great freedom with boiler design and capacity. With boiler and firebox removed from the power unit the wheel diameter and the size and position of cylinders can be varied to suit individual needs with much greater ease, and a variety of types was produced at the Gorton Works of Beyer Peacock.

Orders for twelve Garratts to be known as the 13th class were placed in 1925. Coming into service the following year numbered 160–71, these 2–6–2+2–6–2 articulated locomotives became the forerunners of an eventual fleet of 250 Garratts, which proved a great success on many sections of the Rhodesian system. Nos 170 and 171 were at first fitted with Lentz poppet valves, but these were later replaced by Walschaerts valve gear. Designed for 60lb track with an axleload of 13 tons, they carried seven tons of coal and 4,350 gallons of water. Owned by the MR they replaced the 9th class 4–8–0s and, taking a much greater load, effected considerable saving in train crews.

Experience gained with the 13th class on this climb to Umtali convinced the mechanical and operating officers that the Garratt was the answer for this heavy section. However, as the plate frames of the 13th class had been found unsatisfactory for conditions of continuous heavy work, Gray specified bar frames for an improved design, and in 1929 the first six 14th class Garratts arrived to help handle the growing traffic to and from Rhodesia's port. In their dimensions there was little difference but the boiler was placed higher, giving more clearance below the ashpan, the water capacity was reduced to 3,600 gallons, and the electric headlight was placed on top of the water tanks instead of being on brackets in front. This first batch owned by RR was numbered 215–20, and was followed in 1930 by another ten, nos 231–40. All sixteen were built at Gorton.

When traffic dropped off severely in 1932 the twelve 13th class were stored and the 14th maintained the service from Umtali. As trade picked up the 13th class came back into use as shunting engines at Salisbury and on branch and ballast workings, while later in 1939 nos 161 and 163 were sold to Rhokana Corporation for the ore trains from Mindola to the central plant over its private line at Nkana. No 163 came to an untimely end on a level crossing near Nkana when it collided with a lorry full of explosives for the mine. The Garratt was entirely destroyed in the resulting explosion, pieces being picked up many hundreds of yards away, while the lorry completely disappeared. Everyone on the engine and lorry was killed.

When their maintenance became too costly and more suitable power was available, the remaining ten 13th class were scrapped after World War II.

The 14th class were three tons heavier than their predecessors and nearly 4ft longer. With a maximum axleload of 13.53 tons they proved robust and satisfactory in handling trains up to Umtali. In 1949, when the Portuguese took over the line in Mozambique, eight of the class were sold and RR nos 215–20 and 231–2 then became CFM nos 901–8. The remaining eight moved to Salisbury, Gwelo and Bulawayo, where they soon became established as very useful branch-line power in place of the 9th class.

Gray's next problem was the growing coal and coke traffic which in 1928 was becoming a heavy burden on the Wankie—Dett and Wankie—Livingstone sections of the main line. Double-heading with the 11th class 4–8–2s was an expensive practice and he was asked to provide more effective power. The line from Wankie to Victoria Falls was on a 1 in 50 uncompensated grade with seven chain curves and was notorious for two stiff banks, the Katuna and Fuller banks, of six and seven miles in length.

While re-alignment of the whole section from Deka river, thirteen miles north of Wankie, to Victoria Falls was the answer, it was impossible to await this major deviation. A much heavier Garratt was therefore envisaged by Gray and in conjunction with Beyer Peacock the 16th class 2–8–2 + 2–8–2 type was produced. Eight of these were ordered and in 1930 nos 221–8 went into use on the Wankie—Livingstone run, 78 miles long, where they hauled loads of 675 tons.

The 16th class, built for 60lb track, had a tractive effort of 52,364lb and was by far the most powerful engine on the system, then and for some years after. Having bar frames like the 14th class, these massive locomotives weighed 155.29 tons. Water capacity was 5,050 gallons and the bunker held $8\frac{3}{4}$ tons of coal.

By late in 1932 the Deka—Falls deviation had been opened and 12th class 4–8–2s were able to release the big Garratts for the Wankie—Dett section and some went to the undulating line between Umtali and Salisbury where for many years they worked all classes of trains. On this 1 in 40 graded line they hauled 700 tons with goods trains, while on occasional trips from Salisbury to Gwelo they took 1,200 ton loads.

The 16th class became the mainstay of the Salisbury—Umtali

line for many years and with the upsurge of traffic a second batch
was specified by the new chief mechanical engineer, Major M. P.
Sells, who had come from the Nigerian Railways in 1937. These
twelve, nos 259–70, delivered by Beyer Peacock in 1938 were to
be of great value during the heavy mineral flow of the coming
war.

After some years steaming troubles developed with 'bird-
nesting' in the smokebox, but by re-drafting Sells achieved improved steaming, and reduced coal consumption by nearly 10lb a
mile. A handicap to these Garratts was the need to top up with
coal at the re-crewing depots at Inyazura and Que Que and during
1942–3 the bunker capacity was raised to eleven tons, so eliminating the intermediate coaling time and labour. This class continued on the main line until the arrival of the English Electric
diesels in 1955–6, when some became branch-line engines from
Salisbury and Gwelo, while others went north to the Copperbelt.
Several years later they were placed on shunting, while some
became surplus and were sold to the Benguela Railway in Angola
and to collieries in the Transvaal. No 608 was scrapped after a
head-on collision at Darwendale on the Sinoia line in 1963.

By 1938 the main line between Bulawayo and Salisbury had
been relaid with 80lb metals and heavier stone ballast and while
the 12th class was still coping with the faster passenger trains the
CME was giving thought to a more powerful locomotive. Major
Sells at one stage envisaged a large 4–8–2 designed for a 17½ton
axleload with a tractive effort of about 40,000lb. This would have
had 5ft coupled wheels and would have been a great asset to the
loco stud. Had this design been produced it would have been
the RR 17th class, but the outbreak of war in 1939 shelved the
idea.

His other problem was the provision of a faster locomotive
for the long run between Mafeking and Bulawayo on which the
10th class Mountains were finding the accelerated heavy passenger
trains a strain. Beyer Peacock had recently built for the Sudan
Railway a new design of Garratt with a 4–6–4 + 4–6–4 wheel
arrangement, which might be termed a Double Baltic type. Carrying 10 tons of coal and 7,000 gallons of water, these engines had

proved very suitable for the arid conditions of the Sudan, which were rather similar to those of Bechuanaland where watering points were far apart and unreliable.

This design interested Sells, who asked Beyer Peacock to produce drawings to his specifications for Rhodesian service. Four were then ordered and became the famous 15th class Garratt when they arrived in 1940. This class had a larger boiler than the Sudan design and other features which made it a more attractive and efficient locomotive. The coupled wheels of the unusually large diameter of 4ft 9in were the largest on RR and enabled the locomotive to handle fast passenger trains at speeds of 50mph and over. In full working order the machine weighed 181.23 tons and had an overall length of 92ft 4in. (Picture, p 219.)

An interesting feature was the streamlining of the front tank to give a smoother appearance; they were the first Garratts ever to be built with this innovation. New elements in RR design and practice were roller bearings on all bogie wheels, grease lubrication on the coupled wheels, and the valve gear arranged for chimney-first working, both engine units therefore running in foregear. Originally numbered RR 271–4 they became 350–3 in the renumbering some years later.

The arrival of the 15th class Garratts was, however, ahead of certain engineering works on the Bulawayo—Mafeking line and the four locomotives were shedded at Salisbury to work round trips with the heavy traffic to Gwelo. Allocated chiefly to the Rhodesia Express and well loaded passenger trains over the 187 mile section, they also handled 1,000 ton goods trains. From the start they were an outstanding success, not only running consistently high monthly mileages, which constituted a world record for narrow-gauge steam working, but in their reliability and consequent availability for service. The absence of worry over hot bearings, the comfortable cab and their stability made the class the most popular locomotive on RR.

Their performance was excellent. A load of fourteen bogies, 560 tons, was laid down for the Rhodesia Express but on one trip in January 1941 when running late with eighteen coaches, 687 tons, 18min were made up with nine stops en route. The ruling gradient was 1 in 80 compensated, with curves as sharp as ten chains and the longest bank one of twenty miles.

The mileage run by these Garratts established a record hard to beat for steam and over the first six years all four maintained approximately 6,000 miles a month, including time for tyre skimming or turning, washouts and general repairs. It was one of a later batch, no 379, which established a remarkable record by running 12,270 miles in one month in 1960. There was no nursing of the engine, which was handled by as many as 149 engine crews during the month, and it was out of service for two days for boiler washouts.

By his introduction of the 15th class, Sells gave RR the nucleus of a wonderful free-running and economical fleet of these locomotives, which was recognised by his successor, F. E. Hough, who came from the Nizam of Hyderabad's Railway in 1947. Hough wisely decided to continue with this design as a general purpose engine and a batch of ten, nos 354–63, was delivered in 1947; they differed only in that they had larger tanks, and rear units which were streamlined like the front ones. Another twenty came in 1949, nos 364–83, having a larger bunker to carry $12\frac{1}{2}$ tons of coal instead of 10 tons. This latest order had a maximum axleload of 15.18 tons and weighed 186.74 tons full.

With the boom in postwar traffic two more orders were placed, the only change being that Hough stepped up the boiler pressure to 200lb and so increased the tractive effort from 42,750 to 47,496lb. These were classified 15A. (Picture, p 287.) Beyer Peacock built thirty, nos 384–413, while another ten, nos 414–23, were supplied by the Societe Franco-Belge, Beyer Peacock's associates in France. All these came into service between 1950 and 1952, bringing the total to seventy-four units, which was the second most prolific design of Garratt produced by Beyer Peacock, and only exceeded by the GM/GMA/GMAM class of the SAR.

It was the 15th class that had the honour of hauling the royal train during the visit of King George VI and Queen Elizabeth in 1947. For this duty the locomotives were specially painted in a deep blue livery which looked well with the White Train. Again, in 1953 the 15th class provided the power for the Ivory Train used by the Queen Mother and Princess Margaret during their tour of Rhodesia; this time the engines were specially painted in glossy black.

When in 1955 the new route to the east coast at Lourenco Marques was opened it was the 15th class that worked the train service, hauling 1,000 ton through loads to Malvernia.

Although it was the Bulawayo—Mafeking line for which Major Sells had designed the 15th class in 1940, it was not until after RR had taken over the full operation of this line from SAR in 1959 that these Garratts began to work on the section for which they were originally intended. At first they ran round trips from Bulawayo to Mahalapye but in 1966 the long caboose-worked round trip of 968 miles became the regular stint of the popular 15ths.

Under wartime conditions it was not easy to meet the individual requirements of railways and at the request of the British War Department, to help move strategic minerals, Beyer Peacock built a design calculated to meet the differing needs of the 3ft 6in gauge 60lb rail systems in Africa. An existing basic design was used, as speed of production was vital, and the locomotive that emerged was of the 2–8–2+2–8–2 wheel arrangement, having 3ft 9½in coupled wheels suited for 1 in 30 grades. Rhodesian chrome and copper were essential for war supplies and nine such locomotives were delivered to RR in 1943–4.

These became the 18th class, numbered 281–9, and with a boiler having a grate area of 51.3sq ft they had the highest tractive effort yet used on RR, 58,268lb. Though not built to Rhodesian standards, they were a welcome addition at the time. They were chiefly used on the Wankie—Dett hill section of 51 miles of 1 in 61 uncompensated and handled coal trains of 1,100 tons; but they were slow moving. In late 1947 they were transferred to Umtali, where they were able to haul from Vila Machado fifty per cent more load than the smaller 14th class. Before this the badly designed coupled wheel axleboxes had been replaced with a new design which eliminated much trouble experienced on the road. When the Beira Railway was taken over in 1949 the CFM acquired the nine 18th class and renumbered them 981–9.

278

Soon after his arrival Hough recommended that a modification of the 11th class be quickly ordered to augment the power position. The Montreal Works could give earlier delivery than British builders and twelve 11A class 4–8–2s were delivered in 1948. These were numbered 304–15. Originally they had a boiler pressure of 200lb, giving a tractive effort of 37,485lb, but this was reduced to 180lb when cracks appeared in the frames.

The 11A class had a different appearance from the earlier 11th class, having a capuchon chimney and running plates stepped over the second pair of driving wheels. The cab too was different and the tenders were larger and more angular; for this reason they were 3ft 6in longer than their sisters. (Picture, p 269.) Heavier traffic on the Copper belt took most of these locomotives to the branch lines from Ndola and Nkana sheds. In 1961 all twelve were sold to the CFM and were recently in use on the new Swaziland Railway link with Lourenco Marques.

Looking for more power, CME Hough knew that everywhere locomotive builders were faced with heavy orders and that deliveries were slow; so when he heard that Sudan Railways had ten Garratts for sale he arranged to purchase them. This was in 1949 and it was these 4–6–4 + 4–6–4 Garratts that Sells had considered in 1938 and were the forerunners of his successful 15th class.

These ten Garratts became the 17th class, nos 271–80, and had been built in 1937–8 by Beyer Peacock. They had the conventional square-ended tanks with a high bunker to hold 12½ tons of coal, and the cab was of a more enclosed type suited to the Sudan desert conditions. However, this was not at all popular with Rhodesian enginemen who complained of the heat and lack of ventilation.

Initially they were tried on the Thomson—Livingstone section and from Bulawayo, but they were an unpopular engine with the men and apart from running the Gwelo—Gatooma goods trains were gradually relegated to shunting at the large depots. When more suitable power became available they were stored and in 1964 were sold to the Beira section of the CFM.

The heavy traffic now passing over the Vryburg—Mafeking—

Bulawayo line was next to call for additional power and Hough decided that the SAR 19D class 4–8–2 was very suited for this work, several of them having been working up to Bulawayo since 1948. In 1951 twenty such locomotives were ordered from Henschel & Sohn of Kassel and became the RR 19th class, by coincidence obtaining the same class number as their SAR counterparts. They were the first engines to be built for RR in Germany and were identical to the SAR 19D class, even having the same cylindrical Vanderbilt type tenders. The batch was numbered 316–35 and was mainly stationed at Mafeking, though a few assisted on the main line north and east of Bulawayo for some while.

They weighed 157 tons, of which the large twelve-wheel tender with 12 tons of coal and 6,500 gallons of water was responsible for 75.8 tons. Developing a tractive effort of 36,090lb at 85 per cent boiler pressure they are the most powerful straight locomotives on RR and handle loads of 800 to 860 tons with goods trains. (Picture, p 288.)

It was on a 19th class locomotive that Hough decided to experiment with the steam condensing apparatus patented by Henschel, which had been the subject of extensive tests by the SAR from 1950. Such an economy in water consumption had been achieved that SAR ordered ninety 4–8–4s for use on the dry Karroo section in the Cape and it was felt that this apparatus might be the answer to the water problems in the sand veld country skirting the Kalahari, which had been a headache for the water engineers.

Consequently, a 19th class, no 336, came from Henschel in 1954 with the special apparatus and was designated 19C class. The general appearance of the engine was very similar to the normal 19th with the exception of the steam chamber and large pipe running from the smokebox along the left side to the tender. This latter was very different to the Vanderbilt type, having the section behind the coal bunker roofed and square-shaped with lattice side panels. Three fans were mounted in the roof and were driven by an exhaust steam turbine to provide the necessary draught. It carried ten tons of coal and 3,750 gallons of water, while an underslung condensate tank held 370 gallons; it weighed 82 tons and was longer than the locomotive itself by some 4½ feet. Smoke deflectors of various types were tried and finally a German design, sometimes described as 'elephant ears', was fitted. Considerable difficulties were suffered with this locomotive, particularly with the blower fans, during its early service. To some extent this was possibly due to the pooling practice with engine crews, as it was not until no 336 was allotted to a regular caboose set on the Bulawayo—Malvernia run that better results were obtained. Leaky tubes were another trouble and much time was spent in shed. In 1958 no 336 was involved in a collision with another train and was extensively damaged. The locomotive was put aside for some time until it was decided that, as the condenser experiment had not been very successful, it should be converted to a standard 19th class, after which she went into service with her sisters. (Picture, p 269.)

With traffic continuing to grow more power was needed, first on the branch lines for which a batch of eighteen 2–6–2 + 2–6–2 Garratts of the 14A class, nos 508–25, came from Beyer Peacock in 1953–4. These were a modernised version of the 14th class. For main-line goods work the same builder supplied thirty 16A class Garratts in 1953. For these Hough generally followed the 16th class design but increased the boiler pressure to 200lb psi and gained a tractive effort of 58,183lb compared with the 52,364lb of the original class. As in the 14A class, the front tank and rear bunker were streamlined, while roller bearings were fitted to the eccentric rods and bogie boxes. In Northern Rhodesia their arrival was of immense value in meeting the heavy demand for fuel to the mines as well as the rush of imported goods and plant for the north.

In the meantime Hough had decided on an innovation, the construction of locomotives at Bulawayo workshops from a combination of imported and locally made parts. This resulted from new frames having been ordered to replace suspected 12th class frame breakages, the need for which had been avoided by successful modifications, and boilers supplied from Vulcan Foundry for reboilering being available. Ten tenders were ordered from the

North British Co, which also provided most of the reciprocating and revolving parts, though many other parts were locally fabricated in Bulawayo.

By 1954 all the material had arrived and work was begun on the erection of the first 12B class 4–8–2, the first locomotive to be built in Rhodesia. Hough was responsible for the design and he arranged that the erection of the first be carried out by apprentices under the guidance of an experienced foreman. The engine was appropriately named *Precursor*, the choice being partly because of Frank Hough's early association with the LNWR, but mainly because it was hoped that the local workshops would undertake greater building activity in years to come.

The 12B class had boilers similar to the 11A class but pressed to 190lb. Cylinders were originally 21in by 26in but were later reduced in diameter by one inch to lessen strain on the frames, as these showed signs of cracking in service. With heavier tenders the whole unit weighed five tons more than the original 12th class. These 12Bs spent most of their life at Kafue on round trips to Monze, whence they hauled 1,400 tons on up line goods trains over the easy grades. By 1961 they were displaced by the heavier Garratts and were stabled at Bulawayo until sold to the CFM for use from Lourenco Marques.

For many years the remaining 60lb main-line sections had restricted axleloads but relaying with 80lb material had been proceeding apace and in 1953 Hough was able to call on Beyer Peacock for the heaviest and largest Garratts to be seen on RR. The 20th class 4–8–2 + 2–8–4 had a 17 ton axleload, weighed 223.4 tons and developed 69,333lb tractive effort at 85 per cent boiler pressure. For such an engine it was decided to assist the fireman with a mechanical stoker. They gave an impression of great power and size and were a valued addition to the RR fleet.

Fifteen came into service as nos 700–14 in 1954–5, some on heavy coal traffic from Wankie to Bulawayo with 1,800 ton loads, while others went to Broken Hill for the northern district. Here they were invaluable in clearing 1,400 tons from Kafue over the difficult section to Lusaka and so permitting through goods loads with this tonnage right through Northern Rhodesia to Ndola. Their early success was such that with the continued rise in traffic RR placed its largest order ever, for a further six 20th and for forty 20A class. This was one of the last and largest orders Beyer Peacock secured before closing its Gorton works for steam production. The only difference between the 20th and 20A was that the outer bogie wheels on the latter have the same diameter, 2ft 9in, as the inner wheels, increasing the overall weight to 225.497 tons. (Picture, p 270.)

Of the six 20th class ordered, one was to replace no 700 which had been scrapped after a serious head-on collision at Kasavasa in 1956. Six years later another, no 760, a 20A, was scrapped after collision at Magoye before CTC was completed.

Although the arrival of this second order, which entered service in 1957–8 as nos 715–20 (20th) and 721–60 (20A) made a very appreciable impact on traffic movement, it was not long before trouble was experienced with failures in the boilers and fireboxes and a number of the class had to be withdrawn for lengthy periods. The temporary loss of this power, which was moving the great bulk of traffic in the north, was cause for much anxiety during a time of heavy pressure.

These engines—the largest and last steam order for RR—come close to the dimensions of the giant Beyer-Garratts of both the SAR and the metre-gauge East African Railways. The SAR GL weighs 214.5 tons and develops a tractive effort of 89,130lb compared with the 20A's 225.5 tons and 69,333lb. The giant EAR 59 class Garratts weigh 251.6 tons and have a tractive effort of 83,350lb, and so can claim to be the largest locomotives in Africa, though the SAR GL is more powerful. The EAR locomotives are oil-burners while their rivals use coal.

In very recent years the 20th/20A class has been busy on main lines in Rhodesia and, until lately, in Zambia moving heavy tonnages and proving with their workmates in other classes how valuable a contribution the Beyer-Garratt has made to the motive power of railways in this part of Africa. In all, 250 Garratts came to the Rhodesian system between 1925 and 1958 out of a total steam stud of 516 on the 3ft 6in gauge since the railways began—

a fine tribute to the products of Beyer Peacock, now no more a
builder of steam engines. With the spread of diesels to replace
steam, there will long be nostalgic memories among Rhodesian
railwaymen of the familiar Garratt with her distinctive beat,
though the present survivors still have quite a few years ahead of
them.

Since UDI in Rhodesia, sanctions have made it difficult to
obtain new equipment and with the 10 per cent increase in traffic
in the last two years it has been necessary to hire six 15E class
4–8–2s from the SAR. These are the largest non-articulated locomotives on RR, comparing with the 15th class for power, and work
on the Bulawayo—Gwelo line. Two secondhand 19th class
4–8–2s, built in 1952 for Nkana Mine by Henschel, came into RR
hands in 1968; these have ordinary tenders.

In the early 1950s a small batch of SAR engines was obtained
for the construction of the Rhodesia—Lourenco Marques line.
A shortage of power made it difficult to spare engines for work
trains so the purchase of five SAR class 13 tender-tank engines was
negotiated to run material trains from Bannockburn. Thus it came
about that SAR nos 1314/8/23/4/7 came to Rhodesia in 1952.
These had been built for the CSAR in 1901–2 by Dubs and Neilson
Reid as 4–10–2 side tank engines, but were later rebuilt as 4–8–0
tanks with six-wheel tenders. They were never taken into RR
classification, being treated purely as Engineer's Department
engines and were later sold for scrap.

The standard livery of RR locomotives has always been black with
bright red buffer beams. The engine numbers are shown in brass
letters on the beams and on plates on the cab sides. On some
units, parts of the motion, the jacks on the running plate and the
numberplates are touched up in red. The boilers, generally shining
black, are often enhanced by stainless steel bands which most
sheds manage to keep clean. In October 1961, when the new
motive power depot was opened at Livingstone, the local staff
prepared and painted a 20th class in a livery of Brunswick green
with gold lining on the boiler, the tanks and cylinder casing.
The appearance of this was so attractive that it was then decided
to adopt the green and gold livery for the 20th and 15th classes

as they went through shops but in the event only one other 20th class, one 15th, and one 12th class were done. With the need for economy, and because of cleaning difficulties, black once more became the standard livery.

CHAPTER FOURTEEN

The Coming of Diesel Power

WHILE some thought had been given to the possible use of diesel-electric traction as an eventual replacement of steam locomotives on RR, the ready availability of cheap coal had weighed strongly in favour of retaining the 'steamer', and the initial introduction of diesel power was quite fortuitous and engineered by outside influences. Restriction on chrome exports through shortage of motive power and of wagons, when all traffics were suffering, was of very serious consequence to Rhodesia Chrome Mines at Selukwe, since it led to the accumulation of an enormous stock-pile of chrome awaiting transport. The aid of their American associates was enlisted and as a result the supply was arranged of six diesel-electric locomotives from the United States to assist RR. Late in 1952 the first of these arrived.

They were built by the Davenport-Besler Corporation and had two 350bhp 12 cylinder Caterpillar engines carried on two six-wheel bogies (C–C type). Weighing 75.89 long tons, these Davenports had an axleload of 12.65 long tons and after initial trials as single units they were stationed at Salisbury hauling in tandem (two units with one crew) 750 ton loads to Umtali and back.

They were classed DE 1 and numbered 1000–5 in the RR register. Having a single driving cab, normally at the rear end for operation, the driver had to rely on his mate for hand signals on the left side due to poor visibility. For some years they assisted in the clearance of traffic on the main line, and later were used on

Page 287 Double-headed Garratts on the Zambian Copperbelt: 16A class no 646 and 15A no 401 leaving Kitwe Nkana on the 7.40am freight to Mufulira, May 1971

Page 288 (*above*) A train for Bulawayo leaves Salisbury in June 1980 behind class DE 8 no 1801; (*below*) two DE 2 diesel-electric locomotives head a goods train bound for Malvernia on the Lourenço Marques line. Photo shows train with two staff cabooses attached leaving Westgate Bulawayo

the Shamva and Sinoia branches before being placed on shunting at Umtali and in the Salisbury area.

Serviced originally in the old diesel railcar shed in the station yard at Salisbury, the beat of their engines when idling brought a new noise to the area. They were painted in a chrome yellow livery but this soon became dirty and the DE 1 was never a very attractive machine. Later they were given a green livery but this too was not easy to keep clean in shunting yards and a bright red, to be more conspicuous to motor drivers at level crossings, was then tried but all are now yellow again.

Meanwhile consideration was given to introducing diesel-electric power designed for the hilly Umtali—Salisbury run so that the train service could be completely dieselised. Fuel could be supplied easily at Umtali, only 204 miles from the port of Beira, compared with some 680 miles haulage from the colliery at Wankie. The shorter haul of oil made it more economical than coal, while advantages from the use of diesel-electrics were (a) elimination of water problems, (b) quicker and simplified terminal servicing, (c) more congenial working conditions for the enginemen, and (d) faster overall train timings. An important factor in favour of diesel traction was the tendency of overseas builders to abandon the production of steam locomotives and the making of boilers.

Tenders resulted in the English Electric Co of Preston receiving an order for twenty-three locomotives, the first of which was handed over at Salisbury in June 1955. These DE 2 class diesel-electrics were then the most powerful built for a 3ft 6in gauge railway. They have a V type 16-cylinder 4-stroke diesel engine of 2,000bhp at sea level (de-rated to 1,710bhp at Rhodesian altitudes), the power unit being mounted on two bogies, each with three driving axles with motors attached, and guided by a bissel truck at each end. These 1Co–Co1 type diesels weigh 113 long tons and have a 15 ton axleload. They carry 1,000 gallons of fuel and 135 gallons of lubricating oil. (Picture, p 288.)

English Electric provided staff to supervise the erection of their locomotives at Umtali and for training inspectors and enginemen to handle the units on the road. The contrast to the men sitting in a fully enclosed comfortable cab at the leading end of the unit with excellent view ahead when compared with steam locomotives was most marked. Conversion courses relatively quickly enabled enginemen brought up on steam to handle the new form of power. A diesel engine and electrical workshop was provided at Umtali as well as a running shed, the latter close to the steam shed, which was eventually to disappear. It was, of course, essential to train many steam locomotive fitters in the intricacies of the diesels although some men with diesel and electrical experience were available. These artisans showed a fine sense of adaptability in learning what was almost a new trade and the co-operation of all the staff was excellent.

After initial difficulties had been overcome, very satisfactory service was obtained, and with the order complete it became possible to operate the entire Umtali—Salisbury through service with DE 2s, goods trains usually with two units in tandem. This good record was unfortunately marred by a disastrous head-on collision in September 1956 when a tandem-hauled goods train ran through Eagles Nest siding and met another tandem-hauled goods climbing the bank towards the siding. The two enginemen at fault were killed and two of the four DE 2s involved were so badly damaged that they had to be scrapped.

A further twelve DE 2s were supplied by English Electric in 1957–8 and they replaced some of the steam on the Bulawayo—Malvernia caboose-worked trains over the new link to Lourenco Marques, and were also used on passenger and other trains over the Bulawayo—Salisbury line. The DE 2s proved very successful on the Malvernia run, which involved a trip of 343 miles from Bulawayo through country where the ambient temperature rose in summer to 116°F and dropped to as low as 38°F in winter. A batch of eight DE 2s notched up 657,507 miles in twelve months in 1958–9, giving an average of over 82,000 miles per unit. In a test in January 1961 DE 2 no 1208 ran 14,062 miles in the month over this line and was actually in use for 694 hours out of the total of 744. Comparison with the 12,270 miles run by 15th class Garratt no 379 in 1960 is interesting and shows not so great an advantage to the diesel.

A new diesel running shed was .erected at Bulawayo in the vicinity of the steam shed. The DE 2s were numbered 1200–34, of which 1209 and 1213 were scrapped after the Eagles Nest collision.

By 1961 it had been decided to dieselise the main line between Salisbury and Gwelo and a batch of sixteen 1Co–Co1 locomotives of 1,850bhp were supplied by English Electric from its Vulcan Foundry works. These were classed the DE 3 type and numbered 1300–15, being externally different to the DE 2 class by having a single driving cab instead of cabs at each end. They have a 12-cylinder 4-stroke V engine, weigh 110.2 tons in working order and have an axleload of $14\frac{1}{2}$ tons. In addition to the normal equipment, safety devices and deadman cutout, the locomotives were fitted with the Oerlikon automatic vigilance control system operating on a distance-run basis. Such controls had recently been installed in all the DE 2 class as a precaution against failure of the human element.

The introduction of the DE 3 locomotives resulted in the dieselisation of the main line from Machipanda (the CFM hand-over point) through Umtali and Salisbury to Gwelo and this reduced the booked service on the Salisbury—Gwelo section by three trains a day. The 15th class steam locomotives released from Salisbury were transferred to the Bulawayo—Mahalapye line in December 1962 and there saved one train a day by their ability to take an increased load. To service the larger fleet of diesels stationed at Salisbury a new motive power shed of modern design was provided at Lochinvar. This new shed replaced that at Umtali and centralised the servicing of diesels in the eastern region. Heavy repairs were continued in the Umtali workshops, which in 1965 had ceased to handle steam locomotive general repairs, now concentrated at Bulawayo.

With increasing traffic an order for fourteen Co–Co units was placed with Brush Electrical Engineering Co, Loughborough, and these came into service as the DE 4 class, nos 1400–13, during 1964–5. These 1,730bhp units were the first designed by Brush for the 3ft 6in gauge and have a maximum axleload of 15 tons. The units were designed to be able to work in multiple with the

English Electric units so as to obtain maximum versatility. Indeed the ability to use two diesels in tandem with one crew was an argument for increasing diesel power in place of steam. They have Mirlees-National J-type 12-cylinder engines, weigh 90 tons and have a maximum speed of 60mph. Unfortunately the full benefit of this addition to the RR stud was not experienced at first as these locomotives soon suffered engine trouble and several had to be withdrawn and others run below full power over long periods, while the defects were made good by the suppliers.

This order to Brush is interesting in that it renewed connections with the earliest days of railways in Rhodesia, the Falcon Engine & Car Works of Loughborough, England, which was acquired by the Brush Electrical Engineering Co in 1889, having built the very first locomotives used on the Beira Railway.

Another experiment with diesel power was the introduction of three Wickham-built railcars in May 1966 to operate a fast service for passengers over the Umtali—Salisbury line. These modern cars, 64ft long, with twin Leyland diesel engines giving a total of 310hp, seated twenty first- and forty-seven third-class passengers, the former having a clear view ahead past the driver. A centre kitchenette and bar with gas cooker and refrigerator, enabled a steward to serve light refreshments on the journey. A small luggage-guard's section was provided at the rear end.

The cars gave a twice-daily service between the two towns, taking about 4½ hours for the 170 miles, running comfortably at speeds of up to 65mph. However, with a parallel main road there was insufficient business to justify the high operating costs and in 1968 the railcars were handed over to Zambia Railways.

In the meantime, in order to extend dieselisation, a batch of ten Co–Co heavy duty U20C type diesel-electrics were obtained from General Electric of America and these entered service in 1967 as the DE 6 class, nos 1600–9. It had been intended to order twenty-four main line and twelve shunting engines but, for political and financial reasons, RR was only able to purchase ten units; in consequence Zambia Railways bought twenty-six DE 6 type.

The DE 6 units are slightly more powerful than the other RR

diesels, being rated at 2,040bhp at an altitude of 4,500ft. They have General Electric FDL 12-cylinder engines, weigh 89.4 tons and have an axleload of 15 tons. They differ considerably in appearance from previous locomotives by having the typical American low-nosed leading end with a single driving cab. They went into service without trouble and their advent has enabled RR to deploy its stud of seventy-nine diesels so that they haul most of the branch-line trains out of Salisbury as well as the main-line services to Gwelo, with some through to Bulawayo. The Malvernia trains are almost entirely diesel-hauled and steam power so released augments other sections of the main and branch lines.

Compared with the steam locomotive, the new form of motive power is easier to keep clean and from a publicity angle the appearance of the diesels is attractive. Originally the DE 2s had a livery of cream with the upper portion of the cabs crimson joined by three stripes of the same colour at roof sill, waist and frame, a black line dividing the cream side panels from the lowest crimson strips. A coloured railway crest was affixed below the electric head light on the cab casing and 'RR' in red was on the side panels. Later Brunswick green replaced the crimson on the DE 2s, while the latest livery is green with broad yellow stripes along the waist curving to a point on the cab front. With a passenger train these engines present a colourful picture and a good standard of cleanliness is maintained. Nevertheless, the smell of the oily exhaust and the noise of the motors bring gloom to the lovers of the old 'steamer'. Fortunately for them—and they are many—it will be some years before steam locomotives disappear entirely from RR.

With the imposition of sanctions in 1966, which closed the oil pipeline supplying Rhodesia from Beira, some initial difficulties were experienced, but the supply position was soon assured through other routes and the operation of diesels continued. Some delay to the dieselisation programme has occurred and the retention of steam locomotives has been extended. With the recent rise in traffic, much of it imports for Zambia, more power has been needed but sanctions have made it difficult for RR to purchase new equipment. Seven class 61 Bo–Bo diesel-hydraulic units have been hired from the SAR, 1,420hp locomotives built in 1959 by Henschel, were later bought from SAR and have recently been withdrawn.

The next class of locomotives to be introduced were Bo-Bo diesel electrics of class DE 7, which were equipped with V12 engines with an output of 1,050hp. Thirty six of these locomotives were introduced between the end of 1971 and the middle of 1973, numbered 1700 to 1735. They took over the Salisbury branch lines including that to Umtali. Three were damaged beyond repair after a collision on the Sinoia branch in 1974. The DE 7s were accompanied into service by the DE 9 class, also a Bo-Bo. Initially they were rated at 1,050hp but subsequently reduced to 790hp, at which stage they were regarded as shunting locomotives. They were numbered from 1900 to 1919. Later a new batch of forty-four locomotives were added in 1975/76. They were slightly heavier than their predecessors and had a rated horsepower of 967. Because of these differences they were classified as DE 9A. All were in plain yellow livery, and initially had armour plated cabs, though this latter feature was removed after the end of the war.

All the DE 7 and DE 9A locomotives were basically branch line types, and it was soon discovered that the Somabula-Beitbridge section was seriously deficient in motive power. Therefore two new main line types of diesel-electric locomotives were introduced in 1973. The first are the DE 5 class of Co-Co wheel arrangement. They are very handsome machines and have a tractive rating of 2,266hp which make them ideal for the Rutenga section. They were erected in Rhodesia and the bodies were made in the country. They have proved very successful locomotives considering the difficulties under which they were produced and operated.

The other main line family of diesels introduced at this time was the DE 8 imported from Europe. Initially fourteen DE 8s were commissioned, in a handsome blue and white livery. Twenty identical locomotives of class DE 8A were commissioned in 1974/75, and the only difference to the DE 8s was that they had compressed air as well as vacuum brakes. Finally twenty-four class DE 8Bs appeared in 1976/77. All these locomotives had the same V16 engine and a tractive rating of 2,320hp. The main difference in the 8Bs was that they were 18 tonnes lighter than the two previous types. More recently, due to the fact that trouble was experienced with the engines of the DE 4s they were laid aside for two years, but are now to be re-engined and returned to service.

Abbreviations

BCK	Chemin de Fer du Bas-Congo au Katanga
BMR	Beira & Mashonaland Railways
BR	Beira Railway
BSA	British South Africa (Company and Police)
CFK	Chemin de Fer du Haut Katanga (Sakania-Bukama)
CFM	Caminhos de Ferro de Moçambique
CGR	Cape Government Railway
CME	Chief Mechanical Engineer
CST	Chief Superintendent of Transportation
DNPCF	Direccao Naçionale das Portos & Caminhos de Ferro
MR	Mashonaland Railway
NRZ	National Railways of Zimbabwe
PEA	Portuguese East Africa (Mozambique)
RKJR	Rhodesia Katanga Junction Railway (Broken Hill-Congo Border)
RMS	Road Motor Services
RNTC	Rhodesia Native Timber Concessions
RR	Rhodesia Railways
RR V-B	Rhodesia Railways (Vryburg-Bulawayo)
SAR	South African Railways
TZR	Trans-Zambesia Railway
UMHK	Union Minière du Haut Katanga (mining company in Congo)
ZR	Zambia Railways
ZSMR	Zambesi Saw Mills Railway

Appendices

APPENDIX A

Copy of enclosure to letter from George and Henry Pauling to Major Frank Johnson, Cape Town, dated 1st July, 1891.
Estimated Cost of Construction of 70 Miles Steam Tram Line from M'pandas to Mandegos, gauge 24in, sleepers 3ft, 2ft 9in centres, 18lb steel rails.

	£	s.	d.
Cost of line from England, including sleepers per mile	495	0	0
Cost of freight to Beira @ 50s per ton 43¾ tons per mile	109	7	6
Transhipping freight and barging at Pungwe River: 43¾ tons @ 40s per ton	87	10	0
Earthworks 4 × 1 @ 1s per yard	88	0	0
Platelaying at £40 per mile	40	0	0
Therefore one mile costs	819	17	6
Multiplied by 70	70		
	57,391	5	0
1 Mile Sidings—4 × 200yds—2 × 400—80	819	17	6
16 sets single points and crossings @ £8.15s	140	0	0
2 Engine Sheds @ £100 each	200	0	0
3% Duty on permanent way	1,160	0	0

APPENDIX A

Rolling Stock:

20 Covered Bogie Wagons, 4 tons ea. with brake, £35 ea.	700	0	0
30 Open Bogie Wagons, 4 tons ea. with brake, £25 ea.	750	0	0
3 Passenger cars @ £97.10s ea. with brake	292	10	0
5 Locos 'Wasp Type' 6in cylinder, to draw 80 ton loads	2,600	0	0
Freight, packing and duty, Locos	357	0	0
Trucks	276	0	0
Distribution of Material @ £20 per mile	1,400	0	0
Culverts, etc.	2,000	0	0
Contingencies	1,913	7	6
Total	£70,000	0	0

(*Note: Original in Rhodesian National Archives*)

APPENDIX B

Opening Dates of Sections of Line

1892	September		Construction of 2ft gauge line from Fontesvilla westwards begun
1893	May	10	Construction of 3ft 6in gauge line from Vryburg northwards begun
1894	October	3	Vryburg—Mafeking section opened
1895	July		Construction of Beira—Fontesvilla link commenced
1896	October		Beira—Fontesvilla section completed
1897	March	1	Mafeking—Mochudi section opened
	July	1	Mochudi—Palapye Road section opened
	September	1	Palapye Road—Francistown section opened
	November	4	Francistown—Bulawayo section opened
1898	February	4	Beira—Umtali line (2ft gauge) opened
1899	May	22	Umtali—Salisbury line (3ft 6in) opened
1900	August	1	Umtali—Beira line widened to 3ft 6in gauge, open throughout
1902	June	1	Salisbury—Gwelo section opened
	November	1	Salisbury—Ayrshire line (2ft gauge) opened
	December	1	Bulawayo—Gwelo section opened
1903	March		Bulawayo—Mambanje section of north line opened
	August	25	Gwelo—Selukwe branch line opened
	August	25	Heany Junction—Gwanda branch line opened

	November	4	Westacre Junction—Matopos branch line opened. (Closed June 1948)
	December	1	Mambanje—Wankie section opened
1904	June	20	Wankie—Victoria Falls section opened
1905	March	1	Gwanda—West Nicholson section opened
	July		Victoria Falls—Kalomo section opened
	July	12	Banket Junction—Eldorado section (2ft) opened
	September	12	Victoria Falls bridge opened to traffic
1906	September	1	Kalomo—Broken Hill section opened
1909	June	19	Lyndhurst Junction—Umvuma branch line opened
	December	11	Broken Hill—Congo Border section opened
1911	August		Salisbury—Mount Hampden section widened from 2ft to 3ft 6in gauge
	December	15	Mount Hampden Junction—Jumbo section opened (3ft 6in gauge)
1912	May	16	Eiffel Flats branch from junction near Gatooma opened
1913	April	23	Shamva branch extension from Jumbo opened
1914	June	22	Eldorado—Sinoia branch extension opened with completion of widening of gauge to 3ft 6in from Mount Hampden
	July	10	Umvuma—Fort Victoria branch opened
1928	May	11	Somabula—Shabani branch opened
1929	January	22	Ndola—Luanshya branch opened
	September	21	Mokambo (Congo)—Mufulira branch opened
1930	July	1	Ndola—Nkana branch opened
	July	2	Maryland Junction—Kildonan branch opened
	August	1	Sinoia—Zawi branch extension opened
1931	June	20	Nkana—Chingola branch opened
1932	April	1	Chambishi Junction—Mufulira branch opened
1955	August	1	Bannockburn—Malvernia line opened

1957	January	Luano Junction—Bancroft branch opened
1964	September 28	Mbizi—Chiredzi branch opened
1965	August	Chiredzi—Nandi extension opened
1974	September 18	Rutenga—Beitbridge opened
1981	April 23	Nandi—Mkwasine opened

APPENDIX C

STEAM LOCOMOTIVES OF THE RHODESIAN RAILWAYS: 3ft 6in GAUGE

Class	Nos	Year Built	Builder	Works Nos	Type	Cylinders diam. × stroke in.	Coupled Wheels diam. ft. in.	Boiler Pressure p.s.i lb.	Tractive Effort lb.	Remarks
6th (CGR)	BR. 1-3	1897	Neilson	5157/9	4-6-0	17 ×26	4-3	180	18,780	Ordered by Bechuanaland Rly Co but absorbed in CGR loco stock as 582-4 and 347-50
7th (CGR)	BR. 4-7	1897	Neilson	5160/3	4-8-0	17 ×23	3-6½	160	18,660	
4th (CGR)	MR. 1-2	1882	Neilson	2931/2843	4-6-0	15 ×20	3-6	140	11,250	From CGR/Paulings 1899 CGR W59 and W71
	MR. 3-4	1891	Nasmyth Wilson	423/4	4-6-0	14 ×20	4-7⅞	140	17,515	MR bought direct 1897
	MR. 5-6	1896	J. Fowler	7450/1	4-6-2T	18¼×20	4-0	140	7,160	MR bought 1899 from CGR
	MR. 7	1889	Manning Wardle	1159	0-6-0ST	11¼×17	2-9			MR bought 1899 from Paulings *Jack Tar*. Preserved for RR museum
7th	BM. 1-2	1899	N. Reid	5675/6	4-8-0					
,,	RR. 1-10	1899	,,	5677/86						Considerable re-numbering occurred with first three orders, 1901 and 1906
,,	RR. 11-22	1900	Kitson	5791/5802						
,,	RR. 23-30	1901	North British	4062/9						
,,	MR. 31-50	1903	N. Reid	16085/94 16171/80						
,,	RKJ. 348	1897	N. Reid	5161	4-8-0	17 ×23	3-6½	160	18,660	no 43 preserved for RR museum
	398	1896		4925						
	RR. 19	1900	N. Reid	5817						2nd RR 19 was Imperial Military Rlys 110
6th	RR. 51-52	1903	Kitson	4240/1	4-8-2T	17 ×23	3-6¾	160	18,660	9 rebuilt from 7th class, 1914/23
6A					4-8-4T	17 ×23	3-6¾	160	18,660	4 rebuilt from 7th class, 1918/20
K-M	RR. 53-62	1904	N. British	16216/25	0-6-6-0	15½×23	3-0	180	34,900	
8th	RR. 73-79	1910	,,	19317/9 19356/9	4-8-0	19 ×24	4-0	180	24,370	Originally nos :6/9 and 63/5
8th	MR. 80-97	1912	,,	19743/54 19818/23	4-8-0	19 ×24	4-0	180	24,370	
9th	RR. 105-110	1915	Beyer Peacock	5914/19	4-8-0	20 ×24	4-0	170	25,500	26 rebuilt as 9B class, 1939/50. BP 180 lb
9th	MR. 111-116	1917	N. British	21474/9	4-8-0	20 ×24	4-0	170	25,500	
9A	RR. 117-122	1917	American Loco Co	56724/9	4-8-0	20 ×24	4-0	175	26,250	Tractive effort 30,600 lb
Small	RR. 1-2	1929	Hudswell Clarke	1627/8	0-6-0T	16 ×22	3-6¾	180	17,785	
,,	RR. 5	1901	Chapman & Furneaux	1208	0-4-0ST	12 ×18	3-0	130	7,020	From SAR for Mafeking, 1929
10th	RR. 98-104	1913	N. British	19996/20002	4-8-2	20 ×26	4-6	180	29,466	
,,	RR 153-158	1922	,,	22796/801	4-8-2	20 ×26	4-6	180	29,466	
,,	RR. 159	1924	,,	23089	4-8-2	20 ×26	4-6	180	29,466	
11th	RR. 241-246	1930	,,	23972/7	4-8-2	22 ×24	4-0	180	34,952	
11th	RR. 123-140	1918-9	Montreal Loco Works	59115/23	4-8-2	22 ×24	4-0	180	34,952	
,,	RR. 141-152	1921	,,	59940/8	4-8-2	22 ×24	4-0	180	34,952	
11A	RR. 304-315	1948	,,	62773/84 75468/79	4-8-2	21 ×24	4-0	180	33,737	Originally 200 lb BP, 37,485 lb tractive effort

APPENDIX C (continued)

Class	Nos	Year Built	Builder	Works Nos	Type	Cylinders diam. × stroke in.	Coupled Wheels diam. ft. in.	Boiler Pressure p.s.i. lb.	Tractive Effort lb.	Remarks
12th	RR. 172–191	1926	N. British	23373/92	4-8-2	20 ×26	4-3	190	32,940	
	RR. 192–214	1927–8	,,	23592/4 23724/41 23772/3	4-8-2	20 ×26	4-3	190	32,940	12th class no's 198/212/13 re-boilered with 11th class boilers
12A	RR. 247–258	1930	,,	23996/24007	4-8-2	20 ×26	4-3	190	32,940	Sold to CFM, 1962
12B	RR 260–69	1954/5	RR.	—	4-8-2	20 ×26	4-3	190	32,940	
13th	MR. 160–171	1925	Beyer, Peacock	6269/80	2-6-2+2-6-2	16 ×24	4-0	180	39,168	Sold to CFM, 1949
14th	RR. 215–220	1929	,,	6510/5	2-6-2+2-6-2	16 ×24	4-0	180	39,168	231/2 sold to CFM, 1949. 233-40 re-numbered 500-7
14th	RR. 231–240	1930	,,	6616/25	2-6-2+2-6-2	16 ×24	4-0	180	39,168	
14A	508–525	1953	,,	7581/92 7599/7604	2-6-2+2-6-2	16 ×24	4-0	180	39,168	
16th	221–228	1930	,,	6562/9	2-8-2+2-8-2	18¼×24	4-0	180	52,364	} Re-numbered 600–19
16th	259–270	1938	,,	6877/82 6899/6904	2-8-2+2-8-2	18¼×24	4-0	180	52,364	
16A	620–649	1953	,,	7498/7527	2-8-2+2-8-2	18½×24	4-0	200	58,183	
16A	271–274	1940	,,	6936/9	4-6-4+4-6-4	17½×26	4-9	180	42,750	Re-numbered 350-3
15th	354–363	1947	,,	7228/37						
15A	364–383	1949	,,	7260/79						
15A	384–413	1950/1	,,	7326/40						
15A	414–423	1952	Societe Franco-Belge	7351/65	4-6-4+4-6-4	17½×26	4-9	200	47,496	
18th	81–289	1943/4	Beyer, Peacock	4409/17	2-8-2+2-8-2	19 ×24	3-9¼	180	58,268	WD type. Sold to CFM, 1949.
17th	271–280	1937/8	,,	6798/6801 6870/5	4-6-4+4-6-4	16½×26	4-9	190	41,336	Bought from Sudan Rlys, 1949. Sold to CFM, 1964
19C	316–335	1951	Henschel	27386/405	4-8-2	21 ×26	4-6	200	36,090	
19C	336	1954	,,	27411	4-8-2	21 26	4-6	200	36,090	Converted from condenser to 19th, 1958
19B	337–338	1952	Beyer, Peacock		4-8-2	21 ×26	4-6	200	36,090	Originally Nkana Mine. Bought 1968
20th	700–714	1954/5	,,	7685/7699 7780/7785	4-8-2+2-8-4					
20th	715–720	1957/8	,,	7786/7825						
20A	721–760	1957/8	,,		4-8-2+2-8-4	20 ×26	4-3	200	69,333	

APPENDIX D

15th Class (animals)
370	Ibhalabhala	(Kudu)
371	Inkolongwane	(Hartebeest)
372	Umtshwayeli	(Sable)
376	Ingulungundu	(Bush Pig)
377	Udwayi	(Secretary Bird)
380	Uhelwane	(Goshawk)
381	Ingwe	(Leopard)
382	Iganyana	(Wild Dog)
385	Ingwenya	(Crocodile)
386	Umayelane	(Hare)
387	Imvubu	(Hippo)
391	Ingugama	(Gemsbok)
392	Ithaka	(Roan)
394	Umzwazwa	(Brown Hawk)
396	Igogo	(Klipspringer)
397	Inyathi	(Buffalo)

15A Class (animals)
402	Impofu	(Eland)
406	Ikolo	(Hornbill)
407	Ukhozi	(Eagle)
409	Inkakha	(Pangolin)
410	Inkolomi	(Tsessebe)
414	Ubhejane	(Black Rhino)
415	Itsheme	(Great Bustard)
419	Isambane	(Ant Bear)
420	Indlovu	(Elephant)
421	Intundla	(Giraffe)
422	Inkonkoni	(Wildebeest)
423	Idube	(Zebra)
424	Isilwane	(Lion)

Names yet to be allocated:
Inungu	(Porcupine)
Imbila	(Rock Rabbit)
Umkhombo	(White Rhino)
Isidumuka	(Water Buck)
Umziki	(Reed Buck)
Umathebane	(Kestrel)

20th Class (Regiments)
733	(710)	Imbizo
737	(718)	Ingubo
		Ihlathi
730	(705)	Insuza
		Amaveni
		Isiziba
		Induba
		Enxa

20A Class (Rivers)
742	(726)	Gwaai
		Shangani
		Bembezi
747		Jumbo
		Bubi
		Ingwezi
		Insiza
		Lukozi
		Umzingwane
		Tuli
		Umguza

Bibliography

Clark, Percy M., *An Old Drifter*, 1936

d'Erlanger, Baron Emile B., *History of the Construction and Finance of the Rhodesian Transport System*

Fairbridge, K., *Autobiography of Kingsley Fairbridge*, 1927

Fox, Sir Francis, *63 Years of Engineering*, 1924

Gouldsbury, Cullen, *Rhodesian Rhymes—Ballad of the B.M.R.*, 1909

Lockhart, J. G. and Wodehouse, Hon. C. M., *Rhodes*

Lyon, Polhemus, *Arderne Party Chronicle*, 1904

Muskett, H. B., *Steel Highway*, 1957

Pauling, George, *Chronicles of a Contractor*, 1926

Pooley, H. E., *From Livingstone to Ndola*, 1906

Stent, Vere, *Some Incidents in the Life of Cecil Rhodes*, 1925

Tanser, G. H., *A Scantling of Time*, 1965

Varian, H. F., *Some African Milestones*, 1953

Weinthal, Leo, *The Story of the Cape to Cairo Railway and River Route, 1897–1922*, 1923

West, L. H., *Journal of Finance—Rhodesian Railways*, 1898

Willoughby, W. C., *Native Life on Transvaal Border*, 1900

Wright, E. H. S., *Railways in Rhodesia*, 1904

Other sources included:

Southern Rhodesia—Information for Settlers, BSA Co, 1902

Guide to Rhodesia, BMRR, 1914 and 1924

Rhodesia, 1889–1899, BSA Co, 1899

Rhodesia, London, 1897

Beyer Garratt Articulated Locomotives, Beyer Peacock & Co, 1947

Much detail is available in the reports of the various railway companies, of the Railway Commission of S. Rhodesia, N. Rhodesia and the Bechuanaland Protectorate, and the annual reports of the BMRR and Rhodesia Railways. Of considerable importance for contemporary accounts and comments are the daily and periodical newspapers and magazines, especially: *Umtali Advertiser, Rhodesia Advertiser* (Umtali), *Bulawayo Chronicle, Rhodesia Herald* (Salisbury), *Cape Argus* (Cape Town), *African World, South Africa, Railway Magazine, The Locomotive, Railway Carriage and Wagon Review, Engineering, The Engineer* (all of London), *South African Railway Magazine, Rhodesia Railways Magazine, Rhodesia Annual, Railway Engineering* (Cape Town). In addition, the Rhodesiana Society's publication, *Rhodesiana,* nos 8/1963, 10/1964, and 13/1965 are relevant, while the *Beira Railway Letters* and other papers in the National Archives of Rhodesia (Salisbury) provide much information.

Acknowledgements

As a young LNWR–LMSR railwayman in 1927 I went to London Wall to be interviewed by officials of the BMR for a post on that railway. After working at Euston and various stations within constant sound of trains and locomotives, the quiet, rather Victorian atmosphere of those dingy City offices seemed to me incongruous for a railway head office, for in those days the BMR was ruled from London. Coming out to Bulawayo, I delved into books on the country and then over the years became more and more interested in the history of its railway system.

Time never permitted more than the occasional putting aside of items of historical interest, as over the years I realised their value. However, on retiring from RR, I had time to spare and began as a hobby to seek more from the past. In this I received great help from many serving and retired Rhodesian railwaymen and others whose personal recollections and photographs came in answer to my enquiries. To all these my grateful thanks for willing assistance, with special thanks to Frank Austin and H. B. Muskett for their valuable notes. Helpful information has been supplied by T. P. Gilbert, B. H Johnson, F. E. Chandler, D. C. Sinclair, C. W. Brown, W. T. Bowes, R. A. H. Baxter, D. F. Holland, G. Pattison, H. C. Hawkins, D. H. Stuart, W. H. G. Boot, D. H. Constable, the late S. Tomalin and many others. Of great value was the friendship of the late E. M. Rosher.

I am also indebted for early photographs from Pauling & Co (London), the late J. Pauling, and the late Duncan Bailey of

Chas Roberts & Co (Horbury). The Director (E. E. Burke) and staff of the National Archives of Rhodesia, Salisbury, have been most kind in their help, while G. Ottley, then of the British Museum Library, the staff of the South African Library (Cape Town), and the South African Railways Librarian and staff have given much assistance with my research. I must also acknowledge the kindness of the Rhodesia Railways administration in allowing me sight of old company minutes and documents in RR archives.

Lastly, my thanks to my wife for her great patience in putting up with a husband who spent so much time on research and compiling this book.

ANTHONY CROXTON

Fish Hoek, Cape
1973

PUBLISHER'S NOTE

Since the original edition of *Railways of Rhodesia* by the late Anthony Croxton was published in 1973 much has happened in that country, not least the emergence of the new state of Zimbabwe. The railway system has undergone changes arising from the sanctions imposed during its unofficial period of independence and the ensuing war within the country, which, with the rapid rise in imported oil prices, has led to a resurgence of steam traction with the overhaul of a large number of locomotives to serve during the 1980s. Equally, main line electrification is in hand. For this edition, Anthony H. Baxter, himself employed by the National Railways of Zimbabwe, has added a new chapter eleven to record recent events, and expanded the final chapter on modern motive power. Otherwise Anthony H. Croxton's text has been left as in the original edition apart from one or two places where later information has come to light which clarifies the author's original text.

January 1982

Index

Italic numerals refer to illustrations
(Note: names of countries and places have been used as at the time of the narrative.)

309